' **mountain** /mówntin/ *n.* a large natural elevation of the earth's surface rising abruptly from the surrounding level '

Roseberry Topping

Great Ayton Community Archaeology Project
photography by Joe Cornish

geology

landscape

history

heritage

Explanatory notes

In planning this book we had to agree some physical boundaries to the work. We have included Newton Wood and Roseberry Common, but generally excluded the village of Newton-under-Roseberry, Cliff Rigg and Aireyholme farm buildings. We trust that this, admittedly rather arbitrary, decision does not disappoint any readers. Most, if not all, aspects of Roseberry are covered, from prehistoric times to the present. Although topics are generally set out in chronological order, we did not intend to produce a book that had to be read through from start to finish.

Imperial units are used throughout the book, apart from altitudes, which are in metres. The logic behind this decision is that many dimensions are quoted from historic sources, and it can be misleading to convert these to metric units. So in the interests of uniformity, most distances are given in miles, feet and inches, apart from altitudes. Because readers will, no doubt, refer to modern maps when using this book, all contours and heights are given in metres. We hope that this mix of units does not upset any purists.

In the interests of easier reading, no reference numbers are inserted into the actual text. References are quoted chapter by chapter, which should be adequate for readers wishing to identify specific sources. If an exact source is unclear, we would be willing to supply further details to individual researchers.

One advantage of publishing a book is that it often brings forth hitherto unknown sources of information or undiscovered images. We would be most grateful to hear of any such material. One specific request would be for a print of a banknote issued by the Commercial Bank of Stokesley (1796-1802), which featured the Topping as part of its design.

We have made strenuous efforts to secure the permission of all holders of the copyright of images reproduced in the book. However, we would apologise for any omissions in this regard, and indeed for any errors and omissions in the text. Notification of any mistakes, or possible additions, would be welcomed.

Roseberry Topping

Copyright © 2006 Published by the Great Ayton Community Archaeology Project All rights reserved

No part of this publication may be reproduced, stored in a retrieval system, or transmitted, in any form or by any means, electronic, mechanical, photocopying, recording or otherwise, without the permission of the copyright owner

ISBN 0-9554153-0-6   From 1 January 2007 ISBN 978-0-9554153-0-2

Produced by:

Research, words, maps and image sourcing: Great Ayton Community Archaeology Project

Publishing team: Dan and Hazel O'Sullivan, Ian Pearce, David W Taylor

Principal photography: Joe Cornish

Editor: Ian Pearce

Design and production: Joni Essex

Printing: Falcon Press, Stockton

Typeset in 10.5/14 Garamond and Gill Sans

Endpapers: Christopher Saxton map of Yorkshire from 1577 Copyright The British Library, 2006. Reproduced by permission of The British Library

contents

Introductions

Ian Pearce, Great Ayton
     Community Archaeology Project   7

Joe Cornish   9

Mark Newman, National Trust   10

Graham Lee, North York Moors
     National Park   11

1   Looking at the Topping   14

2   The origin of the name   20

3   Landscape and geology   26

4   Prehistoric Roseberry   38

5   Bronze Age hoard   47

6   Sight lines or leys   55

7   Farming on the slopes   58

8   Fox hunting   66

9   The antiquarians   70

10   Myths and legends   79

11   Roseberry Trinity Fair   86

12   Smoky beacons   89

13   Mystery of the summerhouse   96

14   Industry on Roseberry   106

15   Roseberry's pits   116

16   A Topping radio programme   130

17   Roseberry on historic maps   133

18   Tourism and the Topping   144

19   Accidents and rescues   157

20   Who owns the Topping?   162

21   Roseberry's wildlife   168

22   The Topping today   176

23   Roseberry in art and literature   184

References   200

Index of names   204

Acknowledgements   206

Principal contributors appear at the end of each chapter

introduction —

Ian Pearce
Great Ayton Community Archaeology Project

The distinctive profile of Roseberry Topping is known and loved throughout Cleveland and beyond. Roseberry was familiar to the hunters who trudged across the prehistoric landscape and it provided a home to the first farmers. The mountain was sacred to native Britons and Viking invaders alike, and it protected their descendants from invasions. It inspired writers and poets, and lent its image to artists and photographers. It gave the iron workers of Teesside a breath of fresh air, and yielded ironstone for their blast furnaces. Countless numbers are still drawn to its woods and slopes, and those reaching the summit are rewarded with breathtaking views.

Perhaps it is surprising that there has not been a publication dedicated entirely to the mountain. We hope that this partnership between Joe Cornish and the Great Ayton Community Archaeology Project has produced a book that holds something for everyone, from those who wish to dream over Joe's stunning pictures, to those who desire factual information about all aspects of the hill and its immediate surroundings.

The Great Ayton Community Archaeology Project is a group of twenty-four local people with a consuming interest in the history of Great Ayton. It was started in 2002 by Dan O'Sullivan, and has been funded by the Local Heritage Initiative, the Nationwide Building Society, and the Heritage Lottery Fund. From the start we have enjoyed leadership and guidance from Kevin Cale of Community Archaeology Limited, who has pioneered the formation of volunteer groups to study, record and disseminate information on their local heritage.

Over the past two years all members of the group have contributed to the research and writing. They are David Brook, Alan Bunn, Kevin Cale, John Crocker, Sally Dennison, Mike Dixon, Robert de Wardt, Liz Greenhalgh, Len Groves, Joan Groves, Dennis Herriman, Sue Lane, Bazz Lewis, Peter Morgan, Richard Morrissey, Dan O'Sullivan, Hazel O'Sullivan, Ian Pearce, Cath Small, David Taylor, David W Taylor, Ken Taylor, Dennis Tyerman, Peter Watson, and Ian Wilson. It has been a pleasure for me to coordinate and edit the work, and then to pass it to Joni Essex, who has magically turned the basic text and images into the book you now hold. I apologise in advance for any errors in the text, but would welcome comments and any further information about Roseberry from readers. We trust that you will gain enjoyment, knowledge and understanding from its contents, and help us preserve our wonderful landmark and its heritage for generations to come.

Ian Pearce
Secretary and Treasurer
Great Ayton Community Archaeology Project
1 Dikes Lane, Great Ayton TS9 6HJ
August 2006

introduction –

Joe Cornish
Landscape photographer

By the standards of the earth's great mountains it is a pimple, a paltry 320 metres above sea level. Yet seen rising above the rooftops of the village on a misty morning, Roseberry Topping is no mere hill, but a mythical mountain, the so-called Cleveland Matterhorn.

Roseberry manages to be both great and small simultaneously. Its steep sides, elegant proportions, and its physical isolation imbue it with a certain grandeur. But the patchwork of habitats that cover its slopes, and the easy ascent to the summit confirm its petite proportions. It is by far the most charismatic high point of the North York Moors.

While the pinnacle of Roseberry may at first glance appear to be the focus of many of my pictures, it is often just the finishing flourish in an image mostly revealing a detail of the surrounding landscape. It is literally the Topping on the compositional cake. A drystone wall on Ayton Banks, a harvested field north of Newton, an isolated tree on the slopes of Cliff Ridge, foxgloves near the summer house, or gorse at Gribdale Gate; all these are set in context by Roseberry's distinctive profile.

From its top, Roseberry is no longer a beckoning beacon, but a balcony, offering commanding views over the countryside to every point of the compass. The summit does more than just provide a great lookout point for the photographer, however. The western cliff is a dramatic subject, its vertical face glowing russet, ochre and terra cotta in the setting sun. The sandstone summit slabs retain some of the swirling forms that characterise this rock, but have also been engraved with the names of a thousand graffiti artists over a hundred years.

If we study this landscape, we find its history echoing through the Cumbrian fells, and parallels with the Peak District and the limestone hills of the Yorkshire Dales. These were not the quiet, idyllic rural scenes they may now appear to be, but once rang with the sound of industrial quarrying and mining (indeed, parts of the Dales still do). Roseberry's story is a microcosm of England's north country.

The Great Ayton archaeology group have dug deep to reveal the many layers of this cherished landmark. Their words, work and ideas combine here with my photographs and the graphic design of Joni Essex in this unique collaboration. Shared by North Yorkshire, Cleveland and Teesside alike, this is our tribute to Roseberry Topping, our mountain of the imagination.

Joe Cornish
Photographer
August 2006

National Trust

As a landscape archaeologist, I encounter very few places where the landscape reveals its character at first glance. It usually takes a great deal of research, survey and thought to work out what a place is all about, and to tease out the stories which lie behind it.

Roseberry Topping is that little bit different. True, the detail of its past has taken, and will continue to take, a great deal of unravelling, and these pages are a fine product of a great deal of work starting that process. But the first moment you see it – you encounter it – looming up above the A172, the Topping's essential qualities, its dominance of the landscape, its mystery, complexity and ancientness – stare you directly in the face. This is a place that invites exploration, and thanks to the National Trust ownership, everyone can do just that.

Much of the history and archaeology on Roseberry is of national significance, and this first comprehensive telling of the hill's story in one place is very welcome. But just as important is the fact that the Topping is perhaps more significant regionally than it is nationally; it is a place that the people of the northern fringe of the North York Moors and the southern side of the Tees valley look on as being theirs. So what could be more appropriate than a study conducted and produced by the local archaeology group? What a welcome example of a community seeking to understand and value its environment.

It has been a great pleasure to offer a little help and support to the Great Ayton Community Archaeology Project's voyage of discovery on Roseberry Topping, and I hope that this book will inspire its readers to enjoy, protect and sustain this wonderful place into the far distant future.

Mark Newman, Territory Archaeologist, North, The National Trust
January 2006

North York Moors National Park

Images of Roseberry Topping seem to be just about everywhere these days! Wherever I look, at home, at work, in town, I am surrounded by wonderful images, from all seasons of the year, of this impressive whale-backed hill. Many are taken, of course, by Joe Cornish and appear on cards, calendars and even the cover of former editions of the Ordnance Survey Explorer maps.

Standing at the north-western extremity of the National Park, Roseberry Topping announces our presence from miles away, signalling the boundary of one of this nation's very special places. It draws people like a magnet, inducing many who would normally only venture on foot to the nearby corner shop, to fight their way breathless to the top, to enjoy the staggering views; back across the Moors, along the Vale towards Stokesley, over Guisborough Forest to the sea and towards the industry of Teesside, gleaming through sunlit steam.

I generally approach the Topping as the pivot point of a walk, for a view of the lowlands before swinging back across the Moors, the view changing with direction and distance. When viewed from the north-east, Roseberry Topping presents a similar profile to Freebrough Hill, but from most other directions it is the dramatic scar which draws your attention, caused by the landslip of 1912 which produced the landscape we know today.

The archaeology of the area is also fascinating, a mix of prehistoric and modern exploitation, particularly around the flanks of Roseberry Topping itself, as this book will reveal. Given the vast geographical area of the National Park and the relatively limited resources available to research and report on the history and archaeology of places of particular interest and importance within the Moors, it is wonderful to be able to support the Great Ayton Community Archaeology project in their enterprise. Groups such as this make a real and significant contribution to understanding and raising the profile of the archaeology of their area. I wish the book, and further enterprises by the group, every success!

Graham Lee, Archaeological Conservation Officer, North York Moors National Park Authority
February 2006

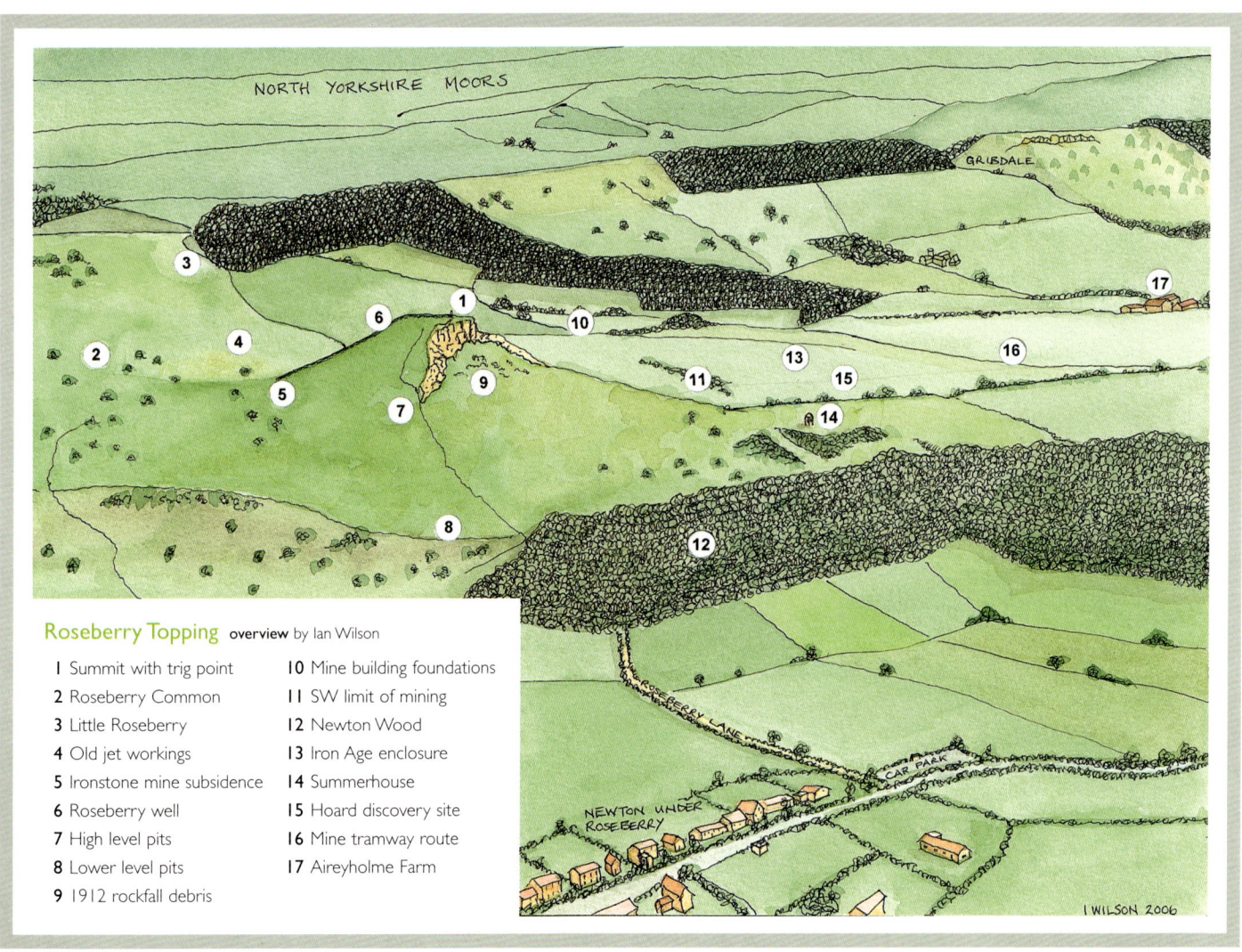

so long as
Roseberry Topping stands,
so long will its special
place in the affection
of people endure

looking at the Topping

1

For most people their introduction to Roseberry Topping is through its dramatic appearance, whether seen at first hand or in an illustration. So it seemed appropriate to begin this book with images of the mountain from the past four centuries. The earliest known pictures depicting Roseberry are the pen-and-ink sketches by George Cuit, produced around 1788. His series of eight scenes associated with James Cook included three with the Topping in the background. Two of these are shown here, the third can be found in Chapter 7.

Above left: The cottage built by Cook's father, now dismantled and rebuilt at Melbourne, Australia, in 1934. *Above right:* A view across Low Green at the western end of Great Ayton.   Images reproduced by kind permission of the Wakefield Art Gallery and Museum

Left: Possibly the earliest newsprint image, from an 1881 *Illustrated London News*. The hand-colouring is a later addition. The whinstone bulk of Cliff Ridge dominates the centre of the picture. Cook's Monument can just be seen on the skyline to the right.

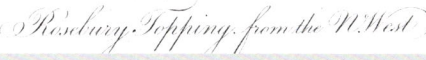

Most of the early depictions of Roseberry are engravings, usually produced to illustrate published books. Nineteenth century engravings generally show Roseberry as being symmetrical and volcano-like, often viewed from the south-west. Most pictures today show the distinctive profile resulting from the 1912 rockfall.

Top left: Engraving from *The History of Cleveland* of 1808 by Rev John Graves. The other two hills are Langbaurgh and Cliff Ridges, both prior to the extensive extraction of whinstone following the arrival of the railway in 1864.

Middle left: 1855 engraving printed by Rock & Co of London, taken from a viewpoint which today would show a distinctly different profile.

Bottom left: Engraving by Todd, commissioned by the printer Thomas Heaviside of Stokesley around 1874.

Below: A late nineteenth century engraving printed by Tweddell of Stokesley. The prominent line from Newton Wood to the summit was the stone boundary wall between the parishes of Ayton and Newton. On the original the summerhouse can just be made out above Newton Wood.

LOOKING AT THE TOPPING

An 1855 postcard, the earliest known photographic image of the Topping. The 'King's Head' public house, at Newton-under-Roseberry, is to the right and can still be recognised today in spite of many later modifications.

Copyright The Francis Frith Collection SP35QP
© www.francisfrith.co.uk

2006 digital photograph of the King's Head. This view, which excludes modern developments, can be compared with the above postcard. The profile of Roseberry Topping has been dramatically changed by the 1912 rockfall.

Left: A public view of … the sign outside the Roseberry Public House on the High Street in Stokesley features hikers about to ascend the Topping. It was commissioned by a previous landlord, Gary Simm.

Left: A private view in …
Arncliffe Hall: this is a wonderful scene of the Goddess of Plenty hovering above Roseberry Topping in one of the plaster ceilings. The Hall was built in 1753-54 to the design of John Carr. In his classic series on the buildings of England, Pevsner described the house as a 'fine ashlar job' and was most impressed with the plasterwork. 'Inside, the house has some of the most spectacular Rococo plasterwork in the country. The staircase hall has a figure of Plenty hovering over Cleveland represented by Roseberry Topping, the characteristic peak, and by a cow and a cottage. The job is attributed to the York plasterer who worked in St George's Hall.'

Photograph reproduced in this book with the kind permission of Sir John and Lady Bell

Suggitt's Ice Cream The great-grandmother of the current owner, Peter Suggitt, started making ice cream in her kitchen on Waterfall Terrace in 1922, perhaps inspired by the success of Italian immigrants' ice cream parlours in Middlesbrough. The design on the cartons, featuring Captain Cook's Monument and Roseberry Topping, has remained unchanged from its inception. Two tubs are shown here, a 1950s' waxed paper tub by Mono containers and the current tub.

Roseberry Catering of Great Broughton specialises in catering at large public events such as Stokesley Show. Although the business had been established for a number of years it was renamed Roseberry Catering in 2004, with a new logo.

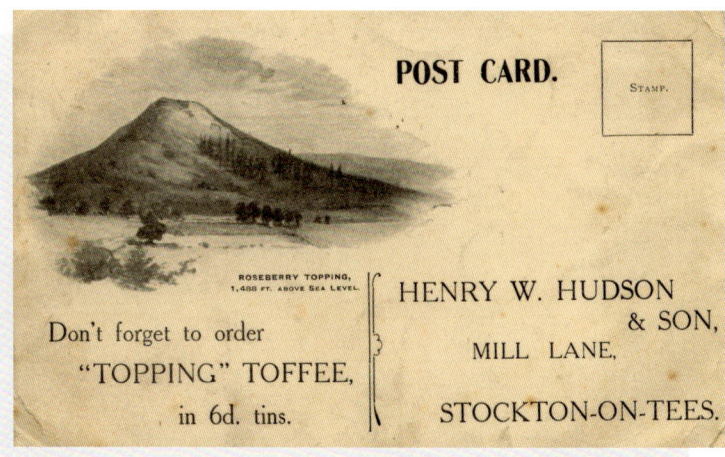

HW Hudson & Son ran a wholesale confectionery business in Mill Lane (which later became Dovecote Street), Stockton, from the end of the nineteenth century to the 1930s. Before the Second World War they used Roseberry Topping to advertise their Toffee. Presumably because either Graves or Ord was used as a reference, the advertisement unwittingly exaggerated the height of the Topping by 50%.

Fruit and Veg

The Rosebery potato is a second early redskin and the Lord Rosebery is a red dessert apple. Both were originally cultivated on the Earl of Rosebery's estate at Dalmeny, on the southern shores of the Firth of Forth. In Buckinghamshire, 'roseberry' is a dialect version of raspberry. Intriguingly, Mentmore Towers, the Rothschild's grand mansion that became Lord Rosebery's home after his marriage, is in Buckinghamshire. No doubt they had roseberry jam for tea.

A published view on ... the cover of a book. Roseberry can be seen in a variety of advertisements and publications, which often have no specific relevance to the Topping itself. This view from the summit forms the cover of the British Geological Survey publication *Britain beneath our feet - an atlas of digital information*.

LOOKING AT THE TOPPING – written by Alan Bunn, Hazel O'Sullivan and David Taylor

Lord Rosebery

Until this book was about to go to press, it was believed that there was no connection between Roseberry Topping and Lord Rosebery, apart from both having public houses named after them. But recent correspondence with the Dalmeny Estate, the seat of the Earls of Rosebery, has revealed that there is indeed a connection.

The Earldom of Rosebery was created in 1703 in Queen Anne's Honours List, apparently in recognition of Sir Archibald Primrose's support of William of Orange against James II. Primrose's family owned land near Roseberry Topping, and it is family folklore that he chose the title because of the hill and also because he liked the play on the words, Primrose and Roseberry. According to the present Seventh Earl, Neil Archibald Primrose, the variation in spelling arose because 'they weren't very fussy about spelling in those days'.

Succeeding generations inherited the title, the best known being Archibald Philip Primrose (1847-1929), Fifth Earl of Rosebery, often referred to as Lord Rosebery. Looking back on his life it is not difficult to see why this particular aristocrat became famous. In his youth he was a great gambler, was thrown out of Oxford for keeping a racehorse, and was rumoured to have had an affair with the elder brother of Oscar Wilde's 'Bosie'. But he is chiefly remembered for his three ambitions: to marry the richest woman in England, to become Prime Minister and to win the Derby. Surprisingly, given his youthful inclinations, he achieved all three. He married Hannah de Rothschild in 1878, became Liberal Prime Minister after Gladstone resigned in 1894, and his horses won the Derby three times!

His political and racing interests were continued by the Sixth Earl of Rosebery, Harry Primrose, who was Secretary of State for Scotland in 1945 and who owned two Derby winners.

Above right: Lord Rosebery as portrayed by the *Illustrated London News* 18 September 1909

Image supplied by John Weedy of Lancaster

Roseberry Topping in Jamaica

The town of Roseberry, with a population of some 18,000, lies in the Parish of Saint Elizabeth in south-west Jamaica. In 1837 the Estate of Roseberry, in the Parish of Saint Elizabeth, was owned by John Longlands. More intriguingly, since there must surely be a connection with North Yorkshire's Roseberry, in 1840 Thomas Hansill owned thirty-five acres of land in the Parish of Saint Dorothy which he called 'Roseberry Topping'.

Roseberry Topping in Wales

Between 1989 and 1991 the Brush Electric Company of Loughborough built a hundred Class 60 diesel locomotives. They were named after famous people or mountains, and the fiftieth in the series, 60050, was 'Roseberry Topping'. Today the Talacre garden railway layout in North Wales includes a model version of this locomotive. So there really is a 'Roseberry Topping' in Wales.

the origin of the name

A rose by any other name

To those unfamiliar with the North Yorkshire landscape, 'Roseberry Topping' tends to conjure up a vision of some 1960s' whipped-up dessert. The name has certainly gone through many twists and turns to arrive at the present form, and its derivation has exercised many Cleveland scholars and writers. Old manuscripts and Scandinavian history have been the common starting points for researchers; some theories are based on logical deductions from these sources, but some seem to owe more to imagination than reason. Delving into the origin of the name has been a pastime favoured by the clergy; half of the references used in this chapter were written by such gentlemen. In the end, one work stands out above the rest. In 1913 Major Robert Turton of Kildale Hall listed forty versions of the name, along with their sources and dates. Careful consideration of each led him to deduce that 'Roseberry Topping' was almost certainly derived from *Othenesberg*, conventional Old Norse for Odin's Hill.

Earliest records

The first mention of the name that would become Roseberry was in the Guisborough Cartulary, the foundation charters of Guisborough Priory, dating from about 1120. A translation of the description of the boundaries of land controlled by the Priory included the phrase 'as far as the great road of *Ohensberg*'. Today's bridleway from Aireyholme, past Roseberry and on to Hutton Lowcross, was probably the main route between Ayton and Guisborough in those times. The charters also referred to Roseberry as *Othenesberg*. A little later, in 1239, a legal document used the name *Outhenesberg*. These variations should not be seen as too significant; at that time it was not uncommon for the spelling of names to vary, even within the same document.

From Old Norse to today's name

Dialect variations account for the initial changes to *Othenesberg*, particularly from the thirteenth century. Locally, the English version probably became *Ouensberg* or *Ounsberg*, with occasional returns to the long vowel as in *Onesberg*. There were also regional variations in dialect, specifically *ou* to the north of the Cleveland Hills and *au* to the south. A good example is in the different pronunciations of Broughton, 'Browton' in Cleveland, 'Brawton' to the south. Finally, the Normans had difficulty with the *th* sound, and they probably transformed *Othenbergh* to *Osenbergh*. An example of this variation, with two versions of a place name, one used by the better educated and the other by the common people, is with the neighbouring town of 'Stokesley' or 'Stowsley'.

' For who can climb thy summit, and from thence
Behold that prospect, so enchanting, spread
Before his wondering gaze, nor feel its power
To cheer the mind and elevate the soul? '

Rosebury Topping John Ryley Robinson 1827

Between 1340 and 1424 several surviving legal documents used *Osenbergh*. These documents were probably written by educated people who did not live locally. When a local jury had to record a verdict in 1424, the written document used *Ounesbergh*. These two versions can be taken as synonymous. The next time the name occurs was in a list of beacons towards the end of the reign of Elizabeth I, as *Oseburye Toppinge*, the *n* of an unaccented syllable having dropped out. Although Newton village had became known as Newton-in-Cleveland by the sixteenth century, it was later coupled with Roseberry. This led to the change from *Osebury* to *Rosebury*, a particularly easy change when the words followed 'under'. Newton-under-Osebury and Newton-under-Rosebury are practically indistinguishable in everyday speech.

The transition from the old to the new name may have occurred during the seventeenth century. At the beginning of that century the Cottonian manuscript referred to 'Roseberry toppinge', and later Camden named the hill as 'Ounsbery or Rosebery Topping'.

Discredited ideas

The classic writers on Cleveland's history have put forward several theories for the origin of the name, usually slanted towards their personal view of history. George Young asserted that the ancient name of Roseberry was *Ohtneberg* or *Hogtenberg*, Norse for high-hill. John Graves offered two explanations; he favoured a derivation from the British word *ros*, meaning a heath or common, and the Saxon *bury* or *burg*, a fortress. Less likely, in his opinion, was a derivation from Odin. John Walker Ord believed that there were two possible origins for the name, a hill fort or a sacred hill, and while he correctly favoured the latter, his reasoning was suspect. Ord attached 'the highest degree of credit' to the Rev G S Faber's view that Roseberry was a corruption of *Ros-baris*, in turn derived from the high ground in Armenia where the biblical ark had come to rest, and applied to other hills by the Celtic Druids.

Canon Atkinson was pretty blunt in expressing his disdain:

> 'I find myself totally unable to regard the derivation put forward in Mr. Ord's quotation from Faber's Origin of Pagan Idolatry as other than entirely fanciful, and entirely unsupported by any scrap of tangible evidence, while Mr. Graves' etymological attempts in the matter can only excite a smile at their naïve simplicity & unconscious self-contradiction.'

After this one might have imagined that Atkinson would lend his support to one of the more plausible explanations of Roseberry's derivation. Instead he proposed an obscure route starting with the Anglo-Saxon *Hreosebeorh*, meaning the hill of the one who rages. The god Wodan used to chase through the sky in a raging storm. This was converted by the Danish invaders to *Othenesberg*, since their equivalent of Wodan was Odin. Finally, in some collective amnesia, this version was forgotten and the original reappeared, but in the anglicised form of 'Roseberry'. To support this idea Atkinson quoted the theory that *Hreosnabeorh*, from the poem of Beowulf, was Roseberry. All of this was dismissed by Turton, but in gentler terms than those used by the good Canon to dismiss his predecessors:

> 'It is equally difficult to believe that an old Anglian name like *Hreosnabeorh*, as that a Celtic name like *Ros*, could have lain hidden for six, seven, or more hundred years, no trace of it during that period ever having come to light, and then suddenly be reproduced, in the seventeenth century, by a people to whom Celtic, Anglian, and Danish were alike sealed languages.'

More recently A H Smith wrote that the forms beginning with *Ou-* suggested that the first element of the word was from the Old Norse personal name *Auðunn*. This is most unlikely since the *Ou-* spellings only appear in the thirteenth century, long after the Norsemen.

There are still occasional debates in correspondence columns and letters to editors disputing the derivation of the name. It is even possible to find generally discredited views, such as those of Faber and Atkinson, quoted as if they were accepted wisdom.

So we return to Turton as giving the most plausible explanation; based on similar Scandinavian names, *Othenesberg* was derived from the Old Norse word for Odin's Hill, Odin being the Scandinavian god of wisdom, poetry, war, agriculture and the dead. Roseberry Topping may have reminded early Norse settlers of some hill in their old country, where possibly sacrifices were offered to the god, or perhaps its majestic shape and isolation seemed a fitting place for the abode of the god. The existence of the old hermitage cut into the rock may give weight to origins in the worship of a god. *Othenesberg* was then transformed into Roseberry. The vagaries of place name derivations can be seen in Langbaurgh, a nearby ridge, and Roseberry. It is possible that they share the common root of *berg* or hill.

And Topping?

Topping probably derives from the Old Norse *toppinn* for hill-top. It became an old Yorkshire dialect word for a high hill, and also for a standing-up roll or curl on the forehead. Ironically, this second meaning seems more appropriate to the present-day profile. The presumed omission of a final *g* was 'corrected' by later scribes. The term appears elsewhere, for example as Blakey Topping, and can still be seen in Scandinavian place names.

The cult of Odin

Odin was a name that often carried a taboo, and the name is thus rare in both personal and place names. Indeed, the only place where it appears in this direct form in England is at Roseberry, making it a very special place. Where Odin appears directly in Danish place names, it is always associated with a cult site, as at Odense and Onsbjerg. Incidentally Onsbjerg, on the island of Samsø, is the exact equivalent of Roseberry.

Other local place names point to a special significance for Roseberry, for example Upsall on the other side of the vale of Guisborough. Upsall is equivalent to Uppsala in Sweden, derived from the Old Norse for high-placed halls. Bill Pearson, an expert on local place names, has pointed out that Odin had to have a place where he could sit and look out over the world. This could have been Roseberry Topping.

Below: In his diary for 1 October 1768 Ralph Jackson recorded that, at 7am, he rode to the north side of 'Osbury Topping'. From here he walked up to the high side of Newton Wood and through Cliff Rigg.

THE ORIGIN OF THE NAME – written by Len Groves

...a truly magnificent view...
Guisborough can be seen beyond...

landscape and geology

What a view!

Energetic walkers on the Cleveland Way long distance footpath will know that Roseberry Topping is a hill isolated from the main mass of the North York Moors. Their detour to take in Roseberry will mean a 230ft descent followed by an arduous 260ft climb to the summit. Their reward is a truly magnificent view, the Cheviots to the north, the sea to the east, the moors to the south and the Pennines to the west. The sea meets the skyline in a great arc from Huntcliff to the coast of County Durham. Upleatham and the Eston Hills rise to the north-east and north. Guisborough can be seen beyond the flat plateau of the Bousdale promontory. Fields on either side of the River Tees, and industrial Teesside, are laid out like a map. From here it is obvious why for centuries warning beacons and celebratory bonfires were built here. In 1585 the flames from the great fire of Darlington were visible to watchers on Roseberry Topping.

The summit is the best place to see Cliff Rigg and Langbaurgh Ridge, formed from a stream of molten basalt pushed up through the ground some 59 million years ago. A change of view slightly to the south brings the fretted northern escarpment of the moors into focus, as far as Beacon Hill near Ingleby Arncliffe, high above Ingleby Hall. To the south and south-east stretch the higher parts of the North York Moors, the largest area of open heather moorland in England.

Should the weather allow more distant views, Upper Teesdale, Swaledale and Wensleydale, with the distinctive Penhill, may be seen. Penhill was another beacon site. In exceptional conditions it is even possible to see Cross Fell, the highest of the Pennine peaks.

Opposite: Few attempt the Cleveland Way in winter. Those who do, confronted with this view, may decide not to tackle the detour to the summit!

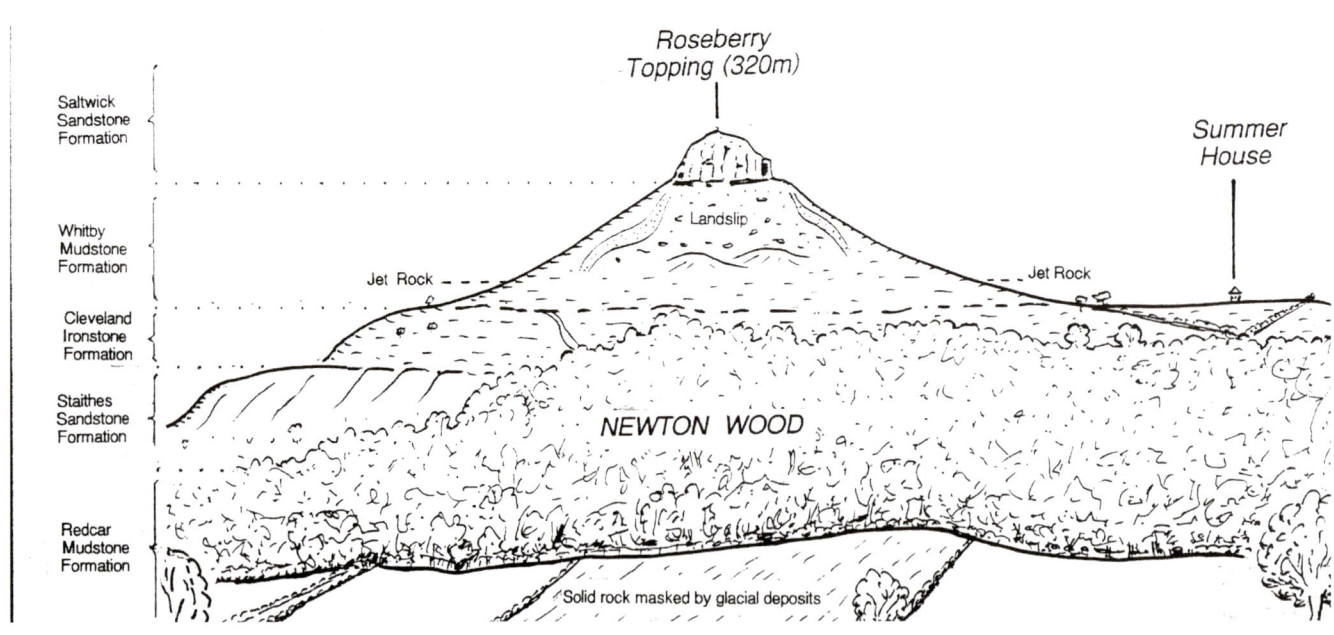

Geological field sketch of Roseberry Topping from the west

Diagram by David W Taylor

28 LANDSCAPE AND GEOLOGY

Two photographs taken from the same position by the Roseberry summerhouse clearly show the effect of the 1912 rockfall. In the 1910 photograph, grass-covered earth extends almost to the summit on the south-west side of the Topping. This material, together with a quantity of sandstone, then slid down the hillside to form a large and irregular mound at the foot of the slope, exposing a much greater rock face at the summit, as seen today.

1910 photograph from the Godfrey Bingley Collection, reproduced here by courtesy of the University of Leeds.
Colour photograph taken in 2004 by Alan Bunn.

The power of the image

The Topping presents a distinctive and memorable profile. It has been described as Cleveland's Matterhorn by many writers, although its present dramatic outline owes much to the rock fall of 1912. Before this time it was generally considered to be more like a volcano, and most old illustrations are from the Stokesley side where this appearance was more pronounced. After 1912 pictures tend to be from Newton, showing the almost vertical cliff edge on the western face. Almost alone among post-1912 authors alluding to the older volcano-like profile was Nikolaus Pevsner, who referred to 'that sudden miniature Fujiyama'.

Given such a striking appearance, it is only natural that the hill has been widely featured in books and guides to Cleveland and the North York Moors. In fact its use goes far beyond the region, and Roseberry has been seen on numerous magazine and book covers. The internet now makes all manner of images widely available, as an image search on 'Roseberry Topping' will readily demonstrate. This means that users of a particular image may well have no idea where it originated, leading to its use well out of context.

A little bit of geology

In geological terms Roseberry Topping is an erosional outlier of the moors. Millions of years of weathering and erosion have separated it from the main mass of the moors. Whilst this feature is not unique in the North York Moors, other outliers are less dramatic. Whorl Hill near Swainby, Freebrough Hill near Guisborough, and Blakey Topping off the Whitby to Pickering road, are all erosional outliers.

The steep slopes of the Topping tell us a lot about the geology and landscape changes over the past 200 million years, right through to some dramatic changes during the twentieth century. Roseberry is a microcosm of the geology of the northern parts of the National Park. Viewed from Newton the hill appears to be built up in a number of layers, with steeper and gentler slopes alternating. These layers are formed by a sequence of sedimentary rock formations, from the oldest at the base to the youngest at the summit the layers seem to lie horizontally, but when viewed from farther along the A173, towards Guisborough, they are clearly inclined from left to right. This inclination happened during their uplift in Tertiary times, when a dip to the east of about 1 in 30 was incurred. The same dip can be seen from Aireyholme Farm.

Jurassic Park

The solid rocks beneath the Cleveland Plain, that low lying ground between the moors and the Tees, originated in the Triassic age. This period ended some 200 million years ago, and was followed by 55 million years of the Jurassic period. The Jurassic rocks of the Cleveland Hills lie on top of the earlier Triassic beds, and include the Lower Jurassic and part of the Middle Jurassic strata. It might be claimed, with a smile, that the North York Moors National Park is the original Jurassic Park. These Jurassic rocks were laid down as sediments in water at the same latitude as central Spain today. The depth of this water varied; sometimes it was a shallow sea, at other times a lagoon and estuary, or a delta. Each environment had its own distinctive plant and animal life, and today these are seen as fossils. Because the beds are nearly horizontal, they appear on a geological map running parallel, almost like contours, round Roseberry.

Within the Jurassic period there are four groups, but only the Lias Group and the Ravenscar Group are present at Roseberry. The Lias Group, which forms the bulk of the hill, owes its name to the almost horizontal layering of the rocks, the name being derived from the Celtic for flat stone. The transition to the Ravenscar Group is high up near the summit.

Devil's toenails, iron, jet and alum

Within the Lias Group the oldest beds were laid down as silts and muds, and are represented today as the dark and relatively soft Redcar Mudstone Formation. It is unusual to see anything of these rocks because they are underneath the lowland fields, masked by the later deposits of unconsolidated material, but at the coast a common fossil in the Redcar Mudstone Formation is the bivalve *Gryphaea*, or 'the devil's toenail'. Later, in more shallow conditions, coarser deposits were laid down which now form the Staithes Sandstone Formation. This stone is of little use as a building material as it is thinly bedded. There are places in Newton Wood where exposed stone shows clear evidence of wave disturbance and current action on the sediments. Fossils found here indicate that there was a rich sea-bottom life with belemnites swimming in the shallow water above. This sandstone is more resistant to erosion than mudstone, and results in the steep slope so well seen in Newton Wood.

Continuing up the hill, and coming out of Newton Wood, there is a more gradual slope before another steep slope. This is due to the harder rocks of the Cleveland Ironstone Formation, a succession of ironstone seams separated by shales. The important seams, in ascending order from the lowest (oldest) to the highest (youngest), are the Avicula Seam, the Two Foot Seam, the Pecten Seam and the Main Seam. All were laid down as a chemical precipitate in a shallow iron-rich sea. Only the Main Seam and the Two Foot Seam were worked at Roseberry Ironstone Mine. The origin of their names is obvious; the other two seams are named after fossils found within them. The upper boundary of the Cleveland Ironstone Formation forms the platform on which the summerhouse stands. There are no outcrops of the seams on Roseberry, but they are exposed and easy to see on the face of the old whinstone quarry at Cliff Rigg.

Above the ironstone the easily-eroded shale and mudstone of the Whitby Mudstone Formation rise about 260ft. Among the fossils at this level is *Hildoceras*, a variety of ammonite. About 33ft up into this formation the Jet Rock occurs. Within a 30ft band of oily shale, pieces of the semi-precious jet are found. Jet was formed from driftwood of the araucarian pine, better known today as the monkey puzzle tree. Dead wood was carried out to sea where, waterlogged, it sank to the muddy sea floor. Jet has been valued for centuries and extensively worked at Roseberry and in the surrounding hillsides.

Still within the Whitby Mudstone Formation, the next rock is a thin-bedded Bituminous Shale, finally followed by the Alum Shale. The upper limit of the Alum Shale marks the end of the Lower Jurassic period. Alum Shale was extensively quarried across north-east Yorkshire for almost 300 years to produce crystalline alum, needed for dyeing wool, treating leather, and a variety of other uses including contraception and the fixing of loose teeth. There was an alum works in the eighteenth century at nearby Ayton Banks, but alum was never exploited in the Roseberry area.

Opposite: The upper boundary of the Cleveland Ironstone Formation forms the platform on which the summerhouse stands

Roseberry's cap

Examination of the next beds shows that there was a distinct change in the environment when these sedimentary rocks were laid down. The massive beds of sandstone forming the cap of the Topping, and underlying the surface of the moors, were laid down in a river delta and later compressed. There are ripple marks on some of the bedding planes and indications that the sand was laid down by strong currents. This sandstone is the Saltwick Formation, the lowest bed of the Ravenscar Group, and is good building stone.

At the base of the sandstone cliff on the west face of the Topping there is a bed of clay and siltstone of national importance. This is the Roseberry Plant Bed and it contains the very delicate remains of Jurassic tree ferns, cycads and horsetail stems, as well as very thin coal seams. Its importance is recognised by its designation as a Site of Special Scientific Interest. As such it has legal protection, and on no account should it be disturbed. In any case, fossils taken from here crumble very rapidly.

After the last Ice Age

The whole area round Roseberry was affected by the last Pleistocene ice advance, during the Devensian Period. Ice from the north and west, hundreds of metres thick, pressed against the North Yorkshire Moors. Deposits of clay, sand and gravel remain on the lower land, hiding the solid rocks of the area. The fields round Newton, and the great natural amphitheatre between Roseberry and Easby Moor, are covered by these deposits, mainly till, formerly known as boulder clay. Within the till, erratics may be found. These are boulders foreign to the locality, giving clues as to the places of origin of the ice sheets that carried them here. Granite from Shap, on the edge of the Lake District, occurs on the slopes of the Topping, dropped by the retreating ice perhaps 15,000 years ago.

The 1912 rock fall

Since the glaciers melted there have been a number of land slips, particularly on the west side of Roseberry. The steep western slope immediately below the summit has been unstable for centuries. As has been explained, relatively weak shales support the heavy sandstone cap of the summit. As the thin covering of soil and the shale are removed by erosion, the edge of the sandstone is undermined and eventually breaks off. As long ago as the seventeenth century the Cottonian manuscript described the passage of stone falling from the summit. In the twentieth century there was a spectacular land slip.

Sometime during the second week of May 1912, a large part of the exposed rock face of the Topping collapsed and slid down towards Newton Wood. We do not know the time or the exact day of the collapse, but it was probably in the early hours of the morning. The incident was covered in the local press, but in a manner that seems quite different from today's reporting. The writer was very concerned that the fall would have reduced the height of the Topping to less than one thousand feet, thus causing it to lose its mountain status. The style is very reminiscent of the nineteenth century Cleveland romantic writers, with more flowery prose and less factual information.

The article opposite was printed in the *North Eastern Daily Gazette* of Tuesday 14 May 1912. It was repeated verbatim in *The Herald*, which was only published every Saturday, on 18 May. The beginning of May 1912 was not a good time for the sights of Cleveland: a week before the collapse of the Topping there had been a disastrous fire at Arncliffe Hall.

Aerial photograph of Roseberry Topping, dramatically showing the effects of the 1912 rockfall. From this viewpoint it is not difficult to visualise how the mountain was originally connected to the main body of the moors by a spur of ground that weathered away leaving the Topping as a geological outlier.

Photo: Robert de Wardt, from an Auster spotter aircraft owned and flown by Peter Wood of Moorsholm

What was the real reason?

Of course we shall never know the real reason for the 1912 rockfall. As in many incidents, there were almost certainly several factors involved. It has been already stated that the west face was inherently unstable because of the geology. Another possible factor was the geological fault that lies directly in line with the disturbance. Although many, then and since, have deemed that the mining under Roseberry was the dominant factor, there may be an alternative explanation had there been prolonged heavy rain.

Forty years previously, at Clay Bank near Ingleby Greenhow, there had been a similar incident. In June 1872, after a period of very heavy rain, part of the upper escarpment broke away and slid down the hillside, obliterating the road from Broughton to Bilsdale. The geological profile here is exactly the same as at Roseberry, with a hard sandstone cap on top of unstable shale. Whilst at Roseberry ironstone mining probably contributed to the instability of the rock face, at Clay Bank extensive jet mining had much the same effect. Today the appearance of the escarpment in the area of the Clay Bank landslip is virtually identical to the area of the Topping collapse, confirming that the mechanics of the falls were similar. At Clay Bank the initiation of the slip was caused by the increased weight of sodden earth and the weakening effects of quantities of running water.

Mr J Theobald Butler of Emerald Lodge, Saltburn, could not forgo an opportunity to correct sloppy journalism in the reports of the collapse. He wrote to the newspaper pointing out that Roseberry was not Cleveland's only mountain, as defined by a height exceeding a thousand feet. There were several higher hills, including the location of the nearby Captain Cook's Monument.

Burton's defence

Joseph James Burton, as owner of the Roseberry Ironstone Mine, was acutely aware that many members of the public held him responsible for the event. Burton answered some of the criticism some years later. He confessed that the landslip caused much heart-burning to many people as being a disfigurement of a much-loved landscape. But he claimed that to others it appeared as adding picturesque interest thereto, and he personally thought that as the surface became re-clothed and coloured by nature it would possess an attractive beauty of outline which had been lacking in the even contours of other days. Perhaps surprisingly Burton's explanation was technically at odds with the now-accepted rotational slip theory:

> 'The landslip commenced by the earthy covering on the S.W. moving forward on the slope and buckling itself on its own material as it reached portions of the hill less precipitous in character. This covering seems to have acted as a strut to support the upper portion of the mass, and its withdrawal left the fissured, faulted and weak alum shales unable to support the heavy Oolitic cap, part of which had at some previous date been quarried. An enormous mass of soil, clay, shale and sandstone then moved forward down the slope, and huge blocks of the cap fell over and rolled on the top of the already moving material for several hundred yards, giving acceleration and force to the movement by added weight and impulse.'

And it's still falling down

If proof were needed that Roseberry would continue to crumble even without mining, small rock falls continue to this day. One only has to stand on the summit and look down at the sandstone blocks lying on the slopes below. There are usually a few that have that characteristic appearance of recent fracturing, before weathering and lichen growth occur.

One of the more spectacular recent falls was in May 1979. For many years there had been a free-standing stone column adjacent to the west face; the gap between it and the cliff had provided 'The Chimney' route for rock climbers. Then it collapsed, and the outline of some of the column can still be seen on the ground where it fell.

Given the nature of the geology of the Topping, it seems inevitable that it will continue to erode, causing more and more of the sandstone cap to break off and fall down the slopes. Indeed at some point in the future Roseberry will probably lose its characteristic profile, and our heirs will lose a powerful icon of the Cleveland landscape.

' geological time includes now '

prehistoric roseberry

Man comes in from the cold

The first evidence of early man around Great Ayton and Roseberry is from the Mesolithic period, about 8000 BC to 3500 BC. After the end of the last Ice Age, the climate during the Mesolithic period improved, with temperatures similar to those of today. This encouraged man to adopt a hunter-gatherer life, moving from one location to another in search of food. Large quantities of flint implements and waste have been found along the old course of the River Leven, west of Ayton, indicating that people set up hunting camps here, feeding on animals, wildfowl, and possibly fish.

Mesolithic people also roamed the higher ground, and flint artefacts have also been found on the moors above Ayton. There is evidence of moorland clearance by fire, a more effective way of removing undergrowth than by the use of stone or flint axes. This clearance may have been intended to extend the range of habitats for animals and birds, in particular to attract grazing animals, rather than for organised farming. Although primarily of benefit to the hunters, burning off vegetation could also have assisted the gatherers. It would have encouraged plants such as hazel, with its crop of nuts, which regenerates quickly after burning.

Careful examination of the surfaces of fields on the southern side of Roseberry has revealed several flint implements dating to the Late Mesolithic period, approximately 5000 BC. With an abundance of natural resources in the area, small Mesolithic groups could have lived in relative ease with no need to travel any great distances. No doubt they did make trips to meet up with neighbouring groups for social and trade purposes, but their longest journeys may have been made to visit ritual sites. The inspiring presence of Roseberry Topping probably drew people from far and wide, and there is little doubt that Roseberry was a very important place during this period.

The New Stone Age

Gradually, people began to herd animals rather than hunt them, and to clear forest and scrub for cultivation. The hunter-gatherer life changed into a more sedentary existence, based on permanent settlements, with an accompanying increase in population. These changes were complete by about 3500 BC, the start of the Neolithic period. Although there is very little evidence of Neolithic settlement sites in North Yorkshire, the chambered cairn complex on Ayton Moor, within a mile of the Topping, probably dates from this time. It continued to be used during the later Bronze Age.

The Bronze Age

Flint blades and tools became highly developed, and their use continued well into the Bronze Age. Copper and gold came into use around 2500 BC, but their use was initially confined to ornamental work due to the softness of the metal. Once it had been discovered that alloying copper with tin produced the harder material, bronze, metal tools appeared. Bronze axes, whether for use in clearing timber, defending property, or purely as high-status items, perhaps characterise this period more than any other artefact. The famous Bronze Age hoard found on Roseberry, which is the subject of another chapter, contained several axes and an axe mould.

Bronze Age dwellings made little impact on the ground, and are thus elusive to detect today. Boundaries were sometimes marked out by a line of shallow pits, and this gives us one possible explanation for some of the pits around Roseberry, which are discussed elsewhere in this book. Bronze Age burial and cremation sites, consisting of clusters of round barrows or stone-built cairns, are a common feature of the moors. Cremated remains were placed in pottery urns, and sometimes grave goods, occasionally including items made from jet, accompanied the burial. Jet could be found under the surface of Roseberry's slopes, and it is quite possible that it was extracted here during the Bronze Age.

As the Bronze Age progressed, there were further improvements in the climate, so that by 1500 BC farming was possible on higher ground. Perhaps because people felt more in control of their own environment, monument building declined. All effort was concentrated on farming, with more organised field systems and animal enclosures.

Increasing populations put pressure on the available resources, turning the settlers' minds to the defence of their property. It is open to question whether the reason for building ditches, banks and palisades during this period was to keep domesticated animals in or to keep hostile humans out. Some later Bronze Age settlements and individual farmsteads were probably located on hilltops for defensive purposes, and inevitably bronze weapons appeared, in the form of swords and spearheads.

The Iron Age

By the end of the Bronze Age, Britain's population had grown far beyond the levels of the hunter-gatherer period. Whilst the majority of people were probably direct descendants of local Neolithic families, there would have been some new blood, either from peaceful immigrants or from invaders. Farming methods were improved and superior tools were manufactured from iron, causing bronze to fall out of common use for tools around 600 BC. The period from this date until the Roman Conquest is known as the Iron Age.

Unfortunately, the increase in population coincided with a time of deteriorating climate across northern Europe. As the temperatures dropped, land became more valuable because less was available for farming and settlement, and there was increasing competition for the remaining usable land. Tribes began to defend their territories, the Iron Age being typified by the appearance of large defensive hill forts. Several hill forts remain in North Yorkshire, but there is no evidence of one at Roseberry, in spite of the dreams of past authors. In any case, the summit would seem far too small an area to be used defensively. The nearest hill fort is on Eston Nab, about six miles to the north. Although the initial appearance of hill forts might suggest an environment of local rivalries and skirmishes, by the time of the Roman invasion virtually the whole of Yorkshire was part of a confederacy of families and tribes known as the Brigantes. The Brigantes, initially allies of the Roman Empire, were later caught up in the civil wars, and found themselves pitted against the legions.

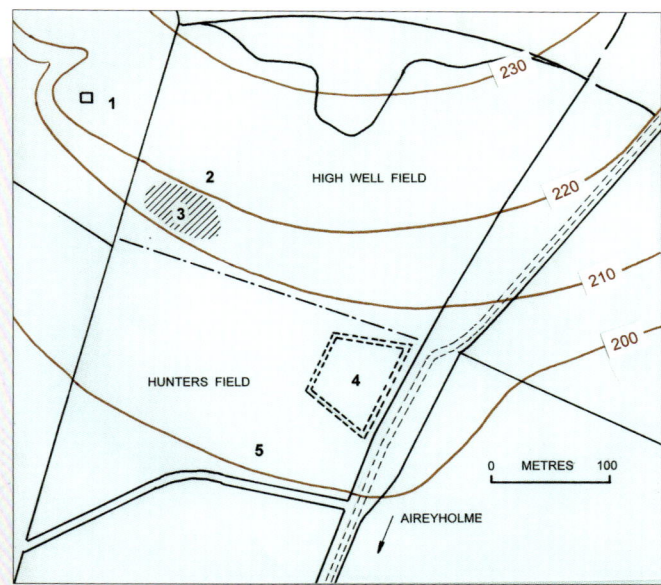

Map showing the position of prehistoric sites to the south of Roseberry Topping. The two named fields, shown in the 1847 Tithe Map, were combined into one during the 20th century.

1 Summerhouse (included only for location purposes)
2 Approximate position of spring
3 Probable region of the Bronze Age hoard discovery
4 Iron Age enclosure
5 Approximate position of quern stones found in hedge

Mapping by Richard Morrissey and Ian Pearce

Evidence of Iron Age settlement sites is widespread across North Yorkshire. Enclosed sites surrounded by earthworks can be seen over much of the moors, including the one at Roseberry described above. On nearby Great Ayton Moor there is a similar enclosure, and a group of five roundhouses near Percy Cross Rigg was discovered and excavated by Roland Close in the 1970s. Field systems considered to date from this period are also evident on the moors, although by this period the soils would have become considerably depleted due to farming since Neolithic times.

Elsewhere, where centuries of ploughing have levelled the surface, crop marks indicate Iron Age sites. With the increasing use of aerial photography, many sites have been discovered in recent years through their tell-tale crop marks. Old ditches, originally dug into clay and later filled with topsoil, are moisture retentive. They give the new crop an early start and, more noticeably, yield an extra supply of nutrients for the mature crop. Crop marks are most visible as areas of green during summer droughts while cereal crops are ripening. The Roseberry Iron Age enclosure can only really be seen by its crop mark at certain times of the year.

Roseberry's Iron Age enclosure

A typical Iron Age site would consist of a rectangular bank and ditch enclosure, containing one or more round houses. Agricultural activity would have almost certainly extended well beyond the enclosures, but generally few traces remain. At Roseberry, aerial photographs show a roughly rectangular crop mark in the field to the west of the existing bridleway up from Aireyholme. There is also a second, less well-defined, linear crop mark to the southwest. The route of the bridleway itself may even pre-date the enclosure. Whilst no burial or ritual monuments have been found in the vicinity, there are the sites of several other dwellings, showing up as circular crop marks.

The enclosure is situated on what is now cultivated farmland. At an elevation of 210m, the area is protected from northerly winds by the Topping and also by the terrace of the ironstone series immediately above. The entire site has a south-facing aspect with a large area of manageable land, ideally suited to mixed farming. Early farmers would have benefited from deep soils built up over several thousand years of vegetation. They often divided up the land following natural features, as is likely to have been the case here. To the north lies the slope of Roseberry, to the east is Howden Gill, and to the west the steep hillside within Newton Wood. These boundaries enclose enough useable land to make sustainable living possible.

Design of the enclosure

The aerial photograph shows the main feature to be the enclosure, which is some 300ft along its longest edge. There are several linear crop marks close by, but there does not appear to be any discernable central circle indicative of a dwelling within the enclosure. However, this does not prove the absence of such a dwelling, since a hut would require far less excavation than the ditch marking out the enclosure. The ditch could well have been up to six feet in depth, from the evidence of other local sites, and this would ensure its survival as a crop mark today. Excavated material would have been used to form a large bank, probably on the inside of the ditch, although enclosures do exist with external banks, such as the example on Great Ayton Moor. Even a six foot ditch and corresponding bank, possibly surmounted by a wooden palisade, would only serve to keep livestock inside, with perhaps some defence against wild bear and wolves. It would not really have been proof against human attack, and in any case the proximity of the overlooking terrace would present an excellent vantage point from which to launch any attack.

Photograph showing the crop mark made by the Iron Age enclosure to the south of Roseberry Topping. The outline of the enclosure can only be seen from the air, and then only under certain growing conditions. *Photograph by courtesy of Blaise Vyner*

much like pieces of natural sandstone. The upper bun-shaped piece would have been held in position on the base by means of a metal pivot, with wooden handles fixed into the holes on the sides. Grain was poured into the hopper in the upper stone, which was then turned back and forth allowing the grain to fall down the hole in the centre onto the grinding surface. The ground flour would then escape from around the edges of the quern.

Excavations at Thorpe Thewles, to the north of Stockton, have provided some information about animal husbandry, although unlike Roseberry this is a low-lying site. Celtic Shorthorn cattle, now extinct, provided milk, beef, leather, bone, horn and manure, as well as pulling a simple plough. Iron Age sheep, such as the Soay which still survives on Scottish islands, were used for milk and wool, rather than meat. Goats and pigs were also kept.

Horses may have been status symbols as much as farm animals, and equine designs occur frequently in Celtic art. The modern descendant of the Celtic horse is probably the Exmoor pony, a tough, independent animal. Caesar wrote of the fearsome prowess of the Celts in their two-horse chariots, during battles fought in south-east England, and described the Brigantes as horse-riding warriors.

Dogs, too, have been an essential companion to man since the early Mesolithic period, the native wolves having been first domesticated at that time. An asset on hunting expeditions, dogs also proved their worth at home. With far more acute senses than man, they would give an early warning of visitors, whether welcome or not.

Above: These two beehive querns were found some years ago in the hedge forming the southern boundary to the field containing the Iron Age enclosure, and within a hundred yards of the enclosure.

Any old iron?

Excavations of Iron Age sites have shown that the skill of iron smelting had developed into a well-practiced craft. Evidence of bowl furnaces, constructed from clay, has been found at several sites on the North Yorkshire Moors, and a whole furnace survives at Levisham Moor. Locally, evidence is limited to the single piece of cinder from ironworking, found on the floor of a hut during excavations on Great Ayton Moor. Since there would have been easy access to ironstone, and because the ironstone was of better quality than ores used elsewhere, it is disappointing that no evidence for early iron working around Roseberry has yet been discovered.

Life at Iron Age Roseberry

Despite the possibility of tribal warfare and invasions from the North Sea, the Iron Age people settling around Roseberry would still have managed to live a reasonable life, being fairly self-sufficient. There was fresh running water and plenty of wood. They enjoyed a varied diet, and were proficient in making most things necessary to their lives, no doubt benefiting from living in extended families where skills could readily be passed on to the next generation. When goods from outside were needed, there was a well-established barter system, and itinerant merchants would pass by. Roseberry, a notable landmark, perhaps with religious significance, may have encouraged passing traffic. Also, being near the coast, the area around Roseberry would be convenient for any new continental imports. Locally-mined jet may have been a valuable exchange commodity.

Finally, at the end of a hard day, the Iron Age families living at the foot of Roseberry could watch the setting sun over Cliff Rigg, colouring the western slopes of the Topping a fiery red.

Prehistoric society, ritual and religion

To return briefly to the Mesolithic period, it is true that the move to fixed settlements provided a more secure, predictable lifestyle. But such a lifestyle did have a cost. In the hunter-gatherer society a group was limited to the number that the natural environment could support, and food was relatively easy to come by. Farming, however, required much more human input. Although organised farming produced an overall increase in available food, leading to population growth and inter-group trading, the old ways were never completely abandoned. Even today, the drive to hunt and gather is still present within us, whether shooting grouse or picking bilberries.

Population growth had increased the demand for land suitable for cultivation. Initially, the better drained soils would have been used for farming, but gradually, through forest and scrub clearance, boundaries were expanded. Land and property ownership, and the organisation of labour, became important aspects of the economy. Formal boundaries appeared, as did social hierarchies to control the local population. With property and ownership came status, and with status came divisions within society. A sudden deterioration in climate around 1150 BC may have caused harvests to fail, leading to widespread hardship and famine. Very likely, trade between communities was replaced by aggression, leading to boundaries being reinforced, strategic sites being fortified, and bronze being used to manufacture spears and swords, as well as agricultural and domestic items.

Whilst we may make some reasonable deductions about prehistoric society, dealing with ritual and religion is much more difficult. The danger of reading too much into the limited archaeological evidence is illustrated by the nineteenth century fascination with the Druids, extending to a suggestion that there were human sacrifices on Roseberry Topping. With this caveat in mind we must proceed with caution. It is likely that the Mesolithic world was defined by the landscape, and that important features within the landscape assumed particular importance. If so, Roseberry Topping could have played a key role in any common belief system at that time.

As people increasingly controlled their environment and organised themselves into larger social groups, more formalised rituals probably emerged. At first these may have been focussed on natural objects such as trees and springs, sun and stars; a worship of creation rather than a creator. Later, more organised cults might have appeared, with some individuals assuming a leading role in the ritual practices. This new organisation would have enabled the massive building programmes of the later Neolithic and Bronze Age periods.

Some nineteenth century authors were much taken with what were seen as pagan religions, especially that of the Druids. The mysterious engraved plate found with the Roseberry hoard does seem to have some ritual connections, although it is difficult for us to be as certain as Faber that it was the Archdruid's breastplate.

The Roman invasion brought the state religion of the Roman Empire, initially in the form of a range of deities each with specific roles, followed by Christianity with its single god and creator. By that time there would have been a heady mix of beliefs in northern England, including contributions from indigenous traditions, from later invaders and settlers, and from the Roman Empire itself.

It is difficult to know how closely Roseberry was linked with some of these beliefs. There are several reasons why the hill could have been a site for rituals. It was certainly a significant landmark and it contained valuable minerals. Much later references to a hermitage at the summit and to the Holy Well, hint at a possible religious significance in earlier times.

. . . colouring the . . . slopes of the
Topping a fiery red . . .

. . . about halfway up the hill south of the summerhouse . . .

The Bronze Age hoard

5

Roseberry's hoard

Probably the most exciting archaeological find around Great Ayton was the Roseberry hoard discovered in 1826. It was a collection of bronze implements, including a two-piece mould, axes, and gouges. The hoard was discovered by a labourer working for George Jackson on the slopes of Roseberry Topping. Jackson, who lived at Tanton House, near Stokesley, owned land around Great Ayton including Aireyholme Farm. He kept the hoard for several years, knowing it was valuable, but having little interest in archaeology he passed it to William Nicholson of Egglescliffe. Nicholson, after lending the hoard to John Walker Ord, later sold it to Thomas Bateman of Derbyshire, who was to build up a large archaeological collection. After Bateman's death much of this collection was bought by the Sheffield City Museum.

Bronze smiths and their hoards

As the Bronze Age progressed, the industry became more organised. Mining and smelting were concentrated on a few large sites, whilst the bronze metal was worked by many local smiths. At least some of these bronze smiths were itinerant, operating rather like travelling salesmen. The casting of the metal did not need any fixed equipment; a supply of bronze, some moulds and finished items for sale could readily be carried in a sack. These itinerant smiths would travel from one community to another, casting and selling tools, ornaments and weapons, and collecting worn or broken items for recycling. This method of working gave rise to at least some of the forty or so hoards of bronze found buried in the Yorkshire region alone. A comprehensive study of over one hundred hoards found in Britain and Ireland, by John Evans in 1881, showed that the items found at Roseberry were all typical of a late Bronze Age hoard, apart from the curved knife.

Why such hoards were buried can only be guessed. Suggestions have been to protect them from theft, or simply to store them in a secure place. Many reasons have been put forward as to why hoards were not recovered by their owners, ranging from simple forgetfulness to sudden death. There may be another explanation for their non-recovery. The first iron implements arrived by 700 BC and quickly replaced bronze. It is possible that it simply became uneconomic to retrieve all the bronze hoards and some, including that at Roseberry, may have been just abandoned. The Roseberry hoard has been dated towards the very end of the Bronze Age.

The original depictions by Mr Cartwright of items from the Roseberry hoard are reproduced here by the kind permission of the Society of Antiquaries of Scotland and the National Museums of Scotland. It is believed that they have never before been published. Cartwright's paintings show damage to the socket-heads of the axe and chisel, damage which is mysteriously absent in Ord's engravings and in the items displayed at Sheffield. Another doubt is raised by the illustration of the axe: the flank of Cartwright's axe appears smooth, whereas the flanks of the axe at Sheffield are ribbed. Cartwright's hand-written captions are as follows:

Fig 1   This fragment has been gilt (a) is a wire loop and there has been a corresponding one on the opposite corner. The three holes above the lunette have probably been for the purpose of affixing some other ornament.

Fig 2   This has also been gilt.
(Faber wrote that Cartwright supposed it to be a portion of a buckle. A hundred years later Elgee suggested that this item was probably a dagger sheath.)

Fig 3   There is an appearance of gilding near the edge of this.
(This is an axe head, open at the top to accept the stock, and with a securing loop. There is a fragment missing.)

Fig 4   This is nearly the colour of the metal which appears to have had a small portion of tin mixed with the copper.
(This appears to be a mould, with the two halves pushed together.)

Fig 5   Not unlike a gouge. Metal very soft.

48   THE BRONZE AGE HOARD

Rev G S Faber

George Stanley Faber, the Rector of Long Newton, has already made an appearance in this book in connection with the origins of the name of Roseberry Topping. Long Newton is a journey of some eighteen miles from Newton-under-Roseberry, but Faber heard about the Roseberry hoard and he approached George Jackson, hoping to acquire it for himself. Faber's version of what happened is important as it is the earliest description of the discovery and some of the items found. He presented an account to the forerunner of the Society of Antiquaries of Scotland in 1828, only two years after the hoard was unearthed. His paper was published much later, in the 1857 edition of *Archaeologica Scotia*. Typically of Faber, he was only interested in the hoard so far as it provided evidence for his own ideas of prehistory. He began his paper with his fanciful theory about Roseberry's name as the 'Hill of the Lunar Ship', and then went on to describe the manner of the hoard's discovery.

> 'About two years ago a labourer accidentally discovered, beneath a rock not far from the summit of Roseberry, and (as his expression was) *looking to the twelve o'clock sun*, a very considerable quantity of copper implements, some of which contain a portion of tin, and others of which have evidently been gilt; a circumstance which may serve to indicate their appropriation to sacred purposes. They are at present in the possession of an opulent farmer, on whose land they were found, and who unfortunately refuses to part with them.'

Jackson was clearly not going to give up the hoard just then, but he did allow a Mr Cartwright of Norton to produce coloured drawings of five of the items that Faber considered the most significant. Faber gave pride of place to a fragment of flat plate, which he said had been gilt, with engravings of lunettes and circles. He asserted that it was 'if I mistake not, a consecrated breast plate, worn by the Archdruid' and claimed that it exhibited the astronomical impress of the sun, moon, and various deities. Ord was probably referring to this when he related how Nicholson had told him that there had been a brass plate with an inscription, but that it had fallen to pieces on exposure to the air. Faber had a more plausible explanation for its fate, angrily railing:

> 'Unluckily, all the fragments, which I should think must be well nigh twenty in number, were much damaged, particularly the very curious gilt breast-plate, by the roughness of the ignorant labourer who found them; for, even after the discovery, without the least care or regard, and almost (as it were) through wanton mischief, the unlettered barbarian, I am informed, repeatedly struck his spade into the very midst of them.'

Captivated by his archdruid's breastplate, Faber did not even describe the other four items drawn by Cartwright, merely referring to them as fragments.

Much of the high quality of Cartwright's coloured illustrations was lost in the engraving included with the printed paper, and his descriptive captions were omitted. Fortunately, the originals have been preserved, and are reproduced here. Faber had to apologise for the long delay in producing the illustrations due to Mr Cartwright's absence in the West Riding on business, but the wait seems to have been well worthwhile.

John Hixon

There was a second contemporary account of the Roseberry hoard. In 1832 John Hixon, an attorney living in Skelton-in-Cleveland, submitted an 'Account of some ancient Instruments found in quarrying Stone on the South Side of Roseberry Topping in 1826' to the secretary of *Archaeologia Aeliana*. Hixon included an engraving of the same five items illustrated by Cartwright, but this cannot have been copied from Cartwright since it reveals additional details. There was also a sketch of a whetstone. Most importantly, Hixon's drawings showed exactly the same damage to the sockets of the axe and gouge as did Cartwright's.

William James Nicholson

William Nicholson ran a market garden in Egglescliffe. It was famous for its strawberries, which included a variety called Captain Cook. Nicholson seems to have developed an additional interest in collecting and trading antiquities. By the time Ord was writing *The History and Antiquities of Cleveland* Nicholson owned the hoard, and he sought the opinion of the authorities of the time, including John Graves, as to the origins and purposes of his bronze items. It was only natural that he should also consult Ord, and indeed he lent him the bronze artefacts for an extended period. Ord's opening sentence, at the start of the eight pages devoted the hoard, reads 'Several singular relics have come into my possession through the liberality of the owner, Mr Nicholson of Egglescliffe, which will be found peculiarly interesting to the antiquarian'.

The hoard was returned to Nicholson who, nine years after the publication of Ord's history, sold nine bronze items from the hoard to Thomas Bateman. In November 1855 he had written to Bateman offering him a stone axe, the two-piece mould and axes, for ten pounds. Bateman wasted no time in agreeing the purchase and in December Nicholson wrote advising Bateman that nine bronzes and a stone axe were in a box being sent by railway. He added a note saying 'I do not have any other things found at Roseberry Topping'. This implies that the other items found with the hoard, the engraved flat plate, lumps of copper and jet, and the whetstone, had already been lost by 1855.

John Walker Ord

John Walker Ord and his epic work of 1846, *The History and Antiquities of Cleveland*, are the subjects of other parts of this book. Ord was familiar with the new science of archaeology. He had explored the contents of tumuli near Eston Nab in 1843, and he had studied the many hundreds of pits between Hutton Lowcross and Roseberry, which he believed to be the remains of a two-mile long British village. With his eminence and interest in the antiquities of Cleveland, it is not surprising that Nicholson should have entrusted him with the care of the hoard for a few years. Ord recorded the circumstances of the find in William Nicholson's own words.

'In March 1826, as a labourer in the employ of George Jackson, Esq., of Taunton in Cleveland, was engaged in clearing away some blocks of stone on the south side of Rosebury Topping, about half-way up the hill south of the summerhouse, he discovered a number of ancient implements lodged in a cleft of the rock, about a spade's graft below the surface, many of them in high preservation, and others in a somewhat mutilated state.'

Ord was obviously very impressed with the collection. He commissioned an engraving showing nine items from the Roseberry hoard and, rather strangely, a stone axe. This axe had been found by Nicholson's father, possibly at Skinningrove, some time around 1815. It seems to have been associated with the Roseberry hoard and was sent

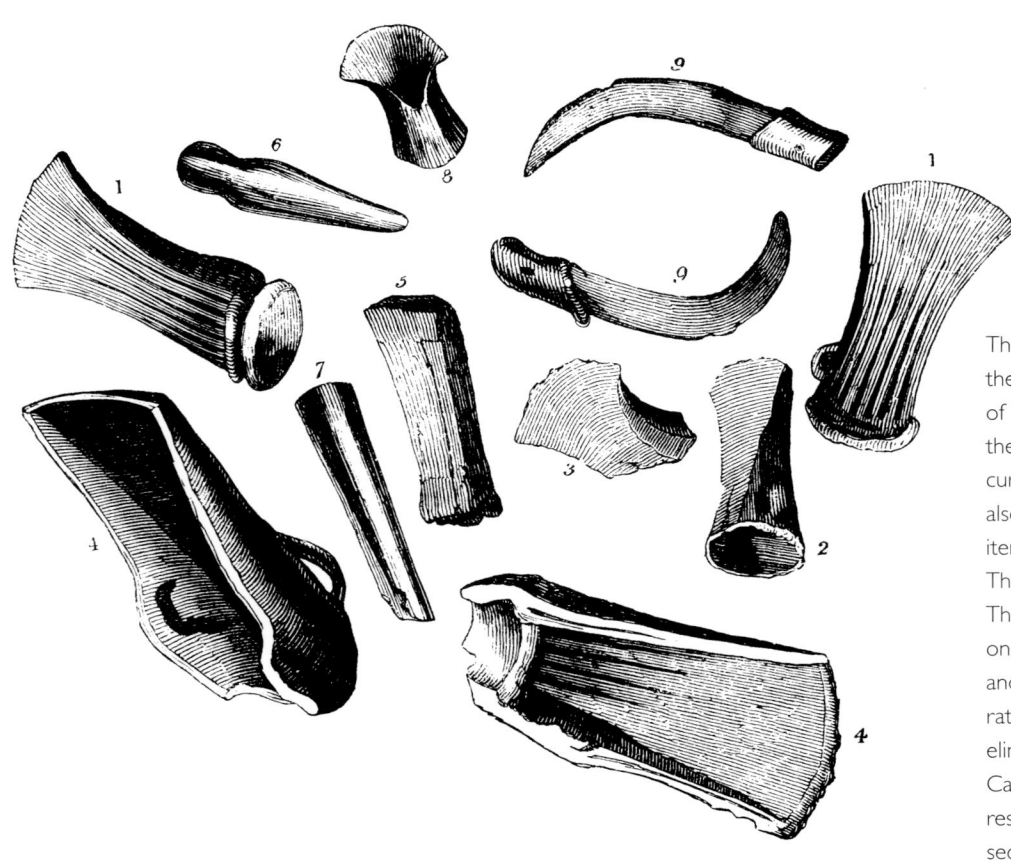

The anonymous engraving of nine items from the Roseberry hoard included in Ord's history of Cleveland. Note that there are two views of the axe (item 1), the mould (item 4) and the curved knife (item 9). The original engraving also featured the Skinningrove stone axe, as item 10, but this has been omitted here. The accuracy of some of the engraving is poor. The mould (item 4) omits the internal loop, one of the axes (item 1) has no socket, and another axe (item 2) is shown with a circular rather than a square socket. By a process of elimination, Ord's item 5 must correspond to Cartwright's Figure 4, yet it bears little resemblance to the actual rectangular cross-section hammer.

THE BRONZE AGE HOARD

down to Thomas Bateman with the nine bronze items from Roseberry. Ord described the bronze items as three celts (a term for socketed axes), one being a broken fragment, a two-part mould for casting celts, a hollow tube, three pike or spear ends and a curious curved blade. He also described, but did not illustrate, two of the items shown in Cartwright's paintings; a brass article in the form of two tubes, and a brass plate. Brass, an alloy of copper and zinc, had not been invented at the time of the Bronze Age, but contemporaries of Ord seemed to use the words bronze and brass interchangeably. The article in the form of two tubes had been considered by Cartwright as a buckle, and would later be thought by John Evans (a nineteenth century authority on bronze hoards) to be some form of clasp and by Frank Elgee (the celebrated twentieth century archaeologist) to be a dagger sheath. The brass plate was about eight inches square and the thickness of a shilling. It was said that it had carried an inscription and that it was much corroded. On exposure to the air, it fell to pieces.

Ord also mentioned that a large piece of copper and a whetstone were found with the hoard; both provide evidence that the hoard belonged to an itinerant smith. An accompanying lump of jet had probably been picked up by the smith during his travels around Cleveland. Although unconnected with bronze working, jet was already valuable at this time.

Ord's ideas of their use

Ord took a delight in dismissing some of the wild opinions as to the purpose of the items in the hoard. It had been suggested that the three axe heads might have been the heads of British arrows, Roman catapult projectiles, spears, or even the tops of walking staves used by 'civilised Britons'. Alternatively, they might have been chisels for cutting stone, for splitting timber, for sacrificing small animals, or for cutting inscriptions on ancient monuments. Ord reminded his readers that William Camden, that 'Aladdin's lamp of distressed antiquarians', had said that many spear heads, axes and swords had been found prior to the sixteenth century, wrapped in linen, and that they had been cast from moulds. But true to form, Ord could not let matters rest with the simple explanation that they were axes cast from moulds. He went on to pronounce them British battle axes, wielded in close encounter to defend the hill-fort on the summit of Roseberry.

Thomas Bateman

Thomas Batemen was born in 1821 at Rowsley in Derbyshire. His father was an amateur antiquarian and young Thomas soon developed a passion for barrow digging. He joined the newly formed British Archaeological Association, set up as a reaction to the rather stuffy Society of Antiquaries which found it hard to accept some unconventional aspects of the new archaeology. Thomas himself was anything but conventional, engaging in a long-standing affair with Mary Mason, the wife of a boatman on the Cromford Canal. At the Canterbury Archaeological Congress in 1844 he passed her off as his wife whilst finding time for some barrow digging around Canterbury!

Bateman also collected antiquities, and he purchased the Roseberry hoard in 1855 from William Nicholson. He had probably learned about it from *The History and Antiquities of Cleveland*, and he may even have met Ord. At the time the book was published Bateman was digging in York, where part of the walls were being demolished to make way for the new railway.

After Bateman's death the hoard passed to his son, who squandered his inheritance in easy living and became an alcoholic. Much of the archaeological collection was sold off to raise money. The Roseberry hoard, along with many of Bateman's papers and field notes, was purchased by the Sheffield Museum in 1893 for £1600. That is how the Roseberry hoard came to be at the Sheffield City Museum in Weston Park.

Where was the hoard found?

We have the two descriptions of the discovery, one from Faber and one from Nicholson, via Ord. By careful analysis of the accounts, which have already been included in this chapter, it is possible to locate the site where the hoard was actually found.

To the south of the summerhouse there is a steep slope, between the 220m and 210m contours. The steepness of the slope is due to the underlying erosion-resistant ironstone beds. This slope continues across the large field between the summerhouse and the bridleway between Aireyholme Farm and Roseberry Common.

The 1847 Tithe map shows two smaller fields here, Hunters Field and High Well Field, which have subsequently been combined into a single field. Hunters Field ended at the foot of the slope, and an old stone gatepost can be seen where this old boundary would have met the bridleway.

Between 1780 and 1831 the British population doubled, and from 1815 to 1846 the Corn Laws kept the price of grain artificially high. So farmers had a real incentive to increase the amount of cultivated land, often by 'intaking' an area of moorland by clearing away stones and vegetation. It is probable that in 1826 George Jackson was creating a new field beyond Hunters Field, the incentive to gain more cultivated land overcoming the natural disadvantages of the steep slope and the spring in the new High Well Field. While his labourer was clearing away the stones and vegetation prior to ploughing, the hoard was discovered. The description 'lodged in the cleft of the rock' seems to imply that it was discovered in a crevice in the ironstone, under the surface of the slope. It would be logical for the bronze smith to bury the hoard near a landmark, in this case near to a spring, in order to aid its recovery. The whole area has been extensively searched with a metal detector in the vague hope that some small pieces of the original hoard might remain in the ground, but absolutely nothing has been found. The location is on privately-owned agricultural land.

Reality, replica, or wrong?

For the past few years the Sheffield City Museum has been undergoing a major refit and the actual hoard has not been accessible. However, replicas of the Roseberry hoard were produced for the County of Cleveland Schools Archaeology Service. At the dissolution of Cleveland County in 1996 there was lively debate about which of the new boroughs should inherit them. By the toss of a coin Middlesbrough won ownership, and the replicas can now be seen in the Dorman Museum.

Assuming that the Dorman Museum replicas are exact copies, serious questions can be raised about the authenticity of some of the items in the Roseberry hoard. Contemporary illustrations, in the papers written by Faber and by Hixon, show five identical items. Faber also commented that the paintings were executed with 'perfect accuracy'. Three of these five items survive, the large axe, the hammer and one of the gouges. Only the hammer is recognisable as featuring in the collection at Sheffield.

The axe shown by Faber and Hixon is of a different design, and had a damaged socket. Their gouge was similarly damaged. Reference to Ord's engravings does not help since they are poor representations of the actual items. While discrepancies in Ord's engraving may be dismissed as poor draughtsmanship, the evidence in the papers by Faber and Hixon calls into question the provenance of some of the 'Roseberry hoard'.

It is possible that some of the original Roseberry items were mislaid either during the time they were with Nicholson, or when they were in Bateman's large collection. Certainly there was confusion in the period between Bateman's death in 1861 and the sale to Sheffield in 1893. About this time Evans was researching his authoritative work on bronze implements, and he was told of both a Roseberry hoard and a Cleveland hoard in the Bateman collection, although he suspected that they were one and the same.

Fact and fiction

Many authors, from archaeologists to the authors of local guide books, make reference to the Roseberry hoard. Surprisingly, they often manage to disagree with the only two vaguely contemporary accounts of discovery, by Faber and Nicholson (as quoted by Ord), setting off a literary version of Chinese whispers. Thus the date of the discovery, actually 1826, became 'about 1830' and later 'in the 1830s'. The location has moved from the south to 'the Topping's western flank' and even up to the summit. In other accounts the discoverer is described as a quarryman, and the present day location of the hoard has even been given as Hull!

Finally, there has been much speculation as to the purpose of some of the items in the hoard, particularly the small curved knife. This seems quite rare; indeed Evans wrote that only one other similar item had been found in Great Britain. Some claimed it was a sickle, proving that Late Bronze Age people were cultivators, while others said it was too soft to be a practical tool and was ornamental. There have even been suggestions that it was used by the Druids for the ceremonial cutting of mistletoe. This is one issue which is unlikely ever to be resolved.

The Roseberry hoard was inaccessible while this book was being prepared because the Sheffield City Museum was undergoing extensive renovations. The excellent replicas shown here are at the Dorman Museum in Middlesbrough, and reproduced by permission of Ken Sedman, the Senior Curator at the museum.

Items in the upper row, from the left, are as follows (references quoted in brackets are from illustrations by Cartwright on p48, and Ord, p50):

Hammer (Cartwright fig 4, Ord item 5). Ord described this as a hollow tube, whilst the Dorman Museum strangely refers to it as a handle for an implement. Height 3".

Gouge or chisel (Ord item 6). According to Ord, who described it as a pike or spear end, it still had the remains of a wooden shaft in it when first found. Height 3½".

Gouge with slight lip at the top (Cartwright fig 5, Ord item 7). Cartwright showed a fragment broken off the side of the socket. Height 3".

Gouge with splayed end (Ord item 8). Height 2½".

Curved blade with socket for a handle (Ord item 9). Elgee thought it to be a knife. Height 6".

In the lower row, again from the left, are:

Socketed axe (Cartwright fig 3, Ord item 1). Cartwright showed a fragment broken off the side of the socket. Ord depicted a solid axe, without the socket. Height 4¾".

Two-piece mould for casting axes with ribbed flanks and a securing loop (Ord item 4). The mould is open at the top for inserting a core to form the socket. Height 6".

Socketed axe, square-cross section (Ord item 2). Ord showed a circular socket and omitted the securing loop and flank ribbing. Height 3".

Fragment of axe (Ord item 3).

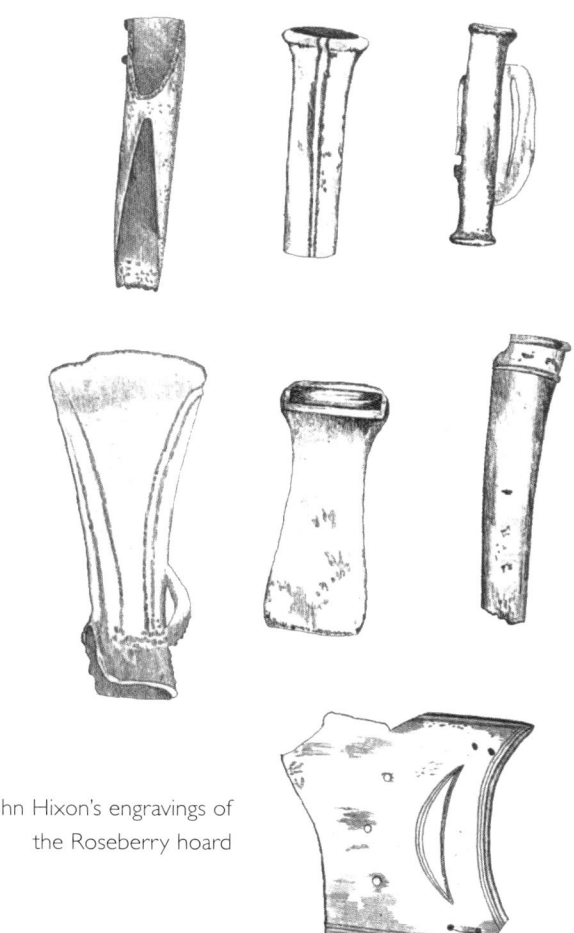

John Hixon's engravings of the Roseberry hoard

THE BRONZE AGE HOARD — written by Ian Pearce

Lino cut by Will Taylor

' Look, you can see Roseberry way over there in the distance '

sight lines or leys

Look, you can see Roseberry

When walking across the North York Moors, there must have been numerous occasions when people have glanced up and exclaimed 'Look, you can see Roseberry way over there in the distance!' One of these people was Brian Smith, a local archaeologist.

For several years before mid-2003, Smith gradually became aware that Roseberry Topping and Freebrough Hill could be seen from many of the Neolithic and Bronze Age burial mounds across the North York Moors. Of course this could be explained simply because such burial mounds were usually sited on high ground, from where it would be more likely that the hills would be visible. However, because of the topography of the moors, particularly at considerable distances from Roseberry and Freebrough, high ground certainly does not guarantee a view of the two summits. In order to see the hill-tops, many barrows seemed to have been deliberately sited where a dip in the skyline allowed a direct line of sight. Smith observed that Roseberry was visible from at least forty groups of Neolithic and Bronze Age burial mounds, although in a few cases the sight line had been partially obscured by tree planting.

The east-west alignment of Freebrough and Roseberry must have held some significance for these prehistoric people, and indeed there is a series of seven cairns and tumuli, all within fifty yards of this line. Although the Topping is not visible from Freebrough Hill, these cairns and tumuli are situated on the highest points along the way, and could be used as markers for a straight line journey from Freebrough to Roseberry. Only one location essential for marking out this route does not have

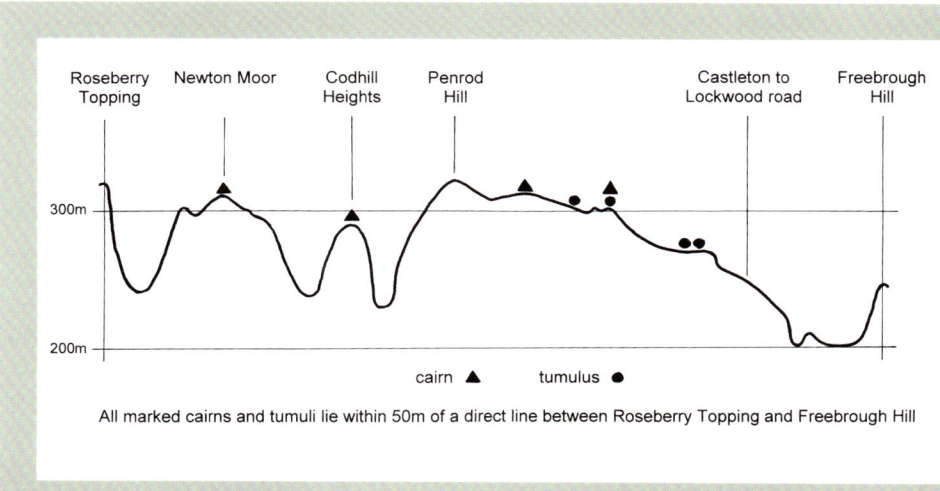

All marked cairns and tumuli lie within 50m of a direct line between Roseberry Topping and Freebrough Hill

There are several examples where a series of surviving tumuli can be seen along a sight-line from a particular monument looking towards Roseberry or Freebrough. Roseberry Topping and Freebrough Hill lie exactly along an east-west line, about seven miles apart. Both hills were almost certainly held in high regard by prehistoric people.

Diagram by Ian Pearce

a cairn shown on current maps. This is Penrod Hill or Pretty Hut Howe, at the head of Sleddale. However Canon Atkinson's excavations in 1864 produced evidence of a prehistoric cremation there. Later, Roseberry would become associated with the god Odin, and Freebrough with his partner Freya.

The information above was based on Smith's personal observations. He has not attempted to make any deductions from what he prefers to call 'sight lines'.

Leys

The observation that many prehistoric sites are in some form of alignment is nothing new, having first been made by Alfred Watkins in 1921. Watkins was a native of Herefordshire, and spent years travelling through the Welsh borders in connection with his father's brewing and milling concerns. After the sale of his father's business interests freed him from the need to earn a living, he devoted himself to photography and nature study, although he possessed no formal qualifications. From studying maps and from personal observation he realised that some prehistoric sites, such as standing stones, burial cairns and lengths of ancient tracks, fell into straight lines stretching for miles across the countryside. Watkins referred to the alignments as 'leys' and, in a paper read to his local naturalists' field club in 1921, he made the plausible suggestion from his evidence that they might have been prehistoric trading routes. He then spent the rest of his life trying to persuade the academic establishment to accept his ideas.

From leys to ley lines

Today Watkins' task to gain academic respectability for his theory would be even more difficult. His original idea of leys has been transformed into the notion of 'ley lines' with mystical significance and imagined forces. Believers have suggested that ley lines not only link ancient sites, but that they are associated with magnetic variations, earth currents, and astronomical positions. They claim that early man was somehow more attuned to nature than we are today and could detect ley lines, and so use them for the routes of tracks and for sites of spiritual significance. Ley lines are also said to be detectable using dowsing rods because of their so-called 'cosmic energy'. In the past few years the internet has given believers in mystery, conspiracy, and the occult, a new means of spreading their ideas and a great many websites are devoted to such topics.

Points where ley lines intersect are believed to have held particular importance, especially where several lines are involved. A notable example on the North York Moors is at Blakey Topping, near the Hole of Horcum, where no fewer than twelve ley lines radiate out to virtually every feature in the surrounding moorland.

Roseberry Topping is another place where several

ley lines intersect. One runs from the summit south-eastwards, following pretty well the line of the whinstone dyke. It goes through Scale Cross near Castleton, along part of Castleton High Street, and then over the moors to Ann's Cross east of Goathland. On this line there is a 'holed stone', a standing stone six feet six inches high with a hole at eye level, allegedly used as some kind of terrestrial or celestial indicator.

What does it all mean?

There are a great many cairns and tumuli on the North York Moors, and no doubt dozens of interconnecting lines could be drawn through different series of such sites. However, the line of prehistoric sites along the line between Roseberry and Freebrough must have been deliberate, as with some other alignments elsewhere on the moors. It is very likely that cairns were used to mark out straight line routes between important prehistoric sites. It is also very likely, given their shape and prominence in the landscape, that Roseberry Topping and Freebrough Hill were sites of spiritual significance to prehistoric peoples, and that they appreciated their east-west alignment. Some other claims of the modern 'ley hunters' are less plausible. For instance, it is true that Canterbury, Glastonbury, Burghead (an old Pictish capital in Scotland) and Tara in Ireland, are all 240 miles from Roseberry, but whether this holds any deeper meaning must remain questionable. After all, if a series of circles radiating out from the summit of Roseberry were to be drawn on a map, it is likely that at least one would pick up several important prehistoric features.

> The question of any spiritual power of ley lines, or whether they exist at all, must be left to the reader

' What shadows we are, and what shadows we pursue '

Edmund Burke (1729 – 1797)

farming on the slopes

Cleveland farming

When Arthur Young, the first secretary to the new Board of Agriculture, rode into Cleveland in 1769 he was impressed by 'an immense plain, finely cultivated, and the inclosures adding prodigiously to the view', but he was appalled by the 'vast waste of desolate moor'.

Heavy clay soils made the Cleveland Plain famous for its wheat and cattle. In 1794 John Tuke commented that no other part of the North Riding, and perhaps even of the North of England, produced wheat in such quantity and quality. Huge amounts of butter and cheese, produced from the milk of the Tees-water shorthorn cattle, were sold through the market at Yarm. In contrast, the thin soils of the moors were only suitable for rough grazing. The southern slopes of Roseberry are midway between the flat, low-lying ground and the moorland, and have been used both for crops and grazing.

Early agriculture

That there is very little evidence of early farming on the slopes of Roseberry does not mean that none took place there. A mile away on Great Ayton Moor there are the remains of Iron Age field systems and animal enclosures. Pollen samples taken from under stones in the wall of the large enclosure would suggest that the moor was then covered with pasture rather than with the familiar heather of today. Querns used for the grinding of cereals have been found at Roseberry and on Great Ayton Moor. Less than a mile away from Roseberry itself there are cairns, probably from the same period. Most notably there is the Iron Age enclosure in the field to the south of the summerhouse. This was probably used to keep animals and may have been a habitation site. All this evidence of human habitation around Roseberry Topping implies that food was produced in the vicinity. It is reasonable to suppose that land here has been farmed since the earliest days of settled agriculture.

By the time of the Roman occupation the Brigantian Celts had abandoned their settlements on the moors. Dramatic climate change had made farming at higher altitudes more difficult, and the richer soils of the Cleveland Plain were found to yield good cereals and pasture. The Romans themselves were excellent farmers. At Ingleby Barwick, eight miles west of the Topping, evidence has been found of Roman grain dryers and a horse-driven corn mill. Their improved techniques were gradually adopted by the local people, and farms became larger and better organised. Remains of these Romanised farms, often and perhaps misleadingly called Romano-British villas, have been found in Cleveland. The moors were at this time probably used only for summer grazing.

After the Roman withdrawal in AD 410 Roseberry's slopes acquired the name *Ergum,* which eventually became

Aireyholme, meaning summer pasture in the mountains. Documents written before the Norman invasion suggest that arable crops were grown up to the 650ft level in Cleveland. This would have included the slopes of Roseberry Topping. Indeed, evidence of early cultivation is shown by an area of ridge and furrow high on the slopes, above the site of the Roseberry Mine drift entrances. The Domesday Book recorded that 'in Aireyholme Ealdraed held enough tilled land that could be ploughed in one year by one plough and eight oxen'.

Normans and medieval times

The scene of pastoral calm changed in 1069. William the Conqueror, tired of northern discontent with Norman rule, sent his troops to harry the northern counties. Probably based at Whorlton, his soldiers sallied out to destroy farms and houses, burn crops and murder many of the population. Seventeen years after the harrying, the Domesday survey recorded 'hoc est wasta' across many northern lands. In Cleveland's 120,000 acres there were only eleven farmers and 225 farm workers employed on the land. Half of the villages were left uninhabited with only three, Barwick, Marton and Ormesby, holding more than ten families per manor. Farming on the slopes of Roseberry must have been much reduced, and perhaps abandoned.

The beginning of the fourteenth century saw the flowering of medieval life, nurtured by the monasteries, and North Yorkshire had more monasteries than any other county. As the population increased, the lowlands could not provide sufficient food and areas of previously waste land were taken into agriculture as 'intakes'. The monastic houses of Whitby and Guisborough had established country estates, or granges, and livestock farms, or cotes, on the moors. One of these was on the Guisborough side of Roseberry, extending right across the moors to Baysdale with its priory.

We do not know how farming on Roseberry was affected by the Black Death in the mid-1300s, although the relatively isolated position of Aireyholme Farm may have spared its occupants. Even so, they would not have escaped the extremely wet weather which had flooded much of North Yorkshire about the same time.

Aireyholme and Roseberry, the common pastures of

the parish of Great Ayton, were under the authority of the Manor Court until 1658. Court records from 1647 show two villagers offending against the manorial rules relating to the grazing of animals on these pastures. Richard Mankin was fined for 'putting an unlawful cow in the common pasture', and Robert Ripley was found guilty of 'putting one mare with foal in Ariholm'.

In 1658 Ayton's three-field system was enclosed, including the common land in Aireyholme and Roseberry. Some 484 acres of hitherto unenclosed common pasture, known as Aireyholme or Eriholme, was awarded to John Coulson, the Lord of the Manor. Coulson had been the instigator of the enclosures and ended up owning about half of the newly-enclosed land. New farms, including the present Aireyholme Farm, were built on the common pasture. These new farms were a mix of arable and animal husbandry, and produced far more food than would have been needed locally. Money was to be made by selling Cleveland butter and cheese, beef and wheat to outside markets. Since then, mixed farming has continued on the slopes of Roseberry, although crops and animals have varied over the years in line with changes in demand and, more recently, with agricultural subsidies.

Eighteenth and nineteenth centuries

During the first part of the eighteenth century the upland farming areas were mainly given over to cattle and sheep. Roseberry's slopes would have been ideal for the rearing of sheep. Wool was an important export commodity; not for nothing did the Lord Chancellor sit on the Woolsack. Evidence of Aireyholme Farm's involvement with sheep is seen in the remains of a wall, part of an old sheep-wash, on the northern edge of the farmyard. This sheep-wash is situated at the end of the bridleway from Little Roseberry. The upper end of this bridleway is distinctly funnel-shaped, making it easier to drive animals from the moor and down to the farm. More recently the sheep-wash was used by other farmers who grazed their sheep on the slopes.

However, the main emphasis in eighteenth century Cleveland was on cattle. There was more money to be made from dairy products and beef than from arable crops. We have some evidence for cattle breeding at Roseberry in the second half of the eighteenth century. Bartholomew Rudd the elder (1726-1808) had acquired Aireyholme Farm in 1763, although he seems to have taken little interest in the property. His son, Bartholomew Rudd the younger (1769-1824), did not live at Aireyholme but used it to house his mistress while he lived at Marton Lodge. He was enthusiastic about the selective breeding of cattle, and was friendly with Charles and Robert Colling. Two of their animals, 'Ketton Ox' and 'Comet', achieved national fame for their enormous size, and are remembered to this day in the names of several public houses. Among the bulls bred by Bartholomew Rudd was one named 'Roseberry'.

An early pen-and-ink sketch of Aireyholme which shows evidence of farming around Roseberry, was made by George Cuit in about 1790. Fields enclosed by hedges are shown, on which cattle are grazing, and on the farm there are hayricks for winter feed.

South-east view of Aireyholme Farm, probably drawn around 1788, by George Cuit. Cuit has taken his viewpoint from the top of the bank on the south side of Aireyholme Lane. Evidence of livestock rearing is shown by the hayrick, the pile of manure and grazing cattle. There are crops or pasture in the other fields. In the distance the Roseberry summerhouse can be seen. Today this scene is much the same, apart from some changes to the farm buildings and the post-1912 profile of the Topping.
Image reproduced by kind permission of the Wakefield Art Gallery and Museum.

The end of the century, particularly the final decade, saw an arable revival which extended into the early nineteenth century. This was a result of the Napoleonic Wars, which severely reduced imports of grain and forced up domestic prices. Additional land was brought into cereal production, and it is probable that land around the Topping, previously used for rough grazing, was cleared and ploughed for growing corn. Many of Cleveland's octagonal horse-engine houses, with their threshing mills, date from this period. At Aireyholme the square brick-built horse-engine house probably dates from the early 1800s, and suggests that significant quantities of cereals were being grown on the farm at that time. Cattle and sheep would have still been reared on the highest slopes.

Even after the final defeat of Napoleon at Waterloo in 1815, the Corn Laws kept the price of grain artificially high. With continuing good prices, more land was brought into arable use. In 1826 scrub and stones were being cleared to create the new High Well field, leading to the discovery of the Roseberry hoard of Bronze Age implements. The spring giving the field its name just about survives today, later mining having drained off most of its water supply.

Soon after High Well field started to yield crops, an unusual number of wet seasons undermined Cleveland's agriculture. In a thesis on West Cleveland agriculture, Dr Peter Mitchell commented that during the 1830s much of the region's arable farming was in a poor state due to inadequate techniques, a shortage of capital and the absence of effective drainage. Eventual repeal of the Corn Laws in 1846 dealt an even greater blow to agriculture, with a collapse in grain prices. By 1848 it was reported that there was 'nothing but starvation spread over every parish'. No doubt those extra arable fields at Aireyholme were left uncultivated.

Tithe Map

During the Middle Ages monasteries had enjoyed the one-tenth tax on agricultural output, the tithe. Great Ayton's tithes went to Whitby Abbey, but after the Dissolution the right to Ayton's tithes was purchased by the Marwood family of Busby Hall. There were constant complaints over the centuries about the iniquities of the tithe and its manner of collection. In an attempt to make the tax easier to administer, the tithes were converted into an annual rent in the mid-nineteenth century. The Ayton Tithe Map of 1847 recorded all the fields in the parish, their ownership and tenancy, names, sizes and crops. By then the Rudds had sold Aireyholme to George Jackson, who died leaving Aireyholme in the hands of his trustees. It was being farmed by John Pierson at the time of the Tithe map. The map shows that the highest fields round the Topping were grass and pasture, while the remainder were arable. There was a small triangular plantation on the east side of the bridleway to Roseberry Common, which has now vanished save for a forlorn line of trees along its southern edge.

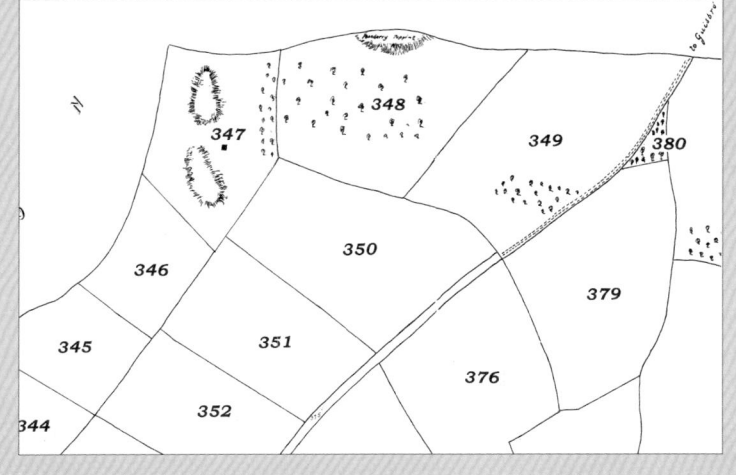

An extract from the Great Ayton Tithe Map of 1847 showing the fields around Roseberry Topping. The apportionment accompanying the map shows the names of fields and their crops at the time.

No.	Field	Crop
344	Great Nanny	Arable
345	Little Nanny	Arable
346	Low Summerhouse field	Arable
347	Summerhouse field	Pasture
348	Roseberry	Pasture
349	High Airey holme	Part pasture, part grass
350	High Well field	Part arable, part grass
351	Hunters field	Arable
352	Stoop field	Arable
376	Low Well field	Arable
379	Low Airey holme	Arable
380	Plantation	

There is a high proportion of arable land. High Well field, with its spring, was probably too wet to be used entirely as arable land.

Food for Middlesbrough, horses for Europe

The decades following the 1847 Tithe Map saw significant improvements being made on Cleveland's farms. Conservative Yorkshire farmers finally started to adopt modern practices pioneered in the previous century. Land was better managed through the widespread use of seed grasses, lime dressing and land drainage. Root crops such as potatoes and turnips were introduced. There were new breeds of animals and important developments in farm machinery. This increasing productivity meant that farming was able to meet the demands of the rapidly growing towns and cities, with produce being carried by the ever-expanding network of railways, which reached Ayton in 1864. Bill Cowley, the well-known twentieth century Cleveland farmer and author, thought that the period from 1850 to 1875 was the golden age of Yorkshire farming. The rapid growth of Middlesbrough resulted in a corresponding growth in local demand for dairy and beef products. Not surprisingly, Aireyholme increased its proportion of cattle farming, with milk being taken in churns from the farm to the new station only a mile away, and thence into Middlesbrough. This, too, was the golden age for Cleveland Bay horses, much in demand across Europe as carriage horses. Like many other local farms, Aireyholme bred Cleveland Bays, and they would have been a common sight grazing on the land around Roseberry Topping.

Golden ages tend to have a limited life, and the atrociously wet year of 1879 resulted in crops failing to ripen and being left to rot in the ground. It has been suggested that this was one of the contributory factors leading to the agricultural depression of the early 1890s. However, dairy farmers supplying milk to towns such as Middlesbrough were shielded from its effects.

Mining disrupts farming

The construction of Roseberry Mine in 1880 must have made the working of the land and the movement of animals around the Topping rather difficult. On the other hand, the horses used within the mine were fed from Aireyholme, and it is more than likely that some of the miners themselves lodged in and around the farm.

The first phase of mining under Roseberry only lasted a few years, ceasing in about 1883. The land around Roseberry then reverted to the production of cereals and the grazing of animals. In 1907 the mine re-opened, this time with a cable haulage system to carry ironstone to the incline by Cliff Rigg in Newton Wood. Wagons running downhill from the mine could de-rail at the tight turn where the line passed under the footbridge carrying the Aireyholme to Roseberry bridleway; apparently farm workers learned not to hang around at this point when a rake of wagons, laden with ironstone, was running down the slope! Mining ceased in the mid-1920s.

Twentieth century

In the first half of the twentieth century there were two detailed farm surveys. The first of these, in 1909, showed similar land use around Roseberry to that of today. Fields to the west of the Topping were arable, the land around the summerhouse was covered in bracken, and the fields around the mine buildings were pasture. The only difference from today was that the field containing the Iron Age enclosure was then pasture, whereas today it is arable.

The Second World War brought many changes to farming. The Ministry of Agriculture and Fisheries undertook a second national survey of agricultural land in 1941. The entry for Aireyholme Farm revealed that in the intervening years since the 1909 survey the proportion of land under the plough had increased by 50%. There were sixty cattle, forty-six hens and sixteen pigs. Six horses worked the farm, but the first tractor had just arrived, a Ford, supplied through the County Wartime Agricultural Committee. These government agencies dictated how farms were to be run and what was to be produced, even over-riding the advice of local farmers. During the Second World War Aireyholme employed more workers than any other farm in Ayton, with support from Women's Land Army girls and German and Italian prisoners. It is possible that the German prisoner of war graffiti at the summit was carved by farm workers during a lunch break in 1947.

Farming on Roseberry today

The southern slopes of Roseberry, and a small area of the National Trust property, are managed by Charles and Mark Phalp of Aireyholme Farm. With improved land rising to over 250m in such an exposed situation, it is not surprising that Aireyholme is classified as a Severely Disadvantaged Area by the Department for Environment, Food and Rural Affairs. The benefits of the southerly aspect are only marginal in such a situation. The land is well drained and ideal for the raising of livestock. Masham sheep produce fat lambs for market. Because of the uncertainties of the weather these lambs are not usually born until the beginning of April. Suckler Limousin-Hereford cross beef cattle are also reared. Wheat and barley are grown in the arable fields with the necessary break crops, such as oilseed rape, to reduce the build-up of pests and disease that would occur if cereals were repeatedly grown on the same ground.

The increase in visitors to Roseberry has resulted in real difficulties in raising livestock on the slopes of the Topping. Litter, open gates and loose dogs all cause problems. The result has been a reduction in grazing on some parts of Roseberry, allowing the landscape to become more overgrown.

Farming is coming to the end of a fifty-year period during which outputs were determined by government policy. In future, real market demand and countryside management will set agricultural priorities. It remains to be seen how these changes will affect the slopes of Roseberry, but it is to be hoped that some form of active farming will continue for years to come.

Graffiti carved by a German prisoner after the Second World War. German prisoners were housed at Undercliffe Hall, not far from Aireyholme. The inscription reads 'PoW, HW, 1947, Essen'. The 'W' might belong to either Wilhelm or Walther, prisoners remembered as working on the farm.

Since the end of the Second World War, farming on the slopes settled into a mix of crops and the raising of sheep and beef cattle. The last working horse went in the 1950s and with it a way of working that had lasted for centuries.

' See on the slope of Rosebury,
Fertile Aireyholm farm,
Mid mountain scenes so beautiful,
To us always a charm.'

The Hills and Vale of Cleveland James Milligan 1881

fox hunting

The Cleveland Hunt

For centuries hounds and huntsmen have pursued their quarry around the Topping. The Cleveland Hunt can trace its history back to the early eighteenth century, and for many years was noted for being a 'Trencher-fed Pack'. This meant that the fox hounds were fed and cared for by individual members at their homes, rather than being kept in a hunt kennels. Cleveland Hunt territory stretched right across the Cleveland Plain to the coast and included the northern moors as far south as the villages on the River Esk. The hunt might meet at Roseberry several times during a season, and the slopes of the Topping were familiar ground. Several of the Cleveland's fox hounds were named after the Topping; the lists from 1837-38 include an 'Old Roseberry' and two called 'Roseberry', all three being bitches.

One that got away

The most famous chase past the Topping took place on 29 January 1785. This was recorded for posterity in rhyme and song, but the tale does not seem to have been published until at least sixty-one years later. Until then the words had been passed on orally, so it was inevitable that several slightly different versions would emerge when publications began to appear. Ingledew's collection of Yorkshire ballads, published in 1860, included 'A New Fox-hunting Song' composed by Kendrick and Burtell. John Jackson, the master of Rudby School, had written 'The Cleveland Fox-Chase' in 1785, but it was not published until 1846 when it appeared in Tweddell's *Yorkshire Miscellany*. Both quoted the same words, but with slightly different introductions. Alfred Pease, in his 1887 history of the Cleveland hounds, printed the song and also what he described as a less polished ballad called 'Cleveland Staunch Pack'. There is yet a further version of the sixty-three mile chase from seven in the morning until four in the afternoon, 'A Song of a Chace with William Chaloner Esqr's Fox-Hounds, Guisbro' in Cleveland'.

The hounds roused a fox at Weary Bank, near Crathorne. They gave chase for sixty miles through many a village and round Roseberry Topping, until they came to the sea at Hinderwell where the fox finally eluded them. Three versions of the fox's flight past the Topping are given below:

> Then Newton, Rosebury, Hutton-Lowcross Gill,
> To each in turn he does go;
> And at Lownsdale, Court Moor, and at Kildale Mill,
> He tries for to clear – Tally-ho!
>
> *John Jackson as published by Tweddell*
>
> To Newton, then to Roseberry,
> To Hutton Lockerass gill;
> To Lownsdale, o'er Court Moor go we,
> From thence to Kildale Mill,
> With the huntsmen Tally ho
>
> *Ingledew*
>
> Through Seymour ward Cars and over Nunthorp deep stell,
> Then ascended the top of Great Roseberry Hill -
> A place of known safety – he scorned for to stay,
> So he chose the wild moore for to show them fair play.
>
> *Cleveland Staunch Pack*

One that didn't

Nineteen years later a fox chased by the Hurworth Hunt after 'a capital run' of fourteen miles over the moors was not so fortunate. It was killed at Roseberry Topping in November 1804. Both this chase and the one described in Ingledew and Tweddell remind us of the old days when the stubble was left on Cleveland's wheat fields until the spring ploughing, and when the foxhunting elite could ride over most land at will since they usually owned it.

Safe at the summit

As suggested in the lines of 'The Cleveland Staunch Pack' quoted above, it was not unknown for a hunted fox to seek refuge in narrow cracks in the rocks near the summit of the Topping. There have been at least three occasions since then when this has happened: in 1843, 1859 and 1971.

On 6 April 1843 the Cleveland Hunt met at Roseberry. The celebrated Cleveland huntsman Thomas Parrington, also known as 'Harkaway', noted in his journal that a fox 'took Shelter in a creek of the Rock on the very Summit of that far-famed hill'. The unfortunate animal was dislodged by a terrier, and after running through Newton Wood once again headed for the summit. He died within a couple of yards of safety.

All of this impressed Parrington, who wrote 'should I hunt in Cleveland all my days it is a thousand to one I ever see a Fox run into the top of Roseberry again'. He also preserved the fox's head in commemoration. Incidentally, Thomas Parrington's father was the last tenant farmer of William Chilton's 480-acre farm at Middlesbrough before it was sold to the new Middlesbrough Owners in 1830. Chilton had paid £15,750 for the property in 1808, and sold it for £30,000.

Tom Andrew, the first Master of the Cleveland Foxhounds This illustration was in Alfred Pease's book *The Trencher-fed Pack*, loaned by John Coverdale

In 1859 an article, 'Extraordinary Run with the Cleveland Foxhounds', was published in the *York Herald*. This described a five hour chase on the 1st December over thirty-six miles from near Hinderwell to Roseberry. Towards the end of this chase the fox went over Little Roseberry and High Roseberry, down through Newton Woods and round to Pinchinthorpe. He then returned to the Topping. 'He once more faced the hills, and in the pelting snow and bitter cold, with nought but darkness visible, on the very summit of Roseberry Topping, he found in a cleft in the rock a secure and well-merited retreat'.

The third incident was in November 1971. The Cleveland Hunt met at Morton Carr and, fortified with hearty refreshments, about eighty riders set off. After losing the trail of several foxes, they picked up a strong scent in the afternoon. The chase was on and led through Newton Wood and up towards the summit of Roseberry. Edgar Pickering, the joint master, and P Gulwell, first whipper-in, managed to ride to within twenty yards of the summit, where the fox lay hidden. But with dusk falling and the ground conditions very slippery, they conceded defeat.

We can now look back to Thomas Parrington's estimate of the odds against a fox hiding at the summit. With three incidents in 128 years, assuming an average of thirty meets per year, the chances work out at about one in 1300. So Thomas Parrington's guess at 1 in 1000 was to prove remarkably accurate. His foresight was plainly better than that of his father, who had thought that nothing would come of the planned development of the Middlesbrough farm.

the antiquarians

Antiquarian status

Five authors have acquired a reputation that sets them apart from others who have written about Roseberry Topping. Perhaps inevitably they are among the earliest sources, and they have been regularly quoted by most of their successors, right up to the present day. They are the virtually anonymous writer of the Cottonian manuscript, who was only identified by his initials, and William Camden, Rev John Graves, John Walker Ord, and Canon J C Atkinson.

The Cottonian manuscript (1604?)

This is a letter, now in the British Library, from an author known only by two initials that can be read as H Tr or F Tr. It is known as the Cottonian manuscript since it was originally part of a collection belonging to Sir Robert Bruce Cotton, a seventeenth century antiquary. The letter, which described the Cleveland countryside with particular reference to alum works, was addressed to Sir Thomas Chaloner the younger (1561-1615), a pioneer in the production of alum in North Yorkshire. It was undated but Robert Turton speculated that it might have been written in 1604. He further suggested, on rather slender grounds, that the author could have been Francis Tresham, a well-educated and much travelled Catholic who would later support – and then betray – the Gunpowder Plot.

The anonymous author provided the very first known literary reference to Roseberry Topping. He attempted to interest his readers by grossly exaggerating Roseberry's size and steepness, as when he wrote

> 'yt is wonderfull to see with what vyolence a stone will tumble from the toppe of the hyll towards a lytle towne called newton the noise that yt makes is soe terryble and the boundes alofte into the ayre soe high that as I am informed when one caste a stone once downe the hyll a horse that was fettered a farre of for feare leaped over a greate gate and onn incounteringe a bigge oulde hawthorne tree which only stoode one the side of the hyll yt dashed yt all in peices as a tempest and ran forward without stay tyll yt came to an earthen fence of a close into which yt perced as yt had bin a great shott, havinge run in a moment from the toppewhence yt was caste to the wall or fence aforesaid at least a large myle.'

He then waxed lyrical about the view from the summit, alleging that it was

> 'a vewe the like whereof I never sawe or think that any travailler hath seene any comparable unto yt albeyt I have shewed yt to divers that passed through a greate parte of the world both by sea and lande.'

The Cottonian manuscript is the original source of many of the oft-repeated stories about Roseberry, including the legends of Prince Oswy, the Roseberry well, the hermitage and Saint Winifred's needle.

' a vewe the like whereof I never sawe or think that any travailler hath seene any comparable . . . '

The Cottonian manuscript c1604

William Camden (1551-1623)

William Camden's *Britannia*, which ran through several editions between 1586 and 1607, might be described as the first guidebook for a tour of Great Britain. It had the imposing sub-title of *A chorographicall description of the most flourishing Kingdomes of England, Scotland and Ireland, and the Ilands adioyning, out of the depth of Antiquitie*. Camden presented, county by county, a wealth of archaeological, historical, physical and other information. In his expanded edition of 1607 he devoted a few lines to Roseberry, which were clearly derived from the earlier Cottonian manuscript.

William Camden had been appointed as second master at Westminster School in 1575, rising to headmaster in 1597. During his tenure he was able to compile his great work, *Britannia*, suggesting that his schoolmasterly duties were none too onerous. Indeed Camden must have spent much time and effort in the work, travelling the length and breadth of the country along the wretched roads of the pre-turnpike period. He clearly intended his massive volume for academic scholars, not least since it was written in Latin.

Rev John Graves (1761-1832)

Although born in Cumberland, the Rev John Graves spent his adult life in Cleveland. By all accounts he was a quiet and industrious man, whose careful research and unassuming literary style gave us the first true history of Cleveland. For many years Graves combined the duties of master at Yarm Grammar School and curate of Yarm. His *History of Cleveland* appeared in 1808 and contained no fewer than eight pages on 'Rosebury Topping'. Although he was primarily writing a scholarly history, Graves also recognised the tourist potential of the Topping. He opened his account with a verbose description of 'a gentleman of a few years ago, on his tour through this part of Cleveland'. His party set out from Ayton and took nearly an hour to reach the rocky summit, from whence the most enchanting prospect opened to their view. This view was of fields and farms, cornfields and country houses, vessels on the Tees and ships out at sea with sails 'fully-bosomed to the wind'. They left with regret, 'highly gratified with our excursion, the impression of which will dwell upon our minds as long as the faculty of recollection remains unimpaired'.

Graves then adopted a more academic style. He quoted from the Cottonian manuscript and from Camden, using Bishop Gibson's edition. There were footnotes adding further details; the stone known as the smith's forge was then called the Cobler's shop, and it carried many initials and dates, the oldest being 1527. This would be the oldest known graffiti carved into Roseberry's sandstone.

Like many churchmen of the time, Graves was much taken with fossils and how their existence could be explained, at a time when the Bible was held to be a literal account. He had found petrified shells, chiefly of the cockle and oyster kind, but occasionally scallop shells and ammonites, or snake stones, about half way up Roseberry in a large laminated rock. Although he correctly identified jet as petrified wood, when it came to the fossils he repeated some of the theories of the learned men of all nations who had 'exercised themselves on this wonder, to shew by what means, animals void of all local motion, or ponderous and mostly living at the bottom of the sea, came to be on high places at a distance from the ocean'. He quoted one of the learned men, Anthony Moro, who believed that the earth was once entirely covered by water in which the sea creatures lived. Sub-oceanic explosions had produced the mountains, and the sea creatures were thrown up from the bottom of the waters, to the summit of the mountains. Based on this theory, Graves bravely challenged the common view that these fossils were a result of the biblical flood.

> 'The vast quantity of petrified shells of different species, in so small a compass, proves that they were suddenly brought and left there; for had the waters, at the deluge, covered these places, and gradually ebbed off, which is the conjecture of some writers, the shell-fishes would naturally have followed the current, and made their escape.'

Graves ended his account of Roseberry with another reference to tourism. He wrote that until recently, on summer Sundays, many young people used to visit the Chapel Well (in the vicinity of the present Thief Lane on the outskirts of Ayton) to drink the clear water. Graves suggested that the hermitage might have been there, rather than on Roseberry Topping itself, giving its name to the Chapel Well. Finally, anticipating Ayton's vigorous temperance campaign at the end of the century, he lamented that his youthful contemporaries now consumed spirituous liquors furnished by the village innkeepers, and that water had lost its appeal.

Classics after Graves

Following fairly closely in the footsteps of Graves there were two writers whose books on Cleveland were to achieve classical status, John Walker Ord and Canon J C Atkinson. But before looking at their efforts the Rev George Young's two publications, *History of Whitby* of 1817 and *Picture of Whitby and its Environs* of 1824, deserve a mention. These were modest works, entirely without the mantle of grandeur adopted by some other authors. Young suggested evidence of a long history of rock falls on Roseberry by writing that the hermitage, cut into the solid rock, had by then fallen down, although later Ord asserted that 'ruthless quarrymen' were responsible. Young also gave us details of some early graffiti on the summit: '1595 Theodocca Cecyll', and 'R.C. 1625'. Ord was to add a Latin inscription carved on a rock which confirmed the 'reciprocal and inseparable friendship' between John Coates and Garbut Dixon in August 1817.

John Walker Ord (1811-1854)

John Walker Ord was a fascinating and complex character. The son of a Guisborough tanner and leather merchant, he abandoned medical studies at Edinburgh and moved to London to embark on a literary career. His charming personality overcame any perceived difficulties with his provincial background, and he was easily absorbed into the literary and social circles of the capital. Within the next few years, in his early twenties, he published a profusion of poetry, including a two-volume work entitled *England – A Historic Poem*. A fervent Tory, he also became heavily involved in political journalism. A mixture of political and other pieces formed *The Bard and Minor Poems*, published in 1842. It included a sonnet, *To Roseberry*, written in the previous year.

Three years later, he published *Rural Sketches and Poems*, which incorporated a nineteen-stanza poem entitled *Prince Oswy: A Legend of Roseberry*. This was Ord's version of the classic legend of the drowning of little Prince Oswy on the Topping.

His reputation established, Ord returned to Cleveland in 1843, and immediately issued a prospectus for *The History and Antiquities of Cleveland* on the first of April of that year. He must have worked at a prodigious rate, publishing this magnum opus in a series of twelve parts, culminating with a complete bound volume in 1846. Ord started with an idiosyncratic British history from biblical times, and a summary of Cleveland and its agriculture. This was followed

John Walker Ord
The handsome portrait on the opening pages of *The History and Antiquities of Cleveland*. This image, obviously chosen by Ord, combines the far-away gaze of the romantic poet with the smart dress of the cultivated academic.

by comprehensive descriptions of all the towns and larger villages in the area. He was rather disparaging of Graves' earlier work, but that did not stop him from plundering it where necessary, even down to quoting the erroneous figure of 1488ft for the height of the Topping. He also used the same spelling of 'Rosebury' as Graves.

Ord's description of Newton-under-Roseberry was somewhat derogatory: 'Newton is a small dirty insignificant village, consisting of a few miserable huts, with a wretched squalid population, and only worthy of notice in connexion with our famed Cleveland Parnassus, Rosebury'. This condemnation was not new, and Ord was merely repeating the poet Thomas Pierson's reference to 'dirty Newton' written over sixty years previously. Why they both painted such an unflattering picture of the village and its inhabitants one would dearly like to know. Ord gave a brief description of the hill's geological features and pointed out that the strata containing fossilised sea shells must have 'lain beneath the waters of the ocean'. Quarrying of the summit rocks attracted some scathing criticism; he thought that this was large scale vandalism. He also speculated on the origins of the name, deciding that it was 'a name of pure Celtic derivation, given by the ancient Britons', and meaning 'fort on the hill'.

The views from the summit were described in typical florid style, including one huge and typically Ord-ian sentence:

> 'The prospect from the summit combines at once the extreme of beauty and sublimity. Nature in her loveliest and most majestic attire: mountains, moors, rivers, ocean, with a vast and almost absolute infinity of intermediate scenery; towns, villages, halls, castles, steeples, towers, and spires – farmhouses, cottages, and simple huts – with forests, woods, groves, corn-fields, pastures, hedgerows, green lanes, - these, with sounds and sights of rural life and rural enjoyment, constitute one of the noblest scenes which it is possible for the mind of man to conceive.'

Ord even managed to top this extravagance with the claim that 'It may be doubted, indeed, whether any scene in Europe presents equal diversity and range of prospect.' Obviously, and in spite of any attractions that London may have held, he was fiercely loyal to the area of his birth. There were quotations from Ebenezer Elliott and Camden, and the first mention of Margery Moorpout's immortal lines on Roseberry, albeit in a footnote. Ord explained that since writing the original text 'we have stumbled upon the old-fashioned little story of Margery Moorpoot [sic]'.

He repeated the legend of Prince Oswy and ended his description of the Topping with comments about the plan to erect a colossal statue in memory of Cook. Ord doubted whether a government and nation that neglected men of genius in their lifetime could be expected to honour them when dead.

Elsewhere in his book Ord gave a detailed description of the bronze hoard discovered on the south side of Roseberry Topping. He was entirely taken with the series of pits around Roseberry, and on this evidence asserted that an ancient British town 'of vast magnitude' had once extended from Hutton Lowcross, near Guisborough, to Roseberry Topping. There is, of course, no real evidence for this.

Ord's work prompted much adverse comment for its pretentious style and obvious inaccuracies. Two examples are typical:

> 'His genius indeed took the most ambitious range, and was not deterred from many a time and oft endeavouring to encompass themes which were wholly beyond its power and ability, and in the execution of which conspicuous failure is only too legibly shown.'
> *W H Burnett*

> 'This work is written in a fulsome style. The author was unfit for such a great work. He is not an antiquary.'
> *Dictionary of National Biography*

Atkinson, too, was openly scornful, especially in his many footnotes. However, Ord's text contained evidence of considerable research, and many of his observations were drawn from personal visits and interviews. Some far-fetched ideas were included, only for him to dismiss them with scientific explanations, and he showed many progressive opinions, particularly on agriculture.

Ord intended his *History and Antiquities of Cleveland* to be a popular work that would encourage a greater interest in Cleveland, and the 600 subscribers to the 1846 edition came from all over Britain. It was also an impressive achievement for a youthful author, but the demands of composing it may well have contributed to the writer's growing mental instability. He died aged forty-two in an Edinburgh lunatic asylum, and was buried in Edinburgh, although there is a prominent obelisk to his memory in the church-yard at Guisborough.

myths and legends

Medieval stories

It is not surprising that Roseberry Topping should be the centre of legends, myths and stories as it sits so prominently on the skyline and can be seen for miles around. As explained earlier, the name is derived from the hill's dedication to the Norse god Odin. It was, in all probability, a spiritual centre for those of Scandinavian origin, who settled in the region sometime between the Roman occupation and the arrival of the Normans. Unfortunately, the tales associated with Roseberry that have been passed down to us do not have any particular association with the Vikings or Odin but seem rather to be of medieval origin. Any account of Roseberry's myths has to rely on the so-called Cottonian manuscript, which was probably written in 1604. This, and the 1607 edition of Camden's Britannia, included popular stories associated with the Topping, and both would be extensively quarried by later historians and travel writers. For instance, the celebrated couplet about the Cleveland weather appears in both:

> 'When roseberrye toppinge weares a cappe,
> Let Cleveland then beware a clappe'

Poor Prince Oswy

The best-known story about Roseberry concerns the young Northumbrian prince, Oswy, and the well near the summit of the Topping. This legend appears in one form or another in many books, even though the author of the first real history of Cleveland, the Rev John Graves, was sternly dismissive. In a terse footnote he asserted 'The traditional story that the Northumbrian Prince, Oswy, was drowned here is too ridiculous to deserve notice'. Later authors were more enthusiastic. John Walker Ord, who considered Graves rather dry, included two versions, a local story and a tale from Osmotherley. Most subsequent writers at least mentioned Prince Oswy. Their accounts were often garnished with quite fanciful detail, even down to quoting the imagined words spoken by the main characters.

In the usual version of the story King Oswald of Northumbria, who was a real person and lived in the early seventh century AD, yearned for a son. Naturally he was overjoyed when his wife gave birth to a boy, who was named Oswy after his father. Then the Queen dreamed that her baby son would die on a certain day and, horrified, consulted the wise men of the time who decided the dream was true, and that Oswy would die by drowning. The distraught Queen took her son south, and up Roseberry, thinking that at this altitude he would be safe. After the long journey she fell asleep near the summit, whereupon little Oswy wandered off and fell into a pool of water by a spring.

Less believable versions described the spring suddenly overflowing, engulfing mother and child or, alternatively, its waters dissolving the walls of their cell, possibly the old hermitage. Whatever the variations, all versions ended on a similar note. Prince Oswy's anguished mother died soon after her baby son, and both were buried in Tivotdale. The name of this burial place then changed to 'Oswy-by-his-mother-lay' which was later transformed into 'Osmotherley'.

The entire tale was captured in an old Yorkshire ballad of nine verses recorded in Ingledew's collection of 1860. In this the little prince is called Oswin, and Roseberry is Ottenberg.

> 'His mother, all eager her offspring to save,
> To Ottenberg high, with the morn did repair,
> Still hoping to rescue her son from the grave,
> For well did she know that no water was there.'

But of course there was water near the summit, and later the ballad described how the spring could still be seen near the summit of the Topping.

> 'On the proud steep of Ottenberg still may be found,
> That spring which arose his sad doom to complete;
> And oft on its verge sit the villagers round,
> In wonder recording the fiat of fate.'

Roseberry well

This brings us to the question of exactly where this spring, central to the Prince Oswy story, is located. According to the Cottonian manuscript, 'at the toppe of a huge stone neere the toppe of the hill drops a fountaine which cureth sore eyes receavinge that virtue from the minerall'; Camden's version is similar: 'neere unto the top of it, out of an huge rocke there floweth a spring of water medicinable for diseased eies'. Roseberry Well can still be seen on the eastern flank of the Topping, just a short scramble down from the summit. It appeared on the 1856 Ordnance Survey map and in 1901 the Folk Lore Society described it as 'a small stream trickling from an arched rock, deeply embedded in the northern part of the

Roseberry Well can still be seen today, it is usually more akin to a small puddle than a flourishing spring

hill, and surrounded with thick sedges'. Burton included a photograph of the well in his 1926 paper, *Roseberry Topping in Fact and Fiction*, with the comment that it was not very imposing because the water had become diverted into another course.

At present there is no known explanation for the well's alleged medicinal properties. Only the smallest puddle of water is present today, certainly not enough to wash one's eyes, let alone drown a prince.

Virgins and a needle

The author of the Cottonian manuscript stated that, on the side of Roseberry, was 'a clefte or cut in the rocke called Saint Winifryds needle'. Apparently a custom existed whereby people attempted to squeeze themselves through this narrow gap, whether for devotional purposes, to attract the admiration of the hermit, or simply for bravado the document did not say, but the result was that 'many a syllie soule' ran the risk of 'a breaknecke tumblinge' when they tried to put themselves to 'a needless payne creepynge through that needles eye'. We do not know exactly where on the Topping this cleft was, although presumably it must have been in the sandstone forming the summit.

Graves claimed that this tradition of Saint Winifred's needle (which he mis-transcribed as Willifryds Needle) was also associated with a passage-way in the crypt under Ripon Cathedral. This was a certain narrow passage described by Camden as a place where virginity might be tested. Graves quoted Camden as follows:

> 'a strait passage into a dark room close and vaulted under-ground, whereby trial was made of any woman's chastity; if she was chaste, she passed with ease; but, if otherwise, she was, by I know not what miracle, stopped and detained there.'

Graves seems to be mixing myths associated with two, quite different, saints. Saint Wilfrid was a seventh century abbot of Ripon, whereas Saint Winifred was a nun beheaded by a pagan prince for refusing his advances. She was then miraculously restored to life, and where the miracle occurred a spring of water gushed out. Winifred went on to become the patron saint of North Wales, and the spring became known as Holywell, and a place of pilgrimage. In medieval times her cult spread, and there are several Saint Winifrid wells in England. So it may be that it was actually the Roseberry spring, with its healing properties, rather than the cleft in the rock, that was originally associated with Saint Winifred. The confusion may have arisen partly because both the Rev Graves and the anonymous author of the Cottonian manuscript were clearly contemptuous of ancient traditions, which they associated with a corrupt and superstitious medieval culture, and therefore they may have failed to record them accurately.

Saint Oswald's Well, alias Chapel Well

There was another well not too far from Roseberry, which was regarded as holy, and which was a popular place to visit for those seeking miraculous cures. This well, labelled Chapel Well on the first Ordnance Survey map, was just to the north of the path formerly known as Thief Lane, running from the Guisborough Road on the outskirts of Ayton to Cliff Rigg quarry. According to the Cottonian manuscript the well was dedicated to Saint Oswald, a king of Northumbria who was martyred by the pagan king, Penda. Coincidentally, or otherwise, it was this Oswald who was the father of young Prince Oswy. It was said that the fate of a sick man could be determined if his shirt was thrown into the water of this well. Recovery could be expected if it floated, but death was inevitable if it sank:

> 'Betweene the townes of Aton and Newton neere the foote of Roseberrye toppinge there is a well dedicated to Saint Oswalde. The neighbours adioyninge have bin seduced with an opinion that if the shirte or smocke were taken of a sycke bodye and throwne into that well a certaine token might be gathered of his life or death, for if the shirt floated alofte yt denounced recovery to the partie, but in case yt sanke then there remaned noe hope of health. And to them that the good saincte for his paynes should not sytt emptye handed they teare of a ragge of the shirte and hange it on the bryers thereabouts whereof I have seene such numbers as might have made a fayre shewe in a paper myll.'

Judging from the comment about the number of shirts hanging on the bushes, many sought the well's prophesies. The reference to paper mills reminds us that paper was made from cloth rags until the end of the nineteenth century.

Later writers questioned whether the Cottonian manuscript was correct when it attributed this well to Saint Oswald, but Young, writing in 1817, reconciled the different titles of the well by explaining that, although the offerings of torn cloth were made to St. Oswald, the well itself was known as the Chapel Well. However some confusion continued; for example in 1889 the Rev Thomas Parkinson of North Otterington referred to 'St Oswald's or Oswy's Well' as being the well at the summit in the Prince Oswy legend. He was later put right by George Markham Tweddell.

Nanny Garbutt

Witches are a fascinating part of past history, some historians believing that witchcraft had its roots in a pre-Christian religion disapproved of by the later Christian Church. It was a punishable offence until 1736 when the laws against witchcraft were repealed, but of course there were witches practising good and evil well into the nineteenth century. Many oral records concerning witches were collected by Richard Blakeborough of Guisborough (1850-1918) and also by Canon John Atkinson of Danby (1814-1900). Atkinson, although a man of God, was clearly impressed by the depth of belief in witches that existed around Danby.

The story of Nanny Garbutt, the eighteenth century Ayton witch, was published by Richard Blakeborough in 1899. It was written in dialect, which makes for difficult reading today. He had been told these tales by a grandchild of Mary Langstaffe of Stokesley, who had survived a nasty encounter with the witch. Blakeborough claimed that the Ayton story went back to 1760, and that there were similar stories from much earlier times. There was also a very similar story originating in Farndale, and another from Borrow Bridge in Westmoreland.

Nanny Garbutt lived in a tumbledown cottage in a corner of the Low Green near the mill, which might imply that her cottage was somewhere near the present entrance to Marwood Drive. She was said to be in league with the

"An' theear he fan three neet-hags set."

One of the original illustrations for Richard Blakeborough's poem *T'Hunt o' Yatton Brigg*. Here Johnny Simpson meets three night hags on the road from Ayton to Newton, with the Topping in the background.

"Then slap doon he cam wiv a bang amang t' steeans."

Another illustration from *T'Hunt o' Yatton Brigg*. This shows Johnny, in the centre of the picture, being dropped from the sky to land among the stones, apparently on Roseberry Common. More tormentors await him on the ground. Nanny's besom can be seen tied between his legs, and rather miraculously his top hat has remained firmly in place throughout the aerial ordeal.

Two signatures appear on the illustration, Richard Blakeborough and Hood. Blakeborough has added 'pinxt et inv' below his name, the Latin 'pinxit et invenit' meaning that he painted and designed it. Hood would be Harold Hood, who ran a photographic business in Middlesbrough. He must have photographed the illustrations prior to printing.

devil. Blakeborough's narrative poem, *T' Hunt o' Yatton Brig*, described how Johnny Simpson of Newton-under-Roseberry called upon Nanny Garbutt's powers. He was in love with Mary Mudd of Ayton, but she would have nothing to do with him and went off with a certain Tom Smith. Johnny visited Nanny to ask her to put a spell on the two lovers. She gave him detailed instructions for the spell, but he failed to follow them to the letter and instead the curse fell upon him.

He had been told to go to Yatton Brig (Ayton Bridge) where he would find Nan's broomstick, then to wave it in the air three times and go backwards into the churchyard. There he should gather some grave mould. Finally, he must wash his hands in the old well and leave the broomstick at its side. But he did not bother to wash his hands and he threw the broomstick into the river. Because he had not washed, and still had the scent of the graveyard on his hands, he found himself pursued by 'three night hags', two of whom grabbed him, whisked him up to the top of Roseberry and tied Nanny's besom between his legs. They told him he would be hunted all that night by a variety of creatures, as described in Blakeborough's dialect lines (with a following translation).

'Wa've ullots traaned,
A cletch o' bats,
Flay-boggles wivoot feet;
Wa've gobblin' dogs,
An' gret big frogs,
An' tha'll all hunt thee ti neeght.'

We've owlets trained,
A clutch of bats,
Flay-bogles (ghosts) without feet,
We've goblin dogs,
And great big frogs,
They'll all hunt you tonight'

Throughout the night these creatures tormented Johnny, chasing him to Easby, on to Kildale, and then back to Little Ayton and Low Green. Then he remembered how Nanny had told him that he would be safe as long as he was on Ayton Bridge; witches cannot follow anyone over a running stream. Unfortunately, as he raced to the bridge the besom fell from his legs and he tumbled into the Leven. He was dragged out and again attacked by the creatures, biting and scratching him. Finally salvation came with the approaching dawn. As the cock crew, all the creatures flew away. Johnny Simpson was just about alive but was put off meddling with witches ever again.

More Roseberry witches

There have been other accounts of witches around Roseberry Topping. David Naitby collected stories about superstition and folklore in Bedale early in the nineteenth century, and many of his writings were saved by Richard Blakeborough, including an account of an aged dame called Benyson who lived at 'the low end of Ayton under Roseberry'. She was a witch who used ointments of fats and herbs to cure sores, 'be they even of two or three years standing'.

More dramatic was his story about three Ayton men who had been out gathering bilberries, when they saw three witches flying astride broomsticks not far from Roseberry Topping.

'These three did watch them circling ower a certain spot, making many oft repeated dolorous cries, as it were in deep distress. They in turns darted downward, lighted upon the ground and were busy at once on some black deed or other, the two mid air at such times, circling with the swiftness of a coach wheel, did the while fill the air with melancholy shrikes, this terrible adventure ending in their scampering off at hell's gallop towards Roseberry Mount. No mortal guesseth at their business.'

The Ayton men claimed to recognise two of the figures as the spirits of dead witches, Nancy Newgill and Hester Mudd of Rosedale. They did not know the third, but David Naitby, Blakeborough's informant, was convinced it was the ghost of Moll Cass, a Bedale witch who had died five years earlier.

> 'When roseberrye toppinge weares a cappe, Let Cleveland then beware a clappe'

Trinity fair

Sunday – that's the best of all

A virtually forgotten aspect of Roseberry Topping is the annual Trinity Mass Fair. There are very few references to this event, although it was still in existence in the early twentieth century and attracted a large number of visitors from industrial Teesside. Trinity Sunday is eight weeks after Easter Sunday, and thus occurs in late May or June. The day apparently began with the vicar of Newton, along with his churchwardens and choir, climbing to the summit and celebrating a Trinity Mass. This was followed by a fair on the lower slopes. At one time the fair was very popular, sandwiched between the Stokesley Fair on the Saturday and Stokesley Races at Seamer Moor on the Monday. The dialect poem *T'awd Cleveland Customs* by Florence Cleveland (otherwise Mrs G M Tweddell) went through the different festivals in the year, including Trinity. Local people who had been away came back home for the Trinity week-end, and Sunday was the highlight of the three days:

> Trenety's t'best tahm we hev –
> There's lots o'Cheese-keeaks meead;
> An' all draw yam 'ats been away
> Te arn ther bit o' breead.
>
> We hev a Fair o' Setterda',
> An' Races teea o' Munda';
> Then there's t'getherin' o' friends –
> That's t'best ov all – on t' Sunda'.

Fun of the fair

According to Jack Fairfax Blakeborough, the fair had its origins in an old woman called 'Old Gag Mally Wright' who held a stall at the foot of Roseberry on Trinity Sunday. It is entirely plausible that she was there to cater for those descending from the Trinity Mass at the summit. Fairfax Blakeborough, probably quoting from his father, said she sold brandy snaps and ale of her own brewing. The fair grew from these humble beginnings into a well-attended event, with food and drink sellers and a variety of entertainments.

Although Roseberry Trinity fair was absent from a comprehensive list of fairs in Yorkshire drawn up in 1770, this list did include Stokesley on the Saturday before Trinity, with its fair for 'horned cattle, horses and linnen cloth'. Fairs required legal status, and so at first sight it appears strange that there was no mention of Newton. However, it may well have been considered as part of the Stokesley Fair. There were other Trinity Fairs in Yorkshire, but none actually on Trinity Sunday.

George Markham Tweddell, the celebrated Stokesley author and printer, visited the fair in 1845. He wrote in his publication, *The Cleveland Repertory & Stokesley Advertiser*, that 'The fair passed off as usual with much animation and bustle, among the fair dames and brawny peasantry of Cleveland'. Local housewives were selling all manner of edibles, and travellers were entertaining the crowds. Tweddell praised the traditional ballad singers, who passed on songs for local people to sing over the coming year, 'the lads going o'er the hills and dales of Cleveland' and 'the maidens tripping o'er the fields in native simplicity or making labour light in indoor pursuits'. He contrasted these songs with the 'whining hypocritical cant' of the Stokesley street singers.

Sacrilege on Sunday

By the mid-nineteenth century the close association of amusements and alcohol with a religious service on the Sabbath was becoming too much for the increasingly censorious Victorians. In addition, the total abstinence movement was particularly strong in this part of Cleveland, supported by the Quakers and other nonconformists. Jack Fairfax Blakeborough's father Richard must have told him about a bill posted a week before Trinity Sunday, probably a year or two after Tweddell's visit, forbidding the sale of intoxicating liquor at the fair. Jack later recalled this in one of his books, but added that in the event none was on sale.

The following year matters went further, with a notice to the effect that anyone attending the fair would be proceeded against. This naturally incensed Tweddell, who championed local traditions and strongly opposed the established church. He saw it as an attack on the common man. Tweddell later told Blakeborough how he had given notice to the Stokesley police that he intended to go to Roseberry on Trinity Sunday, and that he had several persons willing to finance him to defend any action that might be brought. After Sunday lunch he had set off for Newton and the Topping, but found that he was the only person there; a brave but empty gesture worthy of Don Quixote himself.

The end

It seems that after Tweddell's one-man demonstration the fair regained some of its popularity and notoriety. By the early 1900s it was attracting a large number of people from industrial Teesside who, according to Blakeborough, 'cram into one short Sabbath about as much ungodliness as it is possible to conceive'.

This time the banner of public morality was taken up by the Rev E Tugman, the last vicar of Newton. Although he spent much of his time and energies restoring the church at Newton-under-Roseberry, which on his arrival was nothing but 'a little protestant barn', Tugman also succeeded in the permanent abolition of Trinity Mass Fair.

' Ornsbury Toppin Beacon is seated upon a
round hill five miles distant from the sea '

From a list of beacons 1580 – 1590

with Britain on 1 February 1793, although no real action ensued. However, fears grew, not only because an invasion would threaten England's power and prosperity, but also because French notions of revolution could threaten the English establishment. Our coastal defences had been neglected, yet in the absence of any immediate threat improvements were slow to materialise.

Internal defence was the responsibility of the Lord Lieutenant in each county. It took several years to organise local militia, a process exacerbated in Yorkshire by political opposition to William Pitt's government. Gradually, an increasing sense of urgency brought some feeling of national unity and, by the end of the century, volunteer forces across Yorkshire were waiting for the call. Thoughts then turned to how to raise the alarm in the event of an invasion on the Yorkshire coast. In 1801, no less than eight years after the declaration of war, the North Yorkshire lieutenancy deemed it 'necessary that beacons should be erected in proper situations along the coast to give information when the enemy may attempt to land, particularly upon Huntcliff, Rowcliff, Roseberry Toppin, Eston Nab and Hambleton End'. Even then little seems to have been done, and two years later a worried Lord Mulgrave wrote to the Quarter Master General pointing out that no beacons had been built, and that furthermore it would take some time to establish the exact places where they should be positioned. Lord Mulgrave's discontent may have been due to the position of his estate on the east coast, in contrast to the estates of the decision-makers in the lieutenancy. The new Lord Lieutenant, the young Duke of Leeds, appointed following the death of Earl Fauconberg, had only recently acquired estates in the North Riding. And his powerful deputy William Chaytor lived at Spennithorne, at least forty miles inland.

So it was left to Mulgrave to devise a plan for a network of beacons. He wrote detailed instructions for the construction and operation of the beacon sites. A large pile of brushwood and timber was to be placed on each site, together with three or four barrels of tar (to keep the blaze going for at least two hours) and a large quantity of straw (to produce smoke for daytime visibility). The pile was to be thatched to keep it dry, and guarded to prevent accidents. A nine foot pole was to be erected in the centre of the beacon, topped by a small white flag.

This contemporary description of the beacons, as a large pile of brushwood and timber on the ground, conflicts with comments made in 1869 by Samuel Gordon. He wrote that within living memory the beacon on Roseberry was still to be seen. 'It consisted of a high pole, on top of which was placed an iron receptacle for the burning tar, the pole having steps upon it by which the attendant ascended to replenish the fire'. A detailed survey of the East Riding beacon sites was undertaken some eighty years after their inception, when the decaying remains of many could still be seen and people were still living who remembered the beacons in their original state. This survey showed that the general arrangement was indeed for a tall pole, with blocks of wood fixed to its sides to provide a foothold, surmounted by an iron basket to carry the tar barrel. Often the basket was carried on an iron bracket to one side of the pole. Some sites had all three baskets on a single pole.

Since Ayton parish records show that 'fixing a pole upon Roseberry for Beacon' was not carried out until 1807-8, it could be that the pile of brushwood and timber was a temporary measure. Gordon also stated that near the beacon stood a small stone-built house, where a person used to reside to light the beacon in case a foe landed upon our coast. He reported that no vestige of either the beacon or the house existed on Roseberry Topping at the time he was writing, which was some sixty years after the Napoleonic threat of invasion.

The original instructions stated that each beacon was to be under the charge of 'an intelligent steady serjeant and three men' who were to camp near the beacon. They were provided with a telescope by the Quarter Master General, and had to maintain constant watch on the beacons on either side of their position. Lord Mulgrave was at great pains to prevent accidental alarms. The first beacon in a district was not to be fired without the express command of a senior officer, unless others were first seen burning in the neighbouring districts. However, accidents did happen. In March 1805 the men at Penhill beacon in Wensleydale saw a light which they took to be the beacon on Roseberry Topping. The Penhill beacon was lit, the local volunteers mustered and set off on the road to Thirsk, and on the way they were joined by the Masham Volunteers. Although their journey was in vain they were awarded ten guineas for their zeal. It transpired that the burning of heather and gorse on the moors had been mistaken for the burning Roseberry beacon.

1887 Golden Jubilee

By 1887 Queen Victoria had ruled over Great Britain and its empire for fifty years. This great occasion was marked by the lighting of beacons throughout the country, and it was reported that from the summit of Snowdon eighty fires could be seen. It is not known if there was a beacon on Roseberry on this occasion, but it does seem likely.

Coronation of Edward VII

There were nationwide events to celebrate the coronation of King Edward VII on the 9 August 1902. After sixty-five years of Queen Victoria's reign, for most people the crowning of a British monarch was a novel event. How better to celebrate in Ayton than with a bonfire on Roseberry Topping? Robinson Martin, who farmed at Aireyholme, hauled the thirty-two tons of logs required to the summit. He employed a steam engine, normally used for sawing wood and threshing, to drag a sledge loaded with timber up the slopes of Roseberry. The iron bar that Robinson hammered into the crown of Roseberry to hold a snatch wheel is still there to bear witness to the event.

In fact, the celebrations took place the day before the coronation ceremony. There was a service at Christ Church in the early morning, and at 1:00pm the Rev R Withington presided over a general assembly of villagers on High Green. Alfred Edward Kitching and his wife distributed medals and sixpences to children, followed by singing the national anthem. There was a grand procession headed by a band, and a free tea provided for all Ayton's parishioners. In the evening there was dancing on the cricket field with the village's string band, and a bicycle parade, and at ten o'clock a huge bonfire blazed forth on the summit of Roseberry Topping. Those assembled again sang the national anthem, and this was succeeded by a display of rockets. 'God Save the King' was then sung for a third time before the crowd dispersed.

Coronation of George V

At the time of the coronation of King George V in 1911 there was a suggestion that a bonfire should be lit again on the summit of Roseberry Topping. But Mr George Burton, the manager of the Roseberry Mines, refused permission for the fire on Roseberry. Judging by the size of the pile of timber forming the 1902 fire, much heat must have been generated which may have damaged the

Probably the largest beacon-fire ever seen on the Topping – the bonfire to celebrate the coronation of King Edward VII in 1902. Only two of the figures can be identified, both in the central foreground and on a flat outcrop of sandstone. The man sitting on the outcrop and leaning back on the slope to the right is Jimmy Nicholls, head gardener at the Grange, while the man with the child on the left is a Mr Ward, also a gardener at the Grange.

Photo: supplied by kind permission of Mr and Mrs Garbutt of Great Ayton

sandstone at the summit. It was perhaps with further possible damage in mind that George Burton refused to allow another fire. He was probably concerned that pieces of rock could be broken off and fall from the summit, although he could hardly have predicted the massive rock fall of the following year. Turned away from Roseberry, an alternative bonfire site next to Captain Cook's Monument was considered, but the event probably never took place.

VE Day 1945

Victory in Europe was officially declared on 8 May 1945. There was little time to organise any large scale celebrations although the local press reported that a brave show of bunting and flags gave Ayton a gay appearance. There were no official bonfires, but fires were hastily built around the village, including two on Low Green and one

the mystery of the summerhouse

The Roseberry summerhouse

This delightful stone building stands on an area of level ground to the south west of the Topping. It is square in plan, with openings for three windows and a door. It is not possible to tell whether the windows were once glazed, but certainly shutters were once in place since their iron fittings can still be seen. There has also been a door at some time in the past. The highly distinctive roof is constructed entirely of sandstone blocks, surmounted by the remains of a weather vane on a cast iron ball finial. A small flue running up inside the northern corner simply opens at roof level, with no chimney.

This design, which seems to possess a certain oriental feel, is probably unique. Members of the Folly Fellowship, who research and record follies around the world, say that they have never seen anything quite like the Roseberry summerhouse roof. The gazebo in the grounds of Ham Green House at Easton-in-Gordano, Somerset did feature a similar roof, but that building is now alas lost. In any case, it boasted a much more elaborate octagonal design, with elegant window surrounds and a battlemented parapet.

High on the eastern wall of the Roseberry summerhouse a cast metal plaque states:

> 'The shooting box. This building was commissioned by Commodore Wilson of Ayton Hall in the late 18th century as a shelter at lunchtimes and inclement weather during shooting. It was restored in 1983 with assistance from the North York Moors National Park Committee.'

It is now believed that most of this is misleading if not incorrect. The historic name of the building is certainly 'summerhouse' rather than 'shooting box', and there is no evidence to suggest that the building was commissioned by William Wilson, or that it was originally intended as a shelter for shooting parties. It has been impossible to trace the source of the information, although the plaque itself was probably designed by Anya McCracken, the National Park's landscape architect, who died in 1998. Restoration work in 1983 was carried out by Sir Wilfrid Fry of Cleveland Lodge, who was then the owner of the building. Just as with the plaque, much of the history of the summerhouse remains unknown, and indeed, as more research is done, more questions are raised.

When was it built?

There is no date on the fabric of the building, and no mention of the summerhouse in the early nineteenth century books on Cleveland, or in any other writings of the time. The only references are in late eighteenth century sketches by George Cuit the elder, who was commissioned by Constantine Phipps, the second Lord Mulgrave, to produce a series of Cleveland scenes connected with James Cook. Cuit was born near Richmond in 1743, and produced these pictures sometime around 1788. The summerhouse can be seen in two of his sketches, so it must have been built before that time. Although the building is in the distance, it is instantly recognisable with its unusual roof profile.

Did William Wilson build it?

For many years it was believed that the summerhouse had been built by William Wilson. Wilson won fame and fortune as a captain in the East India Company, distinguishing himself in a sea battle with French frigates, and discovering a new sea passage from India to Canton. He married Rachel Jackson, a sister of Ralph Jackson the celebrated diarist. When he retired in 1762 at the early age of 47, he and his wife moved to Great Ayton. His brother-in-law Ralph found them a suitable house, Ayton Hall on Low Green, and from then on Wilson adopted the life of a country squire until his death in 1795.

It was fashionable at the time to enhance the natural landscape with neo-classical buildings, and the absence of any detailed features suggested that the original building on Roseberry was meant to be viewed from afar rather than used as a form of shelter. So it was presumed that William and Rachel Wilson had commissioned the summerhouse, perhaps with an oriental roof design to remind William of his past associations with the east. In the Wilsons' time at Ayton Hall the building would have been visible from the grounds, although today newer structures obscure this view.

This belief originated in a misinterpretation of correspondence to *The Gentleman's Magazine* by the Rev John Brewster of the Stockton Literary Club. In 1787 a letter from 'Cleveland' was printed in the magazine, proposing that a monument be erected to Captain James Cook in or near Marton, where he had been born. Cook was killed in 1779. Cliff Thornton of the Captain Cook Society has shown that 'Cleveland' was in fact Brewster. Nothing came of the idea of a monument, and in 1791 Brewster raised the subject again, still under the name of 'Cleveland'. This time the memorial to Cook was to be on Roseberry Topping, as the following extract from his letter shows:

> 'Not far from Marton, in the range of the Cleveland hills, is the celebrated conical mountain, called Roseberry-Toppin. The proprietors of this mountain, it is reported, have thrown out a hint that they would promote a plan for erecting a monument for this purpose on its summit. The situation seems well-chosen, as the cone of the mountain is visible at the distance of 30 or 40 miles in the counties of York and Durham.'

Brewster went on to discuss various designs for the monument, including a building 'with large apertures in its sides, rather like a Chinese pagoda', but eventually settled on a pyramid. John Graves commented in 1808 that, some years previously, there had been a plan to erect a monument to Cook in the form of a pyramid or obelisk on the summit of the Topping. Nine years later, in the second volume of his *History of Whitby*, George Young included the biographies of several eminent men, among whom was James Cook. Young noted 'it has more than once been in agitation, to erect a monument to his memory on Rosebury Topping; and Major Rudd, the proprietor, has cheerfully consented to the proposal; but no such adequate subscription has yet been raised'.

In 1821 Brewster, now writing under his initials J.B., returned to his idea for a Cook memorial in another letter to *The Gentleman's Magazine*. He began by referring to a proposal made about ten years previously by the Stockton Literary Club, to build a monument on Eston Nab, a high point of the Eston Hills just under four miles north of Roseberry. This proposal had languished and died. Brewster went on:

> 'The writer of this article made a proposal of a similar nature about thirty years ago, in your Magazine: and he is induced to renew the subject, in consequence of a gentleman of family and fortune having erected a prospect-house on the mountain above alluded to, near his own mansion. The building is attended with all of

the effect it was expected to produce, and is visible for many miles both by sea and land. Is it presuming in the writer to suggest to the worthy proprietors to enlarge his building a little, particularly in height, and to adopt the name of "Captain Cook's monument", probably adding an inscription at his own liking, as originally proposed?'

It was originally thought that the 'gentleman of family and fortune' was William Wilson, and that the prospect-house was situated on the Topping. But Brewster's 1821 letter clearly stated that the prospect-house was 'on the mountain above alluded to', in other words on Eston Nab. Another problem with the Wilson theory is that the land where the Roseberry summerhouse stands was owned by Bartholomew Rudd, as pointed out by George Young in his *History of Whitby* and mentioned below. Furthermore, had Wilson been its builder, it would seem almost certain that Ralph Jackson would have mentioned the new summerhouse put up by 'brother Wilson' in his diaries, yet he does not. Finally, there is no mention of the building of the summer-house in the Wilson family letters to their sons, who were in St Petersburg and India respectively. None of this proves that Wilson did not build the summerhouse, but it seems unlikely.

Brewster's final words on the subject of Cook's Monument were printed in 1827, when he praised Robert Campion of Easby Hall for erecting, at his own expense, the now-famous monument on Easby Moor. In this letter Brewster down-graded his description of the building on Eston Nab from a prospect-house to a mere shepherd's hut.

Did the Pease family build it?

There was a view, put forward by at least one local writer, that the summerhouse might have been erected by the Pease family. This however cannot be true. The Pease business interests in Darlington were at a comparatively early stage in 1788, and at that time they had no connection with Cleveland. It was not until well into the nineteenth century that the family started its long association with the area, and acquired the Cleveland Lodge estate.

What about the Rudd family?

It might be expected that the owner of the land on which the summerhouse stood built it. Thomas Skottowe, who was so generous to the young James Cook, owned Aireyholme in the mid-eighteenth century. Skottowe provided the Cook family with a stone cottage on the edge of Cliff Rigg, above Aireyholme Farm, when he employed Mr Cook as his hind at Aireyholme from 1736 to 1755. But Skottowe was plagued by financial problems and sold much of his property in his later life. Thus Aireyholme came into the ownership of Michael Smith of Marske, who made it a gift to his grand-daughter Susan Duck on her marriage to Bartholomew Rudd the elder in 1763. Incidentally, it was during the building of Rudd's residence at Marton Lodge in 1786 that the remains of James Cook's humble birthplace in Marton were destroyed. One of Bartholomew Rudd's sons, Bartholomew the younger, moved into Marton Lodge around 1800, when he would have been approaching thirty years of age. So far as we know, neither of the Bartholomew Rudds ever lived at Aireyholme, which was managed by tenant farmers, although Bartholomew Rudd the younger did install his mistress, Maria Clifford of Myton-on-Swale, there in the early nineteenth century. He was also enthusiastic about breeding cattle, probably at Aireyholme, which might have given him a reason for frequent visits.

Although Bartholomew Rudd the younger may have had a reason to enhance the Aireyholme landscape with a prospect house, it is known that the summerhouse was already there in 1788, years before he started his affair with Maria Clifford. In fact it was probably built before Bartholomew Rudd the elder built Marton Lodge in 1786. It seems unlikely that he would have built the summerhouse himself, with his thoughts on the grander design of Marton Lodge.

... closed never to reopen ...

industry on Roseberry

A post-industrial landscape

Today Roseberry presents a purely pastoral scene, but this has not always been so. Because the geological strata lie in almost horizontal bands, hillsides and escarpments provide easy access for miners. Although largely forgotten today, the extent of past mineral extraction can be seen by looking down from the top of Roseberry, from where the surface of the lower slopes is disturbed by humps and hollows. The seams of ironstone that run through much of the Cleveland area, the shale above and the sandstone cap of Roseberry, have all been exploited. Sandstone was removed in a small quarry just below the summit. The lower levels of the shale were extensively worked over for jet, demanded by the nineteenth century jewellery trade, and the main ironstone seam was mined to feed the Middlesbrough blast furnaces.

Sandstone

The path to the summit from the summerhouse goes up at a steady gradient, before taking a sharp turn to the left, finally passing through an area where there has been some rock cut away. On the left, there is a vertical face of the rock which has been tooled. There are lines of marks forming the typical herring-bone pattern used by stone masons to surface the blocks used in building construction. This face has clearly been prepared prior to splitting into separate blocks.

Examination of the area indicates that stone has been extracted elsewhere, but these more recent operations appear to have been on a small scale. Dating the work is difficult, but one nineteenth century graffiti artist appears to have cut the figures '88' into the tooled face, suggesting that it was worked before 1888. The destination of the stone is not known, but the small amount taken could have been taken for the Roseberry Ironstone Mine powder house. Apart from the summerhouse, this is the nearest sandstone block building and was erected in the first phase of mine operations, commencing in 1881.

Sandstone was quarried from the top of Roseberry. The surface of the stone seems to have been dressed, in the characteristic herring-bone pattern seen on many buildings in Great Ayton, before the blocks were finally cut free.

Stone quarried from the summit of Roseberry would have been brought down on a sled. This means of transport was much easier to control down a steep descent than any wheeled vehicle. The photograph probably shows stone from Cockshaw Quarry above Gribdale, just a mile away from the Topping.

Going further back in time, it would seem that considerable amounts of stone were removed before the seventeenth century. The Cottonian manuscript of 1604 mentions a hermitage, a small smith's forge and the gap known as St Winifryd's needle all being cut into the rock at the summit. Ord was certain that they had all 'been sacrificed by the ruthless quarrymen'. An alternative explanation for their loss might be an earlier rock fall from the unstable western face of the summit.

Although the good quality sandstone on the summit is readily accessible, transport from the site would have been difficult. A sledge, carrying a block of stone, could have been lowered down the footpath running from the quarry; this route appears to have been deliberately constructed on a steady gradient. The sandstone quarry is shown on the 1856 Ordnance Survey map, but no other documentary evidence has been found, either concerning leases or the individuals associated with it.

Jet working

The vogue for jet jewellery was supposedly set by Queen Victoria after the deaths of Wellington and Albert. Whitby became a centre for the jet trade and for the manufacture of jet jewellery. Jet could be found in shale bands in the coastal cliffs, but the increased demand stimulated searches along the visible shale bands on inland sites. Much of the escarpment on the western side of the Cleveland hills remains marked by numerous jet workings.

On Roseberry there were jet workings on the northern slopes. The typical jet mine was a shallow horizontal drift driven into the shale. Today such a mine entrance appears as a trench going into the hillside, often with depressions on the uphill side caused by collapsed drifts, and a spoil heap on the downhill side. In places opencast workings were used and some are visible on Roseberry Common. A more detailed description of the jet workings is given in the chapter on the Roseberry pits.

Little has been recorded about the jet mining industry, and there appears to be no documentation of agreements between land owners and miners. The size of each drift and the apparent lack of any machinery indicate that this was a small-scale industry carried out by groups of a few individuals. It has been suggested that jet mining was a part-time occupation, resorted to when agricultural work was not available. The process probably involved bringing the shale out to the surface and then sorting through it for pieces of jet before discarding it. Again there is no evidence of the commercial organization of the industry, but with a number of small producers spread over quite a large area, it is likely that the output was purchased by a middleman who sold it on to the jewellery manufacturers around Whitby.

The first Roseberry Ironstone Mine

The history of ironstone mining on Roseberry was well-documented by the late Richard Pepper; his enthusiasm and wisdom are sorely missed, and not surprisingly his excellent publication *Roseberry Ironstone Mine* has become the standard reference on the mine today.

When compared with the other industries on Roseberry, the ironstone mining was on an entirely different scale. A large workforce mined and despatched large quantities of ironstone to the blast furnaces along the River Tees. Remains of this enterprise are visible in a number of places around Roseberry. The main surface installations were on

Photograph supplied by Peter Tuffs of Guisborough

Aerial photograph of the Roseberry Ironstone mine site, looking towards Aireyholme. The remaining surface features are continually being absorbed into the landscape, but a great deal remains visible to the careful observer

1. Main drift entrance for the 1880 mine, later used in the second phase of mining, and now filled-in.
2. Secondary drift entrance, now collapsed.
3. Water reservoir
4. Cutting through the ironstone seam to reach a new drift entrance, created after 1910. The wider excavated area is the site of a ventilating fan installed in the second phase of mining.
5. Foundations for haulage engines and boiler house
6. Floor of the stable building.
7. Ground disturbed by mine working subsidence.
8. Line of tramway from mine to the incline by Cliff Rigg.
9. Remains of the stone-built powder house.
10. Old stream bed, originally fed from the spring near the summerhouse. This dried up after 1880 when mining altered underground water courses.

Photograph by Robert de Wardt from an Auster aircraft owned and flown by Peter Wood of Moorsholm

the level ground between Roseberry Topping and Little Roseberry. Here concrete foundations are visible on the east side of the bridleway from Aireyholme to Hutton Gate. Farther to the north are many collapses where the surface has dropped into shallow mine workings. On the west side of the bridleway the collapsed entrance into the main drift of the mine is clearly visible and in the field to the south west of Roseberry a further series of collapses are visible.

Interest in exploiting the ironstone in this area originated during the exploration of the Main Seam of the Cleveland ironstone in the Eston Hills in the 1850s. We know that the hills around Great Ayton were being searched for ironstone at this time, and that the laboratory in the North of England Agricultural School, later the Friends' School, in Ayton was used to analyse samples in 1851. The analysis must have proved favourable, for in 1854 the then owner of Roseberry, Mrs Staveley, granted Joseph Pease 'the mines and seams of ironstone and iron ore under all lands in the parish of Newton with power to search, sink shafts, erect buildings and carry away the ore'. No doubt Mrs Staveley would have been looking forward to some income from her lease, but she was disappointed. The first mining company was taken to court by the Staveley estate for not producing any ironstone or any royalty payments, and was required to compensate the estate for loss of earnings.

Tentative plans were made for a branch line from the Middlesbrough to Guisborough Railway, which would have been laid up Bousdale and thence through a tunnel to the Roseberry mine, but this was never built. No work was done at the mine site until 1873, by which time the railway through Ayton had been opened, and some trial excavations were then made. A letter to the *Guisborough Exchange* in April of that year began 'Guess my horror, when in coming down the hill, I discovered that excavators had been busily at work on one of its gentle slopes'. By 1875 Joseph Dodds and Hugh Chaytor held the lease, and by 1880 the Roseberry Iron Company had been established, with its head office in Coatham, Redcar. It was reported in April 1880 that navvies were working on the tramway and incline from the mine to the main railway. The Roseberry Ironstone Mine purchased a three-foot gauge locomotive from Messrs Black Hawthorne & Company of Gateshead. Naturally enough, this 0-4-0 locomotive was named 'Roseberry'. By the end of the year the work was complete and mining operations were expected to commence in 1881, although the ironstone market was depressed at the time.

At this time the stone powder magazine house was constructed some distance from the mine workings for safety reasons. Explosives were taken to the magazine by a small tramway.

The initial works took full advantage of the geological conditions of the ironstone at Roseberry. The Main Seam was about 5ft 6in thick and sloped gently from north-west to south-east, cropping out on the relatively flat land on the south-east flank of Roseberry. Opening the mine from this point had several advantages. By driving two main tunnels right through to the north-west side and out into the open, ventilation could largely be by natural means. Empty tubs (wagons) could be hauled into

Aerial view of the Roseberry Ironstone Mine, taken from directly above the site. This provides a better view of some of the features in the previous photograph, using the same numbering system. The area of disturbed ground intruding into the arable field on the left is due to the deliberate collapsing of the exhausted mine workings. The edge of this area corresponds exactly to the boundary of the mine as shown in the mine plan.

Distinctive rigg and furrow patterns can be seen running down the hillside. These were formed long before mining operations, when the area was all cultivated land.

Photograph reproduced by kind permission of Tees Archaeology of Hartlepool.

the mine by horses and run out by gravity when loaded. Finally, as the entrance was the lowest point, water in the mine would drain naturally without the need for pumps.

After driving two main tunnels right through to the opposite side of the Topping, the miners commenced working the ironstone on the 'bord and pillar' system normally used in Cleveland. In this system tunnels or 'bords' would be excavated on a grid pattern, working away from the main haulage-ways. The ironstone was loaded into tubs which ran out of the mine by gravity, down a tramway, to a rope-worked incline close to Cliff Rigg where a siding from the main line railway was installed.

Unfortunately, there was no improvement in the ironstone market and, by early 1882, after only about one year's operation, the mine was described as 'resting'. New owners took over the lease, but the small output achieved in 1883 suggests their optimism was misplaced. The mine was officially abandoned in 1887, after some 47,000 tons of ironstone had been mined. At this time only the main haulage ways, the tunnels through the mine to the north-west side of Roseberry, and a few bords near the entrance had been driven. The tramway was dismantled and the locomotive sold. Renamed 'Whittle', it worked on the construction of the Catcleugh reservoir in Northumberland in the 1890s. Today the only evidence remaining of this first Roseberry mine is the tramway track-bed and the powder house for storing explosives.

The 1894 twenty-five inch Ordnance Survey map showed the surface remains of the first mine. The drift entrance was marked as 'Old Level (ironstone)' and the old ventilation shafts were shown, along with the route of the tramway and the stone powder house.

The second Roseberry Ironstone Mine

In 1906 new owners, the Tees Furnace Company Limited, set about reopening the mine. Their managing director, Joseph James Burton, was looking for a much larger scale operation, believing there to be over three million tons of recoverable ironstone. He anticipated employing 200 men to shift 5000 tons per week from the Main Seam. The tramway system was rebuilt on the slightly smaller gauge of 2ft 4in, and a cable haulage system installed. Arnold Martin, from Aireyholme Farm, recalled that the long rake of new tubs was hauled along the road from Ayton Station, and up past Aireyholme, using a traction engine.

A stationary steam engine, located just outside the main drifts, wound the cables used to move the rakes of tubs. This was a sizeable installation, designed to move over 200,000 tons of stone annually from the mine to the incline head and eventually down to the mainline rail siding for loading into trains to the Middlesbrough furnaces. An engine capable of developing over a hundred horsepower would have been needed, and the adjacent boiler house held four boilers.

Underground, the mine reopened by picking up the work that had been abandoned by the earlier owners, proceeding on the same bord and pillar system. The main haulage-ways that had been driven from the drift entrances through to the north-west side were reutilized. The same system of using horse haulage to take the empty tubs into the mine and up the gentle incline, and running the loaded tubs out by gravity, was used. Full tubs were assembled into rakes at the head of the tramway and released once a tail cable had been attached. This cable was used to brake them as they rolled down the gradual slope to a low point in the middle of the route. At this point another cable was attached to the front of the rake to pull them up the rise to the head of the Cliff Rigg incline. All movements were controlled by electric bell signals to the driver of the stationary engine made by riders on the wagon rakes.

In this second period of operation the mine was successful. Its labour force peaked at nearly 400 in 1919. A sharp rise from 200 to 280 employees in 1911 probably reflected the additional labour needed when the mine was extended eastwards to Little Roseberry. This extension followed the dip of the seam and, since it went below the level of the surface works, powered haulage was required to bring the stone to the tramway head. Rather than take a circuitous route through the existing workings, a new tramway was installed running down through a cutting to the east of the existing surface works.

The final stage in the bord and pillar system was to reverse direction, working back towards the entrance by removing the pillars between the tunnels. This process, known as 'goafing', resulted in the roof collapsing. After the Main Seam under Roseberry was exhausted and goafed, an attempt was made to work the Two Foot Seam in the vicinity of the mine buildings. This was short lived, and the mine abandonment plan shows a drift at this level extending only 230ft into the hillside.

The end of mining on Roseberry

Many of the mines in the area were owned by companies which also operated blast furnaces. During the poor economic conditions of the early 1920s, these companies relied on their own mines and did not take ore from independent mines. An additional problem for mines working the Cleveland Main Seam was the relatively poor quality of the ironstone.

Burton himself took over ownership of the mine, but much of the stone under Roseberry was exhausted and that available from the Little Roseberry area was diminishing. These factors led to a fall in the numbers employed, and the mine finally ceased operations in 1924.

The Gribdale Mining Company, which operated a whinstone mine at nearby Gribdale, acquired the mine's assets but were forced to sell off the plant and machinery in 1931, marking the end of Roseberry's ironstone mining history. The notice of the auction by Messrs Farrow and Richardson read as follows.

'Sale by public auction Tuesday February 3 1931. Under distraint for rent against the Gribdale Mining Co Ltd, Roseberry Mines, the whole of the machinery and mines equipment comprising briefly 2 haulage engines by J Tursley, 1 Ingersoll compressor, 1 Robey Fan Engine, 4 boilers, 2 pumping engines, 300 tubs, saw bench, lathe, drilling machines, Haulage Drum and ropes, 120 chains

Thomas Williamson tended the horses at Roseberry. The height of the underground workings was sufficient for horses, rather than ponies, to be used. Since the animals were moving in and out of the mine, they were provided with a leather visor to protect their eyes when coming out into bright sunlight. With their ears protruding from the headgear, any protection from overhead rocks must have been incidental.

Wagons in the cutting at Roseberry Mine. The wires for the signalling system to the haulage cable engine driver can be seen above the wagons. This photograph is part of the Godfrey Bingley Collection of over 10,000 lantern slides, which is housed at the University of Leeds. Bingley sold his iron foundry business in 1884 and devoted his life to his many interests. An interest in geology naturally took him to Roseberry.
Photograph from the Godfrey Bingley Collection reproduced here by courtesy of the University of Leeds

tram-rail with points and switches, the contents of the blacksmith's, joiner's and fitter's shops and the whole of the engine sheds, shops, stores, stables, offices, and office furniture, also the harness for 30 pit ponies, etc. Sale at 11 o'clock prompt.'

The matter-of-fact wording of the auction notice contrasted with the emotional headline in the *North Eastern Gazette:* 'Death blow to Ayton. Sale of Roseberry Mines machinery, 400 men idle, closed never to reopen'. The words were rather over-dramatic, since the figure of 400 referred to the unemployed miners across Ayton and Guisborough; Roseberry mine itself had not employed many men for some years. Because of the sale, and because the surface buildings were generally of simple corrugated iron construction rather than stone or brick, very little evidence of the mine remains.

The official plan of abandonment, dated 6 August 1929, stated that no work had been carried out at the site since the plan had originally been drawn up in June 1924.

One of the very few photographs of the Roseberry Mine buildings, taken at the time of its auction in 1931.

Ex-miners picking up their tools for the last time, before their equipment goes under the hammer. A scene from the 1931 auction of the mine's assets. Photographs from the collection of the late Richard Pepper, and supplied by Peter Tuffs of Guisborough.

Surface remains

As can be seen in the aerial photographs, the outlines of some foundations are still visible in places. The drift entrances on the west side of the bridleway are clearly marked by areas of subsidence in the hillside. Opposite them, in the field to the east of the bridleway, are the concrete bases of the haulage engines with their holding down bolts. Especially noticeable is the platform for the main haulage engine driver to stand on, with a fine edge moulding cast in the concrete rendering. Behind, and to the north, there are other foundations believed to be for an air compressor and its associated steam engine to supply air for power drills in the mine. The boiler house area was further still to the north, but little exists today other than rough ground. When the boilers were sold all the brick mountings were demolished to enable them to be removed, and little is visible on the surface. Further north still, up a slight rise, is a large foundation that was the base of the stable building. Its concrete floor still has the drainage grooves visible. In the aerial photograph this shows up clearly, with rows of vegetation marking the horse stalls. Further to the north-west the embanked walls of the reservoir can be seen up on the hillside. Some pipework is still visible in the surface of the bridleway, where whinstone setts were laid to protect the cast iron pipe.

This is the extent of the remains close to the bridleway past the drift entrances; other remains exist at some distance. The start of the cutting running from the surface works down to the Little Roseberry drift entrance is visible from the bridleway. It runs in a north-easterly direction from the engine house area, and its full extent can be seen by climbing farther up the slopes of the Topping.

Although there is the reservoir close to the surface works, there is no evidence of a water source other than a pipe set to discharge into the reservoir. The 1930 Ordnance Survey map showed small foundations and surface piping in fields to the south of the Little Roseberry drift entrance, revealing a water collection system. The collection pond is still there today. Adjacent are the foundations for a pump, possibly powered by an oil engine, to provide the quantities of water needed by the steam engines at the mine.

The driver of the main haulage engine stood on this platform, which now has the appearance of an altar to the memory of past industry.

The mine buildings were constructed of iron sheeting, and were dismantled and sold after the closure. All that remains on the surface are concrete foundations. This is the floor of the stables, with its drainage channels.

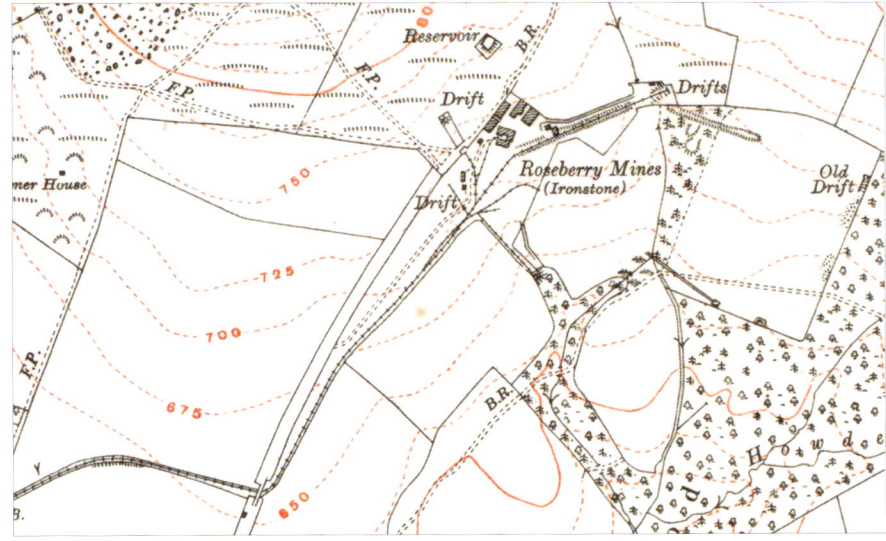

Extract from the 1930 Ordnance Survey map 29NW, original scale six inches to the mile, showing the mine site just after final closure.

Map image supplied by the
North Yorkshire County Record Office, Northallerton

© Crown Copyright and/or database right
All rights reserved Licence no 100046071

Copy of the 1929 abandonment plan of the Roseberry Ironstone Mine. It is immediately apparent that the entire cross-section of the Topping was mined. The early workings are on the left (west) of the plan, and the air shaft is marked. Later workings to the north-east joined up with the Hutton mines at Guisborough and in the south-east with the Ayton or Monument Mine.

Photograph supplied by Peter Tuffs of Guisborough.

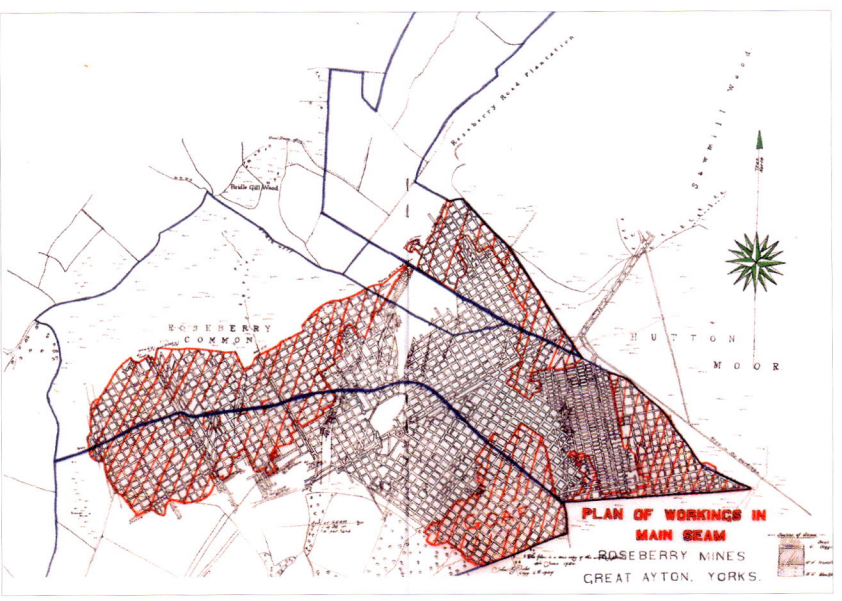

INDUSTRY ON ROSEBERRY *113*

One of the last known photographs of the Roseberry Ironstone Mine workings. The bord and pillar method of extracting ironstone can be seen, with the pillars holding up the roof of the mine. After bords or passageways had been driven throughout the mine, it was the usual practice to work back to the entrance, removing the pillars. About half of the mine workings were 'goafed' in this manner, leading to the collapse of the roof, but at this location the pillars remain.

The width of this passage suggests that the first stages of 'goafing' had taken place, with some of the rock pillars having been removed. The timber props would be a temporary measure to provide some support to the roof, and would later be removed to allow the entire roof to collapse. The state of the workings from both photographs indicates that the mine was not fully worked out.

Photographs from the collection of the late Richard Pepper, and supplied by Freda Phalp of Aireyholme.

Words of warning

The visible features of this large industrial activity can, in many cases, be seen from either the bridleway or the paths up to the summit of Roseberry. Visitors should be aware that all the industrial remains are on private land, which is under cultivation or grazing, and there is no right of access. No part of the site is in the new 'open access' areas.

Subsidence still occurs in the mine workings and further depressions may appear in the ground, possibly even opening into the actual mine workings. Should this occur, it would be very dangerous to attempt to enter. There is always the risk of further collapse and the air inside the mine is probably unsafe, especially as it may be deficient in oxygen and cause suffocation if breathed.

This is no idle warning. In late January 2006 subsidence opened up an entrance to the mine workings on the northern slopes. Shortly after this there were reports of two dogs having gone missing. The National Trust acted quickly to fence off the area, but the incident serves as a reminder of potential risks on the Topping from past mining activities.

Roseberry down under

Bearing in mind the Captain Cook connection, it is pleasing to find some places with the Roseberry name in the Antipodes, although there is absolutely no proof of connection with Yorkshire.

Rosebery is a suburb of Sydney in New South Wales. It was the home of the Roseberry Engine Works, which manufactured a variety of stationary petrol engines that were used in the Australian outback. The small engines were used to drive water pumps, saws, and sheep shearers. Many were marketed under the delightful name of 'Buzzacott' and are now collectors' items.

The Roseberry Mine on the west coast of Tasmania was discovered in 1893 by a prospector, Tom McDonald. It produces copper, zinc and lead, with some gold. Local people in Tasmania say that the mine was named after Lord Rosebery, but since Roseberry was the earliest of the Ayton ironstone mines, dating from 1880, it is at least theoretically possible that Tom McDonald had it in his mind when naming the mine. Another explanation may be through Edward John Rudd, a grandson of Bartholomew Rudd the younger who owned Aireyholme Farm. Edward John Rudd eventually settled in Tasmania in the 1860s, and in 1868 an affair with the 18-year old Martha Whitley resulted in the birth of a son William Edward Rudd.

There are several other mines in the Roseberry area of Tasmania, including the Colebrook Mine. By coincidence, Sir George Colebrooke bought the Cockshaw Alum Works in Great Ayton in 1772.

15

Roseberry's pits

One of the numerous depressions left by nineteenth century jet mining in the area of Roseberry Common. Little Roseberry is the high point in the top right-hand corner of the picture.

Mystery of the pits

One of Roseberry Topping's great mysteries is the origin of the many pits and depressions in the ground across much of the slopes. These have exercised the minds of many who have written about Roseberry in any detail. Most theories have been subsequently discredited, leaving the question substantially unanswered to this day. Part of the problem arises because there are three distinct groupings of pits. These groupings can be differentiated by reference to their elevations: those around the 200m contour, those between the 235m and 245m contours, and those around the 245m contour. There are significant differences between groupings, and also between the individual pits at the intermediate level. To make matters even more complex, the 245m pits run into those at the intermediate level. In addition to the pits there is also a bank and ditch earthwork running along the northern slope.

Although most of the various pits can be seen at ground level, particularly during the early months of the year before bracken and bramble growth, the best views are from the air. The 200m contour pits emerge from Newton Wood and continue in a line along the top edge of Cockle Scar. The 245m contour pits form a semi-circle around the upper slopes, and the intermediate pits are scattered almost at random across the north-eastern slopes and Roseberry Common. None of the pits feature among the *Cleveland County Sites and Monuments Records* or in the 1993 survey *Prehistoric and Roman Archaeology of North East Yorkshire*. Some of them have appeared spasmodically on Ordnance Survey maps, but in general they have been ignored.

This chapter will describe the location of the different groups of pits, review previous references, consider the geology of the area and try to suggest reasons why the pits were excavated. This logical sequence will not be followed exactly in the case of the intermediate-level pits. Because they are so varied, and because in most cases their origins are fairly clear, reasons for their excavation will be considered as they are described.

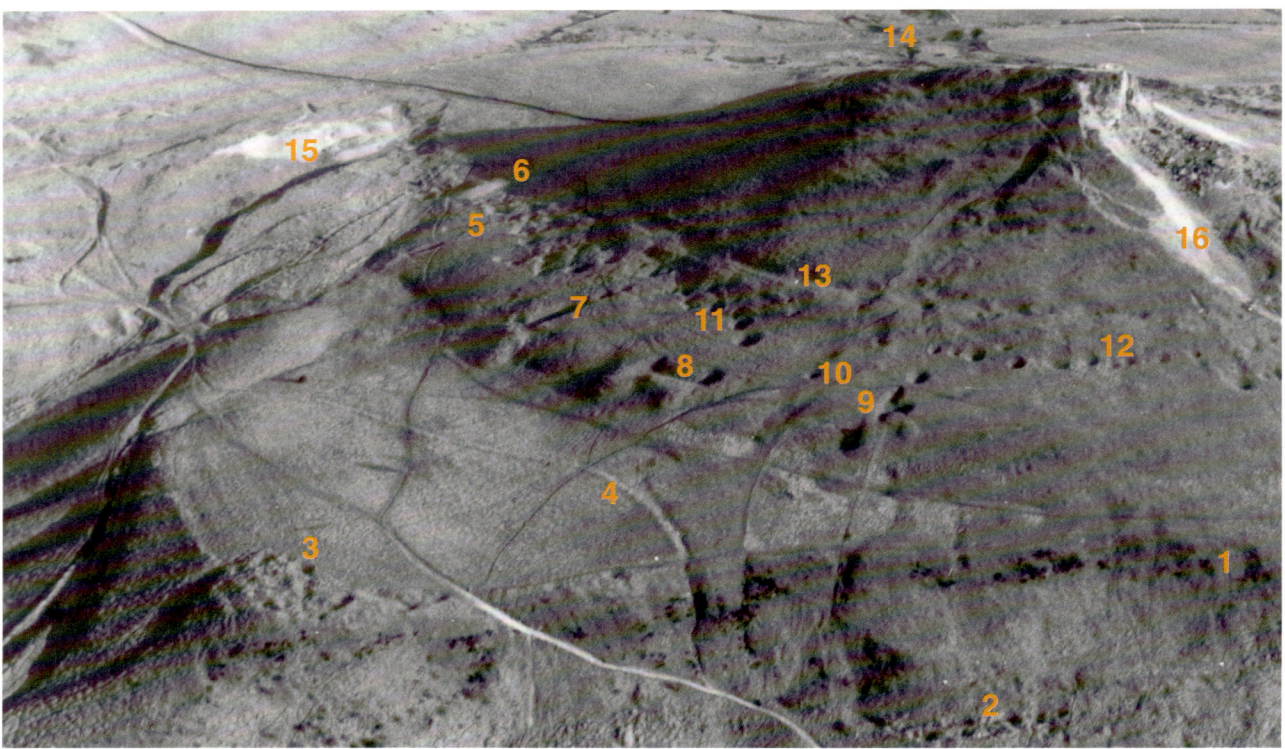

Roseberry's pits are best seen from the air, here from an aircraft flying over Newton under Roseberry towards the summit of the Topping. Brant Gate is the clearly defined path running up from the middle of the lower edge. Some of the features mentioned in the text are:

1 Line of pits at the 200m contour running along the edge of Cockle Scar
2 Some of the above pits that have slipped intact down the escarpment
3 Cluster of pits on the promontory
4 Prehistoric earthwork
5 Jet extraction sites, both mines and open-cast sites
6 Jet mining spoil heap
7 Early trial ironstone excavation
8 Ironstone mining trial excavation
9 Site where the first Roseberry Ironstone Mine drift possibly emerged from the hillside to provide natural ventilation
10 Roseberry Ironstone Mine air shaft
11 Probable ironstone mine subsidence pits
12 Higher level pits running around the 245m contour
13 Series of scoop-like excavations above the higher level pits
14 Site of the Roseberry Ironstone Mine buildings
15 Open-cast jet mining sites on Roseberry Common
16 Debris from the 1912 collapse

Photographs reproduced by kind permission of Tees Archaeology of Hartlepool

Another view of Roseberry's pits taken from an aircraft flying over Pinchinthorpe Hall.

To the south-west, the lower pits lie on the Newton side of the footpath which runs along the top edge of the woods.

The lower pits

There are over forty pits in a line almost exactly following the 200m contour, running along the top edge of Cockle Scar, an escarpment formed by relatively erosion-resistant sandstone. The paved path coming up from Roseberry Lane meets this line of pits at the gate leading out onto the open slopes of the Topping. To the south-west the pits are within Newton Wood, while to the north-east they are in open moorland. Generally they are about 15ft in diameter, between 3ft and 6ft in depth, and in some cases the side facing the edge of the escarpment has been eroded away. Some pits are connected by ditches.

When one walks along the top edge of Cockle Scar, the pits suddenly seem to vanish, only to reappear immediately after the paved Brant Gate path comes over the crest of the escarpment. Unlike the previous pits, which were arranged in a line, these ones form an irregular cluster at the end of a promontory. On this promontory there are, in addition to the pits, two fairly large ditches. Beyond this point, over towards Guisborough, the ground is very uneven and was described by Ord as having a sequence of pits stretching nearly as far as Hutton village.

It seems certain that at one time the pits continued all along Cockle Scar, and that the gap is the result of previous landslips. In 1817 George Young commented on landslips here, and Stephen Sherlock has recently pointed out that aerial photography shows evidence of a landslip. Remarkably, about ten of the 'missing' pits have survived

intact and can be seen today in a large piece of hillside that has slipped en bloc to form a terrace at the bottom of Cockle Scar. These 'missing' pits were engraved on the 1856 Ordnance Survey map, which depicted most of the lower-level pits apart from those under the trees of Newton Wood.

There are three more pits around the 200m contour that are seemingly disconnected from the rest. These are towards the southern end of the array and east of the main alignment, in open ground just outside the Newton Wood boundary fence. These three are the only ones in the entire group of 200m contour pits to appear on some later Ordnance Survey maps, but perhaps significantly they did not appear on the 1856 edition map.

The 200m contour is well below the ironstone and jet-bearing strata, and the underlying rock here is sandstone of insufficient strength for use in building. Early people may have dug exploratory pits in their search for minerals, but it is most unlikely that they would have continued to dig large numbers of pits in close proximity for such purposes.

The earthwork

There are the remains of a long earthwork cutting off the northern promontory of Roseberry Common, enclosing an area of about twelve acres. Sherlock measured cross sections of the earthwork; at the western end it was less than a foot high and just over eleven feet wide, while it was lower and narrower at the eastern end. There were traces of an exterior ditch which he suggested might have been built as a defensive earthwork, or as an enclosure for sheep and other animals as they were taken to and from the high moorland grazing.

The intermediate pits

The numerous pits lying between the 235m and 245m contours are scattered across the north-facing slopes. They vary considerably in size, depth, and profile. Some seem to have been excavated, while others appear to be collapsed underground workings. The pits are in the regions of jet bearing rock and ironstone, and so it is reasonable to suppose that they are associated with the extraction of these minerals. This view is supported by the variation in their elevation. The strata dip at a gradient of 1 in 28 from a high point on the western side down towards the east. This produces a fall of about forty feet across the Topping in the region of the Main Seam ironstone, and the pattern of pit sites tends to correspond with this dip.

Many of the intermediate pits can be seen from a grassy footpath which turns off the paved bridleway leading from Little Roseberry to the summit of the Topping. Immediately opposite the end of the dry stone wall, to the south of the bridleway, this footpath runs round the hill at an almost constant level. Looking across Roseberry Common from the start of the path, the most obvious signs of past mineral workings are the remains of a large open-cast jet working site. Where jet deposits might be found just beneath the surface of a relatively level area, open-cast mining was the most appropriate method. It was used elsewhere around Great Ayton, for example at the large open-cast jet mine at Ayton Banks, near to Gribdale Terrace.

There are also several other open-cast jet sites in the vicinity. More usually jet-bearing rock was reached by tunnelling a drift into the hillside. The remains of many of these drifts or adits can be seen, typically as a trench leading into the hillside with two or three pits, where the drift has partially collapsed, farther up the slope. The 1919 and subsequent editions of the Six Inch Ordnance Survey map print 'old workings' across this whole area, but do not specify what type of mineral was being worked.

Continuing along the path in a westerly direction, we can see a huge excavation. We are now leaving the area of jet mines and entering the region where most of the ground disturbance is due to ironstone mining. This excavation is marked on the 1878 Geological Survey map as an ironstone trial hole; in fact, commercial mining began three years later.

Also in this area are upwards of twenty circular pits scattered apparently at random on both sides of the path. Situated on a comparatively level area, these pits are quite different from those associated with jet mining; they are much larger, up to sixteen feet in diameter and twelve feet deep, with steep sides. They are probably subsidence cones, and are directly above the goafed workings of the Roseberry Ironstone Mine. Goafing was the technical term for removing the pillars supporting the roof of the mine and allowing the roof to collapse.

Two more large excavations are definitely due to nineteenth century ironstone mining, and can be easily identified by gorse bushes near their northern ends. These excavations were also shown on the 1878 Geological Survey map, one described as a second ironstone trial hole. Both were shown on the later editions of the Ordnance Survey map, described as 'old workings'. One of these excavations is almost certainly the place where the whole Main Seam was laid bare to assess its thickness and quality prior to work starting on the Roseberry Mine. The lease agreement for the extraction of ironstone had been signed in 1854, but nothing much was done on the ground until 1873.

The current shape of the second large excavation does not conform to the 1878 map, and is probably another trial hole which was later enlarged when the original 1880 mine tunnels broke out here to provide natural ventilation. Just above the end of this excavation there is a large subsidence cone, the footpath rather perilously passing between the two on a bridge of rock. In January 2006 subsidence re-opened the old mine workings here, providing an eerie glimpse into the bowels of the Topping. Halfway between the two large excavations a pit marks the site of a ventilation airshaft. The initial open-ended tunnel seems to have provided insufficient ventilation, and a chimney was constructed here to boost air flow. In 1912 this pit was filled in, but the material used either settled or migrated down into the old workings, and the operation was repeated in 1952.

Finally, at the place where our grassy path meets the paved path coming up from Newton to the summit, a narrow trench runs up the hillside from the 240m contour. This is probably an old adit for mining ironstone, and perhaps much earlier than the works associated with the Roseberry Mine in the later years of the nineteenth century. It was not shown on the 1878 Geological Survey map, but may have been overlooked by the surveyors.

The higher pits

Running around the upper slopes of the Topping, generally along the 245m contour, is a series of shallow pits with larger scoop-like excavations cut into the hillside above them at regular intervals. The series originally almost encircled the upper slopes, but many of these pits were lost in the ground disturbance consequent on the 1912 rockfall. However, a few remain intact to the south of the edge of the disturbed ground. On the east side of the hill these pits seem to run into the area of ironstone mine collapses.

The first Ordnance Survey map of the North Riding, published in 1856, clearly showed many of the Roseberry pits. These early surveyors produced a very accurate representation of what existed on the ground, in some ways superior to today's maps which generally omit the pits. Contours are shown at 25ft intervals. There are numerous spot heights marked in feet, especially around the summit.
© Crown Copyright and/or database right. All rights reserved Licence no 100046071

The 1856 Six Inch Ordnance Survey map clearly showed over sixty of these pits, generally aligned in two rows, running like a necklace round the hillside. They did not quite encircle the Topping; a sixty degree arc to the south east being devoid of any pits. Nearly forty years earlier Young had written of an entire circle of pits at this level, so it is possible that some had been destroyed in a landslip sometime between 1817 and 1851, when the survey work for the first edition Ordnance Survey map was carried out.

Nineteenth century ideas about the pits

It is interesting to look back at what various experts have had to say about the Roseberry pits, although sometimes this tells us more about the expert than the pits themselves. Young gave the oldest surviving description of the pits in 1817, commenting that they had 'in a great measure escaped the observation of former writers'. He drew on the knowledge of William Bird, who twenty-five years previously had observed that a great many of the hills facing the plain of Cleveland had rows of circular or oval pits or hollows running along their northern sides.

The most remarkable examples of these hollows could be seen on Roseberry Topping. Young made no mention of the intermediate pits, confirming that these were associated with jet and ironstone excavations towards the end of the nineteenth century.

Since similar hollows had been mentioned in a document from the nuns of Baysdale about the year 1200, Young concluded that some of the Roseberry pits could be pre-1200. He initially thought that these were pre-Roman dwellings, but after seven years' reflection he slightly changed his opinion, at least as regards the 200m contour pits. By 1824 he seemed fairly certain that they were military in origin:

> 'Towards the north-east corner of the base, or lower part of the hill, are the remains of an ancient British village; and it is observable, that the lines of hollows, marking the foundations of antique huts, run round the front, not only of Roseberry, but of each of the other large hills that skirt the plain of Cleveland. These chains of military posts, for so we may term them, are always found at some distance from the bottom of the hill; and are in some places single, in others double.'

The next authority to consider the problem was John Walker Ord. He had been told about the Roseberry pits by Mr Thomas of Pinchinthorpe House. Together they explored the entire hillside from Roseberry to Highcliffe, and Ord concluded in great excitement that he had discovered 'the remains of a complete BRITISH TOWN, of vast magnitude'. He excavated some of the pits, although these were almost certainly not the ones in the vicinity of Roseberry, and decided that most had been living quarters:

> 'Here, where human footstep scarcely ever treads, once dwelt a numerous and powerful tribe of Britons, actively engaged in the employments of peace or the necessities of war. They, like us, experienced the joys of love and hate, or the pangs of anguish and despair.'

By mid-nineteenth century the idea that the pits on the 200m and 245m contours were the remains of prehistoric houses was firmly established. In 1869 Samuel Gordon gazed on the pits and mused of 'a barbarous period, long, long ago, when these hills and valleys were inhabited by savage hordes' while rejoicing in the contrast between 'the darkness, cruelty, and Paganism of the dim and distant Past' and 'the light, peace, and civilisation of the Present'.

The Ordnance Survey initially took cautious notice of Ord, and their 1856 map carried the legend 'Remains of Supposed British Settlement' beginning at the higher-level pits on Roseberry and continuing almost to Hutton Lowcross outside Guisborough. But by the end of the century, and with the publication of the Geological Survey

The scarred surface of Roseberry Common is a bleak reminder of the intensive mining of jet over a century ago.

maps, opinion changed to the view that most of the pits were old mineral workings. Accordingly, on their 1895 map the Ordnance Survey referred to 'jet workings', but thereafter avoided controversy by dropping all mention of the pits.

Ord was succeeded as the authority on Cleveland history by Canon Atkinson of Danby. In his 1874 *History of Cleveland* Atkinson accepted Ord's views on the Roseberry pits, and even elaborated on them. Atkinson's acceptance of the habitation theory is surprising since from 1855 several authorities were suggesting that mineral extraction was a more plausible explanation for most of Yorkshire's pits. Perhaps news took a long time to reach Danby. However Atkinson did eventually change his mind, almost certainly because of the Geological Survey. He now turned against Ord, whom he seems to have considered over-imaginative and totally unreliable. As Burton later wrote:

> 'It must be remembered, however, that any statement by Ord, unless capable of absolute proof, seems to have roused in the worthy Canon, the greatest impatience and contempt, and he is therefore in matters of opinion not always a safe guide.'

In 1892 Atkinson described Ord's theory as 'preposterous rubbish'. He was by then convinced that the pits at Roseberry Topping, and indeed all the similar pits across the North Yorkshire moors, were sites where ironstone or jet were mined. He admitted that he had not actually excavated any pits, but he said that if he had he was quite sure he would have found that they were bell-shaped, because when they reached the ironstone, the miners would have dug horizontally, as far as they could. Atkinson even guessed that many pits might be linked underground by a system of interconnecting galleries. May we suggest that Atkinson, too, was perhaps laying himself open here to accusations of over-imagination and unreliability?

Some proper field work

The next local author to consider the problem was Joseph James Burton, in a paper to the Cleveland Naturalists' Field Club. Burton was the managing director of the company operating the Roseberry Ironstone Mine and a keen geologist. It is a great pity that he did not publish more as he was one of the more observant and objective of all the writers on the geology and history of Roseberry Topping. After running through the British settlement theories, he turned to more recent papers written by geologists. Tate and Blake had suggested that the jet used by the Romans could have come from Roseberry Topping. Three other geologists (George Barrow of the Geological Survey, Fox Strangeways, and Dr Veitch) had all been certain that the pits were old jet workings. It was with this in mind that Burton had some of the pits excavated in 1913 in an attempt to clear up the mystery.

From the information in his paper, Burton was certainly looking at the higher pits along the 245m contour, although frustratingly he provided no location map. He did not comment on the disappearance of many of these pits in the land slip one year before his investigations; perhaps he was uncomfortable that a good many people were blaming the incident on his mining operations.

He explained the investigations and results in a letter written in 1916:

> 'I put on two reliable men (old jet workers), to carefully open representative pits over a distance of, perhaps, three quarters of a mile on the N.W., N. and N.E. of the hill, and I spent as much time with them as I could spare and made them leave open every excavated area until I saw it. I had perhaps 20 of these sites fully exposed with the following results:-
>
> In only one case did the disturbed rock (shale) extend more than four feet down, and in most cases not more than two feet. In the excepted case there was near the centre, an irregular, slightly oval shaft of about four feet diameter sunk eight feet. In no case did the old floor of the pits extend horizontally into the jet rock or go down to the ironstone.
>
> There was not the slightest evidence of any "Bell pit" character. The ironstone below the pits was undisturbed and intact, and was worked out by my firm's miners in the regular underground workings.'

Burton sketched a typical cross section which he gave to William Edwards for his book on the early history of the North Riding. There was no scale in either publication, but both men stated that the pits were between two and four feet deep. In many instances Burton found large stones carefully piled up in the centre, as if they had supported a tent pole. In other pits there was evidence of a central hearth, with fire-marked stones and charcoal. In one pit some twelfth or thirteenth century pottery fragments were found, but as others have pointed out all

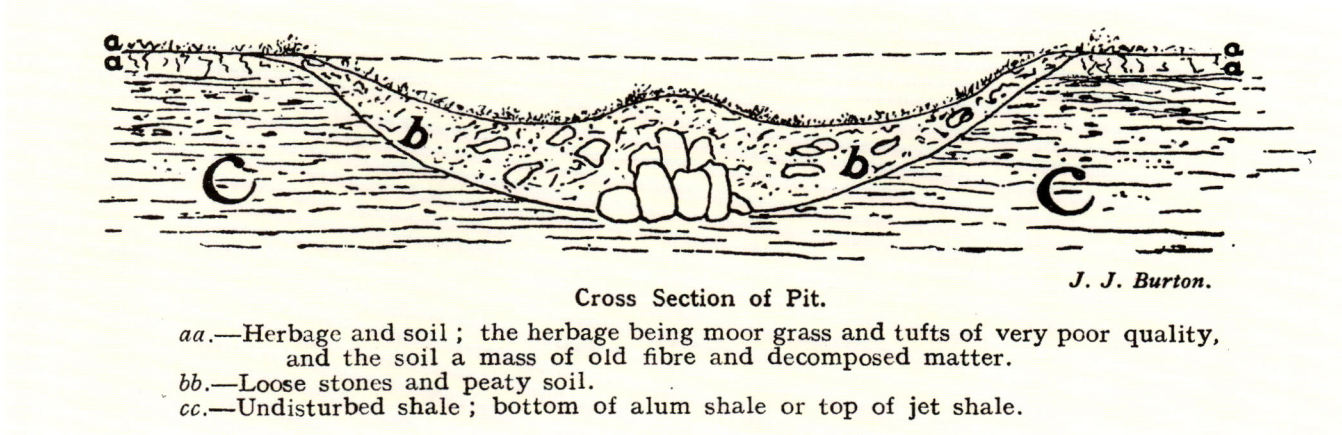

Cross Section of Pit.   *J. J. Burton.*

aa.—Herbage and soil; the herbage being moor grass and tufts of very poor quality, and the soil a mass of old fibre and decomposed matter.
bb.—Loose stones and peaty soil.
cc.—Undisturbed shale; bottom of alum shale or top of jet shale.

Cross-section of one of the pits excavated by Burton's men in 1913. Burton gave this drawing to William Edwards for his book on early man in the North Riding, and this version is taken from Edwards' book. Unfortunately the original carried no indication of scale.

this proves is that the pits were already there by the medieval period.

Burton was adamant that the pits investigated were neither old ironstone workings nor jet mines, and he made no further mention of the pit with the shaft sunk to a depth of eight feet, which might have suggested some form of mine. He had found nothing to prove or disprove the habitation theory, so he conceded that Ord might possibly have been correct in arguing for a domestic origin, but that this could only be 'a working hypothesis'. Burton thought Young's suggestion of military posts to be the most tenable theory, although Young seems to have been concerned only with the 200m contour pits as military posts, and Burton was only considering the 245m contour pits.

Later twentieth century views

In 1924 Edwards made the perceptive observation that it was clear there was no single theory to explain all the pits in North Yorkshire. Presumably referring to the 200m contour pits on Roseberry, he stated categorically that these were not iron workings and that there was no evidence for them to have been pit dwellings. He inclined to the view that they were defensive positions because of their situation.

Shortly after Edwards, Frank Elgee, probably the pre-eminent local archaeologist of the twentieth century, applied his mind to the question of the many pits or hollows found in the district. Elgee was able to take a much wider view than of Roseberry alone. He carefully went through previous publications, and pointed out that authors' changing view of the origin of the pits, from dwellings to mineral workings, was due to the Geological Survey. This began in 1835, and ten years later its field officers gained legal status but lost their blue serge uniforms complete with brass buttons and top hats. By the latter part of the nineteenth century their geological surveys of north-east Yorkshire pits were demonstrating the proximity of many pits to ironstone and jet deposits. Indeed, they specifically commented that jet had been worked in old times along the escarpment to the south-west of Guisborough as far as Roseberry Topping, and that the so-called 'Ancient British Settlements' were nothing but the remains of these pits.

Elgee deduced that the majority of the Yorkshire pit sites were dwelling places from the Urn Period (1110-650 BC), although he excluded Roseberry from this deduction. On the Roseberry pits he concluded that a prehistoric date had not been proven, and that a medieval one was more likely. He simply did not comment on whether they might have been dug for habitation, for mining or for defence.

During the next sixty-five years any author who mentioned the pits merely repeated selected extracts from previous authors. There appears to have been no more serious field study after Burton's 1913 work until 1995. However, there is an important snippet from 1937, when Sir Alfred Pease wrote a letter to John Fairfax Blakeborough recalling his boyhood days around Roseberry: 'I dug up flints and arrowheads from the pits,

which I believed to be the remains of British houses, in view of the burnt stones I came across'. Pease was born in 1857, and so must have found his artefacts in the pits along the 200m and 245m contours, evidence that at least some of these dated back to prehistoric times.

Steve Sherlock's paper

In 1995 the professional local archaeologist, Steve Sherlock, wrote a paper on Roseberry Topping in which he went over the available evidence, in publications and in the field. His on-site investigations only identified a minority of the pits, and he did not mention the higher level pits along the 245m contour at all. However, he did draw a clear distinction between the pits at the intermediate level and those at the lower level, stating that the lower ones formed a fairly regular line along the edge of the plateau, whereas the intermediate ones were part of an untidy complex of 'pits, roadways, terraces and waste dumps'.

When it came to the question of the origin of the pits, Sherlock slightly hedged his bets. Of the intermediate level group he wrote:

> 'Although some of the pits and disturbed ground can be seen to be the result of extractive industries, it is not thought that all of these features are from recent industries, although their origin and function are at present unknown.'

About the 200m contour ones he ventured no opinion, except to say that they could not have had anything to do with ironstone or jet because they were some 35m below these levels.

Getting to the bottom of the pits

We can now present our thoughts on the origins of the different families of pits around Roseberry. The pits on the 200m contour, along Cockle Scar, were probably all excavated at the same time and for the same reason, because of their similarities in size, shape, and location. They might well be at least 1000 years old, and perhaps even prehistoric. The only possible exception is the group of three in open ground to the east of the Newton Wood boundary which, due to their absence from the 1856 Ordnance Survey map, may be much more recent. There are no useful minerals at the 200m contour level. The exposed location and linear alignment seem incompatible with habitation sites, although there would have been water available from springs farther up the hill. From the evidence of flints and arrowheads, it is clear that at least some of the pits are prehistoric in origin. The remaining explanations of their origin include boundary marking, defensive positions or some ritual purpose.

Linear arrays of shallow pits were used as boundary markers elsewhere in Yorkshire during the Bronze Age, but a boundary theory cannot easily explain why the linear alignment should end with a cluster of pits at the northern promontory. Defensive reasons may seem more plausible. The pits are in an excellent strategic position at the top of a steep escarpment, with a commanding view across the Tees and beyond. Some of the pits now in Newton Wood appear to have an embankment wall built up on their western side, facing down the slope. Today it may seem odd that so many defensive excavations would be needed along what is the steepest part of the escarpment, but 2000 years ago the shape of the slope could have been entirely different; we know there have been landslips here at different periods since then. If these pits were originally defensive their origins may well be prehistoric; they may, however, date from the time of inter-tribal warfare after the departure of the Romans, or even from the subsequent years of invasions from the north and from Europe.

The alternative to a defensive explanation is that last resort for anything that archaeologists do not readily understand, some unspecified prehistoric ritual purpose. We can refer to Sherlock Holmes when he told Dr Watson that 'when you have eliminated the impossible, whatever remains, however improbable, must be the truth'. Adopting this principle, and if a defensive role is rejected, we should perhaps conjecture that the lower linear pit alignment may be prehistoric in origin and religious in purpose.

It is much easier to explain the several distinct types of pits at the intermediate level. Most, if not all, of these are associated with the extraction of jet and ironstone, and all the evidence suggests they date from the second half of the nineteenth century. There would be sound reasons for their excavation at that time; the demand for jet increased after the deaths of the Duke of Wellington in 1852 and Prince Albert in 1861, and the exploratory excavations for Roseberry Ironstone Mine were taking place around 1873.

Finally, we come to the pits ranged along the 245m

contour, although here we should probably distinguish between the pits themselves and the slightly higher, scoop-like excavations. Because of their similarities in size, shape, and location these were probably excavated at the same time and for the same reason. There is no ironstone here. Elsewhere, the Dogger seam of ironstone might be expected just below the sandstone of the summit, but in the Roseberry area this seam is absent. Neither is there any jet here. Burton's excavations showed these pits to be well above the jet deposits, and recent auger-borings have confirmed this, with only clay being found to a depth of at least five feet. Surely the location also makes it unlikely that they were habitation sites. Some writers have dreamed of a hill fort at the summit of Roseberry, leading to the vague possibility that the pits may have had some defensive role. Perhaps these pits, too, had some ritual significance; the most striking aspect of the higher-level pits is the way in which they encircled the upper part of the hill, although some have been lost in land slippages. We know that Roseberry Topping was a sacred mountain and it is not difficult to imagine them as having some quasi-religious origin. It has even been suggested that they could be places where corpses were left to decay prior to the bones being given funereal rites.

However the debate continues

Just as the text for this chapter was being finalised, we came across a new theory about the origin of the pits. William Pearson of Stockton-on-Tees has been studying Gaelic place-names in Cleveland for many years. In a recent, and well-researched, paper he devoted several pages to *àirigh*, the early Irish word for 'cow farm'. This word, which is usually spelt as 'erg', appears in various forms in a great many place-names across Northern England, and is associated with the Irish-Norse invaders of the tenth century. An obvious example locally is that of 'Ergum', the Domesday name for the present-day Aireyholme Farm.

Pearson suggested that ergs were hollows, which could be fitted with temporary roofing, for summer occupation to oversee cattle grazing. Ergs are found across Cleveland, for example, near Commondale, near Swainby, and at Sleddale. He initially proposed that at least some of the pits on Roseberry might have been ergs, or temporary shelters for those watching cattle grazing, dating from the tenth century.

In discussion we agreed that it would only be the lower levels pits that might have been used as shelters whilst keeping an eye on grazing cattle; those at intermediate levels were too recent and the higher pits too remote. Although the Cockle Scar pits are well-placed for observing large areas of the Cleveland Plain, they are clearly too numerous to have all been dug as ergs. Bill Pearson then offered an alternative and fascinating explanation. Suppose that these pits were prehistoric, and thus already there when the Irish-Norse invaders arrived. To the newcomers the shape of these hollows would have reminded them of 'ergs'. It would then have been entirely logical for them to call the place 'Ergum', not because it was a place of summer pastures for their cattle, but because the hill was already covered in hollows that looked like old ergs.

It was good to find someone else thinking about Roseberry's mysterious pits, and adding something new to the two-hundred year old debate about their origin. In the absence of any conclusive explanation for the origins of many of Roseberry's pits, the debate may continue for a good many years to come.

a Topping radio programme

Listing from the Radio Times Outside Broadcast Number, dated June 4, 1937

Image supplied by Kelly Books Limited (www.kellybooks.co.uk)

> **8.40 'FINE PROSPECTS'**
> 'The View from Roseberry Topping on the Cleveland Hills'. Roseberry is the only mountain in the Clevelands, and is a landmark for sailors coming to the Tees. You can see from it two distinct aspects of the landscape—natural and industrial. J. Fairfax-Blakeborough will tell you of the country itself, of its people, and of the natural history, and G. H. J. Daysh will talk particularly about the development of Middlesbrough over the delta of the Tees. The Tees, of course, is peculiar among the rivers of the north-east coast in having such a delta. The others reach the sea in steep-sided valleys. Captain Cook spent his boyhood at the farm just under Roseberry. There is a holy well there, too, where they say a royal prince was drowned.
> *(From Newcastle)*

What's on the wireless?

Readers of the Radio Times in June 1937 would have seen the announcement of the first of a series of radio programmes called 'Fine Prospects'. This broadcast started at 8:40 in the evening of Tuesday 8 June 1937, and concerned Roseberry Topping. The programme, *The View from Roseberry Topping on the Cleveland Hills*, involved a twenty-minute discussion between a presenter named Williams, Major J Fairfax Blakeborough and Professor G H J Daysh of Armstrong College, Newcastle upon Tyne. Perhaps surprisingly, but rather splendidly, the original script has been preserved in the BBC Archives in Reading. Although the script was typed, there were many *ad hoc* modifications added in pencil. The style was as informal as contemporary etiquette would permit, the Major being referred to as 'Blakeborough' and the Professor as 'Daysh'.

What's Roseberry Topping?

Much to Blakeborough's surprise the programme presenter, rather disparagingly referred to as 'X', had never heard of Roseberry Topping. In the script he was supposed to respond 'Oh Lord, never admit that to a Yorkshireman' but for the broadcast this was toned down to 'Oh Heavens, never admit that to a Yorkshireman'. Blakeborough quoted from Margery Moorpout's homily to the Topping, reproducing her Cleveland dialect, and also from the Cottonian manuscript. Williams realised that Blakeborough was anything but dispassionate about the mountain, and he turned to Daysh, introduced as a comparative stranger, for a second opinion. Daysh agreed that the view was magnificent, and went on to describe the Topping's surroundings.

The speakers then moved on to consider the view to the north, commenting that Teesside industrial smoke almost always obscured this view. It was only during the 1926 strike, when the works were all idle, that the Cheviots could be seen. Standing at the summit of the Topping today, and looking across to the Cheviots, makes one realise how much cleaner industry is now. Daysh contrasted the people who lived in urban Teesside with the Clevelanders in their scattered villages and hamlets. Cleveland's strong Norse connections were discussed, and

Jack Fairfax Blakeborough, the major contributor to the 1937 programme about Roseberry Topping. This photograph was taken in 1969, when he was 85. Jack Fairfax Blakeborough died in 1976
Photo: Northern Echo and Darlington & Stockton Times

then Blakeborough went through some of the folk lore associated with the Topping; the Holy Well that could cure sore eyes, the Prince Oswy legend, and Nan the witch. He blamed ironstone mining for draining the Holy Well, adding that mining stopped after the war; of course he would have been referring to the 1914-1918 World War. The disused workings had attracted hundreds of visiting youths and so the opening to the subterranean passages had been blocked up.

Industry

The discussion then turned to mining and quarrying. Ironstone was still being mined in Cleveland at that time, although not at Roseberry. Jet was dismissed with the comment 'nobody uses it nowadays. It's quite out of fashion'. Daysh said that the only quarrying then taking place in Cleveland was for ironstone, building stone, road metalling and ganister (this mineral was used to make refractory linings for blast furnaces, and was extracted at Castleton).

Finally, they returned to the contrast between Cleveland and Teesside. Blakeborough claimed that Cleveland had produced some men of vision and brains, but only managed to think of one; inevitably this was James Cook, gazing out to sea from the summit of Roseberry. Daysh championed Teesside, the rapid expansion of its steel and chemical industries, and the reclamation of land at Seal Sands.

This is about where the programme script was planned to finish but Blakeborough, anxious to take listeners back to Roseberry Topping, managed to insert a new final line 'We Clevelanders will always lift our eyes to the hills in pride and affection'.

Broadcast to the nation

It is interesting that this programme was broadcast across the nation as well as regionally. In those days, when television was virtually unknown, one wonders what sort of image of the Topping was created in the minds of the majority of listeners who would not be familiar with North Yorkshire, let alone Roseberry. One might imagine that a few were tempted to seek out and climb Roseberry before the Second World War effectively put an end to leisure travel for so long.

It would be even more fanciful to speculate whether some of the soldiers of the East Lancashire Regiment and the North Staffordshire Regiment, who later found themselves in Great Ayton during the war years, recalled this programme as they looked out on the Topping just a mile away.

Roseberry on historical maps

The first maps of Yorkshire

Not until the sixteenth century did maps of North Yorkshire, drawn to scales large enough to feature what we now call Roseberry Topping, start to appear. It was not long before publishers, anxious to avoid expensive surveys, started to copy from earlier work. In an era before copyright legislation, maps could be given a new look by improved engraving and printing. Of course, this practice meant that surveying errors, or unusual spellings of place names, were often transmitted from one map to another.

Another source of errors, particularly in place names, came about because the most highly skilled engravers were in the Netherlands. Working from documents written in a foreign language about an unfamiliar country, they sometimes made mistakes.

Christopher Saxton 1577

The first definitive survey of England and Wales was carried out by a Yorkshireman, Christopher Saxton. Norfolk, in 1574, was the first county to be completed. Yorkshire, or *Eboracens*, appeared in 1577 and the complete *Atlas of the Counties of England and Wales* two years later. Saxton's maps were engraved on thirty-five copper plates, usually by Flemish engravers. There was

Christopher Saxton map of Yorkshire from 1577. Reproduced here at 13% larger than original size. The structure at the summit of 'Ounsbury' may represent a beacon fire. Elsewhere on this map beacons are shown as a pole with three tar barrels. Copyright The British Library, 2006. Reproduced by permission of The British Library

a general map of England and Wales, followed by thirty-four maps of individual counties or groups of counties. The original proof maps are kept in a bound volume at the British Library.

Yorkshire was distinguished for two reasons: firstly, owing to its size, it had to be engraved on two plates, secondly, because it was engraved by a Yorkshireman, Augustine Ryther of Leeds. The scale was 1:210,000 or just under one inch to $3\frac{1}{3}$ miles. Originally printed in black ink, many of the copies were later hand-coloured. Forests were shown by small clumps of trees, and hills by molehill-like symbols, with their height roughly proportional to actual heights. Great Ayton appeared as 'Enton' and Roseberry Topping as 'Ounsbury toppin hill'. The Topping seems to have been given the honour of being the highest hill in the North Riding.

Saxton's map pre-dates the use of triangulation and little is known about his surveying techniques, but the result was surprisingly accurate. Settlements were shown by symbols according to population, and the place names of Pinchinthorp, Huton, Newton, Gisburgh and Stokesley all appeared on the map, but no roads were given.

Individual sheets of Saxton's map were sold at four pence each. These maps formed the basis for county maps for over one hundred years, sometimes redrawn at different scales, notably in William Camden's *Britannia* of 1586. A complete atlas of Saxton's county maps was issued as a new edition in 1645 and was used by both sides during the Civil War.

John Speed 1612

John Speed was born in 1552 in Cheshire, and initially followed his father's occupation as a tailor. However his true interest was in history and antiquities, and he moved to London where he soon enjoyed the patronage of Sir Fulke Greville, who arranged a post for him in the Customs Service. This gave him sufficient free time to pursue his historical work. He joined the Society of Antiquaries, where he met Camden. Speed's great work was the *History of Great Britaine,* with its accompanying book of maps, *The Theatre of the Empire of Great Britaine*, published in 1612. The maps were to have been engraved by the talented English engraver William Rogers, but he died after only completing the first map, that of Cheshire. Camden recommended the Flemish engraver, Jodocus Hondius, who had worked in London for several years previously, and Hondius duly completed the remaining sixty-six maps. The atlas was printed in black but purchasers could pay to have the pages coloured, although this was expensive and few did so at the time. Given his historical interest, Speed included many notes on antiquarian remains, including some Roman roads, although no actual roads were shown. The maps were clearly intended for library study, supporting his *History of Great Britaine*, rather than as an aid to travel. It is accepted that Speed copied much from previous maps, mainly Saxton and Robert Norden. He was quite open about this, admitting 'I have put my sickle into other mens corne, and have laid my building upon other mens foundations'.

At first sight, Speed's rendering of the area of Roseberry Topping seems to be a copy of Saxton's map, but closer study reveals some important revisions. Ayton had replaced Enton and the profile of the Topping was shown relatively accurately. However, some unusual aspects of the map probably resulted from Hondius's unfamiliarity with English. Ounsbury toppin hill became Cúsbye Toppí Hill. The initial letter 'C' is probably a mistake, but the use of the accent here, and indeed elsewhere on the map, seems to be a convention for dropping the following letter 'n'.

John Speed map from 1612, original scale 1:250,000 or one inch to just under four miles. Reproduced here at 33% larger than original size. With permission of NYCC Record Office, Northallerton

Joan Blaeu map from 1662, original scale 1:220,000 approximately, or one inch to 3½ miles. Reproduced here at 33% larger than original.
With the permission of the NYCC Record Office, Northallerton

Joan Blaeu 1662

In 1638 Joan Blaeu took over the family printing business in Amsterdam after the death of his father, Willem Blaeu, an outstanding map-maker of his age. Blaeu had been engaged in a bitter struggle with none other than Jodocus Hondius, involving accusations of plagiarism and a succession of law suits. Joan Blaeu produced county maps of England and Wales as part of his massive world atlas *Theatrum Orbis Terrarum sive Atlas Novus*, later known as the *Atlas Maior*. Originally published in 1662, in Latin, it was translated into several other languages until the plates were tragically destroyed in a fire in 1672. With six hundred beautifully engraved coloured maps, it was the most expensive book money could buy at the time.

The map containing Roseberry, shown as Cusbye Toppin hill, was never translated into English. A Spanish version has a description of Roseberry on its reverse side, which in translation reads as follows.

'Not very far from here rises the craggy, sharp mountain, Ounsbery Topping, in which abound precipices, although it is always covered with pleasant, continuous green, it is a perfect lookout tower, from which a vast area is visible, and it serves as a landmark for sailors and a guide to those living nearby, given that the summit touches the clouds and from around there almost always fall copious rains. Close to the top, from the rocky crags, bursts forth a spring, the waters of which are a renowned remedy for those with eye infections'.

John Ogilby 1675

Saxton, Speed and Blaeu had not shown roads, their maps being published in large and expensive books and not intended for travellers. Travellers' needs had been met by books describing routes in words only, such as the *Itinerary* by John Leland published from 1535 to 1545, *An Intended Guyde for English Travailers* by John Norden in 1625 and *A Direction for the English Traviller* by Matthew Simmons in 1635. This would change with the work of John Ogilby.

Ogilby had little formal education and worked as a dancing master and theatre producer, before turning to book publishing. Perhaps these wider experiences encouraged his innovative approach to map making, and in 1675 he became the first person to recognise the importance of a pictorial representation of the route, with his famous strip maps. *Britannia, a Geographical and Historical Description of the Principal Roads thereof* contained a hundred maps covering 7500 miles of roads in England and Wales in strip form. Ogilby took great care with the accuracy of his measurements, employing a 'wheel

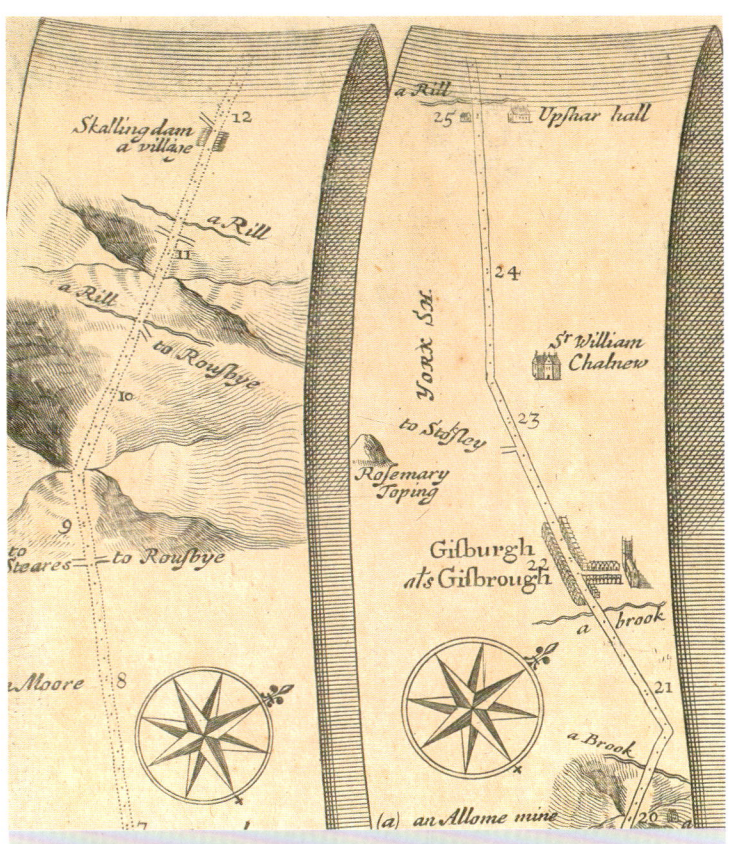

John Ogilby strip map from 1675, original scale 1:63,360 or one inch to the mile. Reproduced here at 40% smaller than original size.
With the permission of the NYCC Record Office, Northallerton

dimensurator'. Not only was his strip format an important innovation, he also used the scale of one inch to the statute mile, which was to be used a map standard for over 300 years.

One of Ogilby's maps was of the road from Whitby to Durham. The seventeenth century road closely followed the east-west alignment of the present A171 in the vicinity of Roseberry. Roadside figures represent increasing distances from Whitby. Roseberry Topping is shown as an isolated hill a mile or so out of Guisborough, near the turning to 'Stoksley', and is described as 'Rosemary Toping'.

John Warburton 1720

Although Ogilby's maps were invaluable for travellers, the strips inevitably showed only features immediately adjacent to the road. There was still a need for a single map covering a large area, and marking roads in addition to the usual geographical features. As a Supervisor of Excise, John Warburton was stationed at Bedale in Yorkshire, and while there he produced his 1720 map of Yorkshire, *A New and Correct Map of the County of York*. He employed a scale of two and a half miles to the inch,

John Warburton map from 1720, original scale 1:158,400, or one inch to 2½ miles. Reproduced here at 60% larger than original size.
With the permission of the Leeds Central Library

and showed roads in great detail. The distances between market towns are given in 'computed' and 'measured' miles, perhaps displaying a slight mistrust of mathematics. 'Rosebutry Toping' is drawn with what looks like Little Roseberry to the east. The title of Warburton's map was always going to tempt providence, and Little Ayton is incorrectly positioned west of Ayton Mag (Great Ayton) whereas it should be to the east. Warburton had somewhat of a reputation for inaccuracy, and he landed in trouble with the College of Arms over errors in reproducing the coats of arms included on some of his maps.

Thomas Jefferys 1771-72

The second half of the eighteenth century was a time of great change. The spread of good turnpike roads reduced

Thomas Jefferys map from 1771-1772, original scale 1:63,360 or one inch to the mile. Reproduced here at 20% smaller than original size.
With the permission of the NYCC Record Office, Northallerton

journey times for post and passengers, while canals provided an efficient way of transporting commodities. Steam power and 'manufactories' revolutionised the production of goods. Agricultural methods improved, feeding the growth of urban areas. Much of the wealth created by these changes went into new estates and country houses. All these changes affected the landscape, and led to demands for better maps. Thomas Jefferys recognised this demand, and he also saw that maps might be surveyed and printed as a commercial investment, rather than their makers needing to seek the support of the government or a wealthy patron. However, his cartography was better than his financial skills, and he teetered on the verge of bankruptcy.

Jefferys worked as an engraver and publisher of maps in London. Initially copying and revising existing maps, he took the considerable financial risk of commissioning new surveys across the country.

His *Large Scale Map of Yorkshire* was published in twenty sheets in 1771 and 1772, at a scale of one inch to the mile. There is no doubt that his maps were the best available until the first One Inch Ordnance Survey maps appeared about thirty years later. A large amount of detail was included, reflecting the new features in the landscape; turnpike roads, canals, mills, mines, and country houses and estates. Thomas Jefferys himself probably never set foot in Yorkshire. The surveying was carried out by Joseph Hodskinson, Thomas Donald and John Ainslie from 1767 to 1770, and it is likely that Hodskinson did the Ayton survey work.

The ups and downs of the landscape were portrayed by hachuring, lines drawn on the map to indicate the steepness of slopes by their closeness. This represented a massive step forward in map-making from the previous practice of selecting certain hills in profile. The technique is well illustrated locally, where the high moors can be distinguished from the lower platform from which the Topping emerges. Not everyone recognised the significance of this innovation and Tuke's maps of 1787 showed high ground only by shading over the entire area.

Charles Smith 1801

As a stationer, and a map and globe seller in London, Charles Smith produced his *New Map of Yorkshire Divided into Ridings* in 1801, printed on four sheets. Distances were marked on some turnpike roads. Locally, distances were shown in miles from Stokesley, an important market town. Langbaurgh Quarry, opened up for the extraction of whinstone, appeared for the first time. The area of 'Cliverick', to the south of Roseberry Topping, was a corruption of Cliff Rigg, as was the more common version, 'Liverick'.

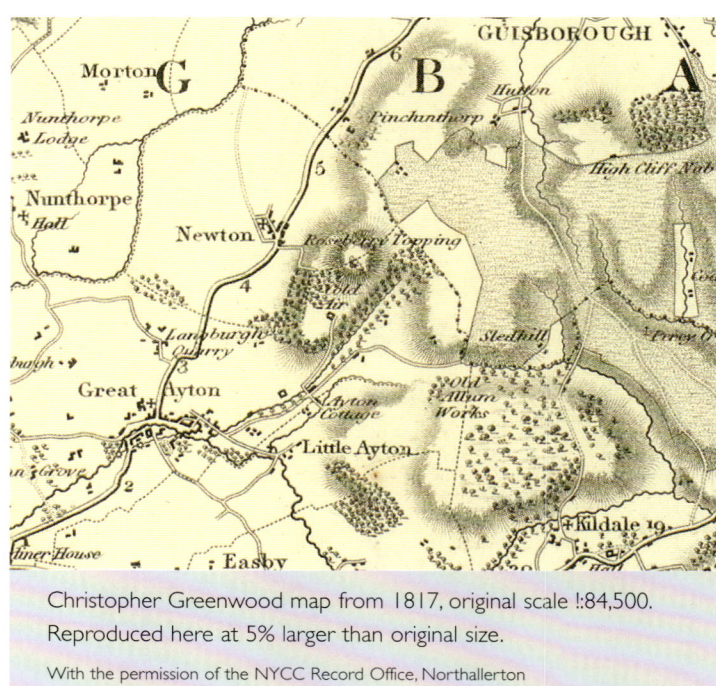

Christopher Greenwood map from 1817, original scale 1:84,500. Reproduced here at 5% larger than original size.

With the permission of the NYCC Record Office, Northallerton

Christopher Greenwood 1817-1818

Christopher Greenwood was a Yorkshireman, born in the West Riding in 1786. By the time he was thirty he was established as a surveyor in Wakefield, although he would later move to London. His first major work was *A Map of the Whole County of York*, published in nine sheets from 1817 to 1818. He then moved on with unbelievable speed to prepare an atlas of forty-two maps of the English and Welsh counties. This is all the more impressive since all the maps were based on surveys by himself and his brother John.

The scale adopted for the Yorkshire map was unusual: one inch to just over one and a third miles. The Greenwood maps were very finely engraved, and are perhaps the first historical maps which are similar to today's Ordnance Survey publications. Strangely, the farm now known as Aireyholme, just south of Roseberry, is marked as 'Cold Air'. A tortuous track, the upper reaches

Charles Smith map from 1801, original scale 1:158,400, or one inch to about 2½ miles. Reproduced here at 90% larger than original size.

With the permission of the NYCC Record Office, Northallerton

Before aerial photographs and satellite-based global positioning systems (GPS) were available, maps were drawn based on the principle of triangulation. This involved accurately measuring the length of a baseline, and then taking a bearing on a distant object from each end of the baseline. Distances from the baseline were then calculated by trigonometry. Bearings of new objects were then taken from the first triangle. The baseline was traditionally measured by the surveyor's chain, twenty-two yards long. This distance is more familiar today as the length of a cricket pitch.

In the mid-1930s Ordnance Survey started the monumental task of re-triangulation, marked out by the construction of the familiar concrete pillars, commonly known as trig points. Each trig point was fitted with a metal socket for accurate location of the theodolite used to take bearings. Britain was covered by a network of trig points, including the one on the summit of Roseberry Topping. The complete re-triangulation was not be finished until 1962, by which time aerial photography had become the established source of data for revisions. Today, GPS has made the Roseberry trig point redundant, but it is still cared for by Ray Pinder of Great Ayton who occasionally freshens it up with a coat of white paint.

JC

of which no longer exist, is clearly shown from Newton to 'Cold Air'. This track ends somewhere near the enigmatic summerhouse, which had been built by the end of the eighteenth century.

Christopher and John Greenwood's maps were to be amongst the last of the county maps produced by independent surveyors and publishers. The Ordnance Survey office was about to revolutionise British map surveying, printing and publishing.

Born out of revolution – the Ordnance Survey

The foundation date of the Ordnance Survey is generally accepted as June 1791, but its origins go back to the Jacobite rebellion of 1745. After quelling the rebellious Scots, George II commissioned a survey of the Scottish Highlands from the Board of Ordnance, the equivalent of today's Ministry of Defence. Hence the description 'Ordnance Survey'. Later in the eighteenth century, another rebellion provided the impetus for an Ordnance Survey of England. This was the French Revolution, which raised real fears of a cross-Channel invasion. Preparing for the worst, the government ordered a detailed survey of the southern coast, and within ten years maps had been printed of Kent and Essex, at the familiar scale of one inch to the mile. When Nelson and Wellington effectively removed any threat from France, the military imperative for accurate maps lessened. Fortunately, at the same time there was an increasing demand for definitive maps required in connection with the management and transfer of land and for civil engineering schemes, from sewers to railways.

Roseberry on Ordnance Survey maps

The first Ordnance Survey maps, known as the Old Series, started to appear in 1805. Progress with extending the maps northwards was slow, and unfortunately for Roseberry Topping the early surveys stopped at a line from Preston to Hull. It was not until 1840 that surveying recommenced northwards. In 1851 a botany party from the North of England Agricultural College, later better known as the Great Ayton Friends' School, encountered some 'Royal Engineers' on the Topping. At that time the Ordnance Survey was using companies of Royal Sappers and Miners for survey work; in fact they would not be transferred to the Royal Engineers until 1856. The sappers told the scholars that they were engaged in the most complete survey of the country since the Domesday Book.

The 1856 edition of the Six Inch maps of Yorkshire showed Roseberry Topping in some detail. Roseberry Well was marked just below the 1000ft contour, with another spring on the northern slope just below the 900ft contour. There was a sandstone quarry near the summit. The lower southern slopes, above the summerhouse, were shown as wooded. Those mysterious pits, in a double line running round the upper slopes, were clearly depicted between the 800ft and 850ft contours.

The 1892 Twenty-five Inch map showed Roseberry in even greater detail. A band of conifers ran round the

Ordnance Survey map from 1919. Original scale six inches to the mile. Reproduced here at 33%. Roseberry Topping is covered on two of the Yorkshire (North Riding) sheets, XVII SW and XXIX NW. Map images supplied by the NYCC Record Office, Northallerton
© Crown Copyright and/or database right All rights reserved Licence no 100046071

entire southern slope. The boundary between Ayton and Newton was designated as 'Union Boundary', a reminder of the unpopular nineteenth century workhouse system for poor relief. By this time, the first phase of ironstone mining at Roseberry was over, and the site was marked as 'Old Level (Ironstone)' along with two shafts, the route of the original tramway, and the stone-built powder magazine.

For many, the Ordnance Survey will always be associated with maps printed to a scale of one inch to the mile. The first time that Roseberry Topping was seen on such a map was when the Old Series Sheet 104 for Whitby was published in 1860-61. More advanced hachuring brought out the detailed relief of the hill and its surroundings. In 1872 the first maps of the New Series appeared, based on a new survey. They were available either as 'hill' format with hills shaded, or as 'outline' with contours shown for the first time. The New Series brought another innovation; the maps were folded inside covers so that they would fit into a pocket. Colour printing began with the 1895 editions.

The 1919 map dramatically revealed the effects of the 1912 land slip, with a large area of disturbed ground covering much of the south-west slopes. This map also included the buildings and tramways associated with the second phase of ironstone mining.

Greater demand for maps

At the beginning of the twentieth century the rapid increase in cycling, and later in motoring, led to a much greater market for civilian maps. The Popular Edition of the 1920s was specifically designed for motorists, cyclists and tourists, with a splendid red cover appropriately featuring a cyclist in a Norfolk jacket and plus fours, studying the map. The Fifth Edition of the 1930s had a hiker in a similar pose.

In the mid 1930s the monumental task of re-triangulation was started, marked out by the construction of the familiar concrete triangulation pillars on high points across the land, including the one on the summit of Roseberry Topping. The complete re-triangulation would not be finished until 1962, by which time aerial photography became the established source of data for revisions.

Although the armed services had been overprinting maps with a purple grid system for map references for many years, the metric National Grid did not appear on commercial Ordnance Survey maps until the 1950s. Metric scales, initially at 1:50,000, were being introduced, but the ever-popular One Inch Series was to continue for some time, culminating in the Tourist Maps of the 1970s. Maps of tourist areas were nothing new, but this was the first time that the Ordnance Survey had considered the North York Moors as sufficiently important to warrant their own tourist map. With Whitby Abbey on its black cover, it indicated picnic, camp and caravan sites in small red symbols. Tinting and hill shading were added to the usual contour lines. However, the typical tourist,

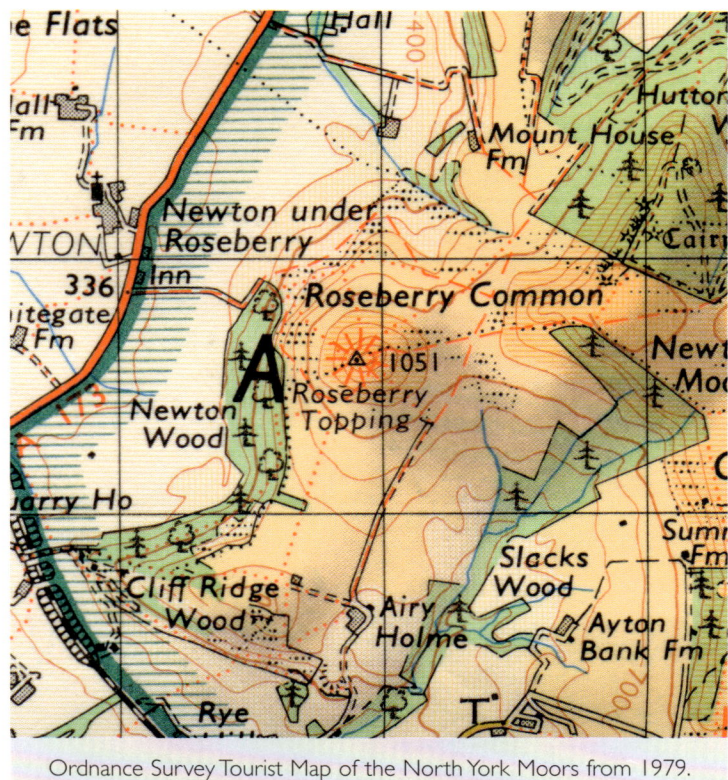

Ordnance Survey Tourist Map of the North York Moors from 1979. Original scale 1:63,360 or one inch to the mile. Reproduced here at just over twice the original size.
© Crown Copyright and/or database right All rights reserved Licence no 100046071

apparently incapable of understanding contours, was thought to have mastered six-figure map references. Selected places of interest, including Roseberry Topping, were listed and only identified by map references. In later editions the new Cleveland Way long distance footpath was marked, with a detour to the summit of Roseberry.

The final change to metric scales was made by the 1:50,000 Landranger Series with its pink covers, introduced in the mid-1970s. By 1995 the Ordnance Survey had digitised all its maps, making Britain the first country in the world to have completed the transition to electronic mapping. Paper maps were now mainly purchased by the leisure user, and many of them considered the scale of 1:50,000 to show insufficient detail. To answer this criticism, the 1:25,000 Outdoor Leisure Series, covering tourist areas, was introduced, with distinctive yellow covers. Two North York Moors maps were published in 1995 and included footpaths, bridleways, field boundaries, picnic and caravan sites. In recognition of the increasing number of foreign tourists, information was printed in three languages.

These 1:25,000 scale maps were well-received, and work started on extending the series across the country, in the form of the orange-jacketed Explorer Maps. These excellent maps included even more tourist information, such as way-marked long distance paths, cycle trails and nature reserves. The changing emphasis of paper maps towards leisure users was dramatically shown by the treatment of Roseberry Topping on the recent Explorer OL 26 map for the western area of the North York Moors. This map even featured Roseberry Topping on its cover. The thick purple line of the National Trust land boundary, the green of the Cleveland Way, and the blue 'viewpoint' symbol completely obliterated all administrative boundaries running across the Topping. Sadly, this map omitted the summerhouse, whether deliberately or accidentally is not clear.

The end of maps as we know them?

It seems probable that new technology will make the much-loved paper maps virtually obsolete, even for leisure users. Modern global positioning systems based on satellites provide an electronic image of someone's surroundings with their exact position identified. Old cloth and paper Ordnance Survey maps are already collectors' items, and this may be their ultimate destiny. But then, ever since the advent of radio, and later television, the death of newspapers has been predicted. They are still with us, so perhaps there are a great many years of life left in the Ordnance Survey paper maps.

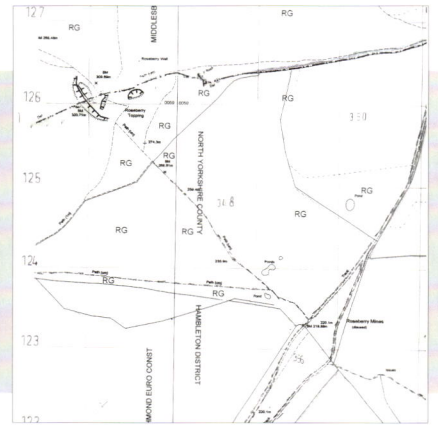

Extract from the digital Ordnance Survey map used as a working document by the Great Ayton Community Archaeology Project. Reproduced here at approximately 1:10,000. Whilst this format provides great accuracy and flexibility of use, it undoubtedly lacks the aesthetic qualities of the older printed maps.

Map images supplied by the NYCC Heritage Unit, Northallerton. © Crown Copyright and/or database right. All rights reserved Licence no 100046071

Looking over the Cleveland Plain, with Roseberry Topping on the distant skyline. Fields and farms, roads and woodland are presented to the viewer almost as if printed on a map.

tourism

Early tourists

What is a tourist? With its distinctive profile and imposing height, Roseberry Topping inevitably catches the eye and the imagination, and has drawn people over many centuries. Prehistoric people placed enormous importance on landscape features such as the Topping. Roman soldiers certainly passed through Cleveland, and no doubt some went up to the summit. The Cottonian manuscript described numbers of people visiting the Topping by the start of the seventeenth century.

That indefatigable traveller of the eighteenth century, Daniel Defoe, certainly climbed the Topping. In the third volume of his splendid work *A Tour through the Whole Island of Great Britain*, published in 1726, he recalled seeing the Cheviot from the summit of 'Rosemary-Top', nearly sixty miles distant. His reference to 'Rosemary-Top' appeared in his letter on south-west Scotland, although he apparently thought that the peak was situated in the East Riding.

We have seen that Graves made specific mention of a party of tourists in his *History of Cleveland* of 1802, and it is really in the nineteenth century that tourism, as know today, really began. Tourists required a means of transport and a source of information about an area, and this century would provide both in forms increasingly accessible to ordinary folk.

Books for travellers

There was really very little to guide visitors to Cleveland until the early nineteenth century. Works such as Camden's *Britannia* were meant for academic reference, and certainly not for tourists. Printed gazetteers were available, but these tended merely to list places and their populations with few details that might interest the casual visitor. John Walker Ord, however, intended his *History and Antiquities of Cleveland* to have popular appeal, and to encourage interest in the area. Having read Ord's claim that 'it may be doubted, indeed, whether any scene in Europe presents equal diversity and range of prospect', readers unfamiliar with the Topping might have been encouraged to travel to Cleveland, climb its slopes and admire the view. They might, however, equally have been discouraged by his description of Newton-under-Roseberry as 'a small, dirty, insignificant village, consisting of a few miserable huts, with a wretched, squalid population'.

The learned Canon Atkinson certainly did not write his *History of Cleveland Ancient and Modern* for tourists, being much taken with medieval history and serious study. He merely noted that the Topping was 'certainly worthy of a passing notice'.

The Victorian business traveller in the North Riding, as opposed to the tourist, might have used one the several

Directories (Baines 1823, Pigot 1834, White 1840, Slater 1848, Bulmer 1890). These publications gave useful information for every town and village, typically a potted history, important residents, businesses and tradesmen, carriers and coaches. Newton-under-Roseberry generally only merited a few lines, sometimes with a brief mention of the Topping.

Modern tourism dawns

For centuries North Riding folk lived predominantly in small villages surrounded by countryside. The fields, hills and moors were rather taken for granted, and it was left to the odd teacher or vicar to see the landscape as something of value in its own right. Then nineteenth century industrialisation and urbanisation spread across much of England. To the people working in the rapidly expanding towns of Middlesbrough and Stockton, the distinctive form of Roseberry Topping, barely visible through the smoke, must have seemed remote and inaccessible. However, as the century moved towards its close, smaller families, reduced working hours, increased leisure time and the availability of transport meant that the country became within reach of the town-dwellers. It was a means of escape from everyday urban life. With fresh air and exercise for the body and new sights and sounds for the soul, mass tourism had been born.

Contemporary writers, apart from Ord, seemed to be oblivious of this developing phenomenon. Ord alone sensed the enormous potential level of interest in local history and local sites. He almost certainly saw that the alienation of urban dwellers from the countryside would build up an appetite for memories of traditional rural life, and that the advent of the railways could bring Cleveland within easy reach of those far beyond its borders.

Arrival of the railway

If visitors were to get out onto the moors and climb Roseberry Topping, a means of travel was essential. With the expansion of Teesside there were many who wished to escape the industrial smoke and grime to seek the healthier outdoor environment offered by the moors. Whilst the northern fringes, particularly Eston Moor, could be reached on foot, places farther away needed some means of transport.

Railways were born in the north-east of England. In 1853 the Middlesbrough & Guisborough Railway opened, with a station at Pinchinthorpe, virtually at the foot of the Topping. It was normal to alight at Pinchinthorpe for an ascent of the Topping, passing the King's Head at Newton, so conveniently situated en route to the climb. An alternative station would have been at Hutton, but as local folk advised visitors, this was 'Mr Pease's station; built for hisself, and not for everybody'. Five years later the North Yorkshire & Cleveland Railway started, but with no station within easy reach of Newton-under-Roseberry. It was not until both of these railway companies were taken over by the North Eastern Railway, and new track put down between Battersby and Nunthorpe, that the railway came to Ayton in 1864. Even then the new line was initially only for goods traffic, mainly Rosedale ironstone, and it was not until 1868 that Ayton Station opened for passenger traffic. Now visitors had the choice of Pinchinthorpe for Newton and the northern side of the Topping, or Ayton for Aireyholme Farm and the southern side.

The railway companies were quick to realise that tourism represented a new source of ticket sales beyond goods traffic and 'necessary' passenger journeys. The North Eastern Railway was printing a guide to hotels and furnished lodgings across the north of England by the early 1860s.

Arrival of the safety bicycle

Development of the bicycle into a practicable means of transport gave a further boost to tourism. The Bicycle Touring Club, later to become the Cyclists' Touring Club, was founded in Yorkshire in 1878. However it was not until the 1890s that the safety bicycle, running on pneumatic tyres, became widely available. The importance of pneumatic tyres for the cycling tourist can be gauged from the price of second-hand machines; a second hand bicycle with solid tyres could be had for twelve shillings and sixpence, whereas one with pneumatic tyres was at least five times as much. The Cyclists' Touring Club recommended hotels for their touring members, and the CTC sign with its winged wheel can still be seen outside the Blackwell Arms at nearby Carlton-in-Cleveland. Those visiting the Topping might have stayed at the Buck in Guisborough, where they could indulge in another new aspect of tourism, the photographic dark-room, or at the identically named Buck in Great Ayton. Later, the King's Head at Newton would also receive CTC recommendation. Cyclists' guides appeared in bookshops, often featuring routes starting at railway stations. *Jackson's Cyclist's Guide to Yorkshire* of 1896 gave details of 138 outings, including a 22½ mile trip from Saltburn to the Cleveland Tontine, going past Roseberry Topping.

Group outings

The nineteenth century tourism described thus far was undertaken by individuals, but some organised group tourism did exist. Railway excursions went to popular holiday destinations, generally at the seaside. Day trips to Newton-under-Roseberry from Stockton or Middlesbrough, using wagonettes drawn at a slow pace by heavy horses, would allow the town-dwellers to sample the famous draught porter from the King's Head, if not to climb the Topping.

Later, in the early part of the twentieth century, the motor charabanc brought cheap and easy day trips into the countryside. Early postcards of Osmotherley show charabancs lined up outside the public houses of the village. Although there are no similar views of the Kings Head at Newton-under-Roseberry it is reasonable to suppose that this too was a favourite stop, with a climb up the Topping for the more energetic. Why else would there be so many different postcards of Newton produced at this time?

It is worth pointing out that, even with the train and charabanc, Roseberry Topping could only be seen as a local tourist destination. The numerous railway posters, that did so much to foster an interest in Britain's geography and heritage, tended to feature places seen as of national interest, and in North Yorkshire they concentrated on the coast and coastal resorts. Possibly the only representation of the Topping is on a British Railways poster by Estra Clark in 1949. This portrayed the whole of Yorkshire in great detail, with vignettes of local scenes and events. The Topping is shown between a lively Stokesley Fair and the serene Guisborough Priory. Although the scenes on the map are not drawn to any scale, Roseberry is tiny and appears as a molehill in the foreground of the Priory!

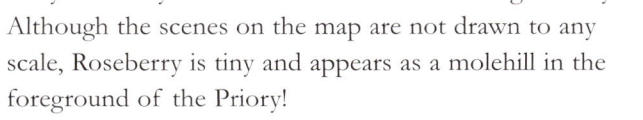

Above: Part of poster reproduced by courtesy of the The National Railway Museum

New writers

In parallel with the changing views of the countryside, and the developments in transport, publications mentioning the Topping changed to cater for a new readership. The romantic poetry of Pierson and Tweddell, and the scholarly voices of Graves and Atkinson, were gradually replaced by a more factual approach. Often these were in the form of descriptions of the author's own travels.

Walter White was the pioneer of this new style of writing. He was a Berkshire journalist who spent a number of years travelling around Britain and Europe after the break-up of his marriage in the 1840s. He spent a month visiting Yorkshire on his own, staying in farmhouses and little roadside public houses, and he published an account of his experiences in 1858 as *A Month in Yorkshire*. One long day's walk started at Hutton Lowcross, on to Guisborough Moor, and then to the summit of Roseberry Topping. Descending to the King's Head at Newton under Roseberry, he walked on to Stockton via Nunthorpe and Marton, finally boarding the train to Darlington. He mentioned the patches of gorse, which then as now, grew on the lower slopes of the Topping. At the summit he met up with two families from Middlesbrough 'come up from the murky town to pass the Sunday on the breezy hilltop'. In a telling comment on the conditions then prevailing in Middlesbrough he quoted one of the women saying 'Tis frightful to see how fast the graves do grow in the new cemetery. It can't be a healthy place to bring up a family in. That's where we live, is it – down there, under all that smoke? Ah! If we could only come up here every day!' This sentiment would be echoed by many even today, although Teesside is no longer enveloped in a pall of smoke.

He approached the Topping from Guisborough, and on reaching the summit threw off his knapsack and lay down in idle enjoyment at the view. In contrast with later travellers whose view north was obscured by Teesside's smoke, White was on the Topping just after the birth of modern Middlesbrough. The first blast furnaces were fired up in 1852 at Bolckow and Vaughan's Eston Iron Works, and Gladstone would not make his famous comment about Middlesbrough being an infant Hercules until 1862. White's view north was dimmed by the smoky atmosphere of the Durham coalfields, and he could see the first iron furnaces here and there across the landscape.

One of the first true walking guides was the 1866 *Walks in Yorkshire* by W S Banks. This set the pattern for many future publications by including snippets of relevant history gleaned from existing learned works. In these early days of travel Banks, a visitor from the West Riding, expected Clevelanders to be significantly different to himself. In the event he found 'they have, in regard to gross oddities at least, ceased to be so'. As with White, Banks was seeing the last of pre-industrial Cleveland, and he observed that the area would be less interesting for tourists after further development of its mineral wealth, when its 'quiet dales would be busy with iron furnaces and black with their smoke'. He arrived in Stokesley, expecting it to be full of ironworkings and smoke, and then went on to the Topping. At this time Roseberry's profile was 'singularly pointed as seen from all sides but the south-east'. Banks had clearly studied Ord, and ingeniously linked two facets of the hill's supposed past by suggesting that the inhabitants of the British village drank at the well near the summit.

Another work aimed at tourists was *The Watering Places Of Cleveland*, by Samuel Gordon, published in 1869. Gordon had been born in the Potteries, coming to Stockton to work as a journalist in 1861. This was very much the tourist guide but with copious amounts of the old romanticism. He devoted a chapter to Roseberry Topping, the beginning of which asserted that it held a special place in the hearts of all true Yorkshiremen. Although there were higher peaks, this was the mountain of Yorkshire. His trip to the Topping began in the modern era, as he described taking the train from Stockton and alighting at Pinchinthorpe Station, but then he retreated into the flowery language of the pre-industrial age. After a drink at the King's Head in Newton, he ascended the Topping. The lane leading to the foot of the hill was bordered by masses of primroses, alas, no longer to be seen in such profusion. In his account, anticipating the massive rock fall of 1912, he noted 'here and there were masses of overhanging rock, which seemed ready at any moment to become detached, and then roll, avalanche-like, down the steep'. At the summit he 'gazed in rapture at the mighty panorama that was stretched beneath and around us' and then poured out several pieces of poetry. Middlesbrough and Stockton, however, lay under a pall of smoke, and all beyond was obscured in a

' if we could only come up here
every day! '

A Month in Yorkshire Walter White 1858

greyish mist. Although Gordon had talked of May sunshine and an almost cloudless sky at the start of the walk, he now rather optimistically thought that this aspect of the view might have been better given 'a more favourable condition of the atmosphere'. Hastening away from industry and back to the earlier romantics he reproduced in full a poem by John Ryley Robinson of Dewsbury, no doubt another early tourist to the summit.

By the end of the nineteenth century tourism was well established, albeit with a clear differentiation between organised parties of working class trippers and the more seriously-minded (or self-righteous) individuals from the middle classes. The 1897 book *Beautiful Cleveland* commented in its introduction that the rural gems of Cleveland were away from the haunts of the 'tripper' and the other inevitable jarring things one associated with watering places where there was 'something going on, and plenty of life'. This book described a series of walks, including a week-end tramp over the Cleveland hills. Setting off from Redcar with nothing but a walking stick, the anonymous author went through Guisborough, past Hutton Hall, over the railway bridge at Pinchinthorpe, past the Topping and into Ayton. Here he came across 'a waggonette of noisy, profane, muscular, Middlesbrough excursionists'. He continued into Stokesley as the sun set and on to Carlton in the moonlight, all the time casting his eyes back to the beautiful scene of Roseberry Topping.

The twentieth century

Two authors stand out at the start of the early twentieth century, each bringing a very different perspective to their writing. John Fairfax Blakeborough was perhaps the last of the traditional Cleveland authors; born in Guisborough, passionate about horses and country sports, and part of the Yorkshire establishment. Michael Heavisides personified the modern tourist, coming from urban Stockton, travelling on train and bicycle, and taking photographs.

Blakeborough's father Richard already had a large collection of unpublished folk tales, and Jack carried on this work, recording local dialect and stories. He published several books, some with references to Roseberry Topping, using much of his father's material. In 1900, when he was only seventeen, he produced a small guide to encourage people from Teesside to take their holidays in one of the Cleveland villages. In his 1901 notes on *Great Ayton, Stokesley and District, Past and Present* he opened the chapter on the Topping with the words 'Roseberry: were every verse that has been written about thee, a yard, it would be a mountain that would make thee blush at thine insignificance'.

Michael Heavisides produced a guide to Cleveland that owed nothing to its predecessors. He used the railway to get away from his home in Richmond Road, Stockton-on-Tees, taking his Coventry Eagle bicycle with him, for days out in the countryside. Sometimes he was accompanied by his son, invariably referred to as 'the young scion'. In 1901 he published *Rambles in Cleveland and Peeps into the Dales on Foot, Cycle and Rail*. An enlarged second edition appeared in 1903, and a re-print in 1988, demonstrating the esteem that this book enjoys. Route descriptions were interspersed with anecdotes, poems, extracts from other authors, and photographs mainly taken by Heavisides himself with his No.5 Poco camera.

The trip to Great Ayton in 1902 was memorable for two reasons. It was the first excursion with his son, the young scion, and the first outing for his new bicycle, a brand new Coventry Eagle with a back-pedalling brake and free wheel. He left his son watching the village cricket match whilst he cycled over to Newton to take a picture of a farmer feeding calves, and returned to 'again enjoy the delightful view, as old Roseberry and the red

Michael Heavisides used his camera to capture the rural idyll. This illustration appeared in his classic book *Rambles in Cleveland* with the accompanying caption 'Feeding calves under Roseberry'.

' While others on Rosebury rocks
Delight to carve their names '

The Hills and Vale of Cleveland James Milligan 1881

mounds stand out resplendent on this perfect summer's afternoon'. The red mounds were the mining tips on the side of Cliff Rigg, now covered with vegetation. He described routes to the summit from the Ayton Station via Aireyholme, from the village through Cliff Ridge quarries, and from Newton. Those of mature age were recommended to take the gentle ascent by way of the shooting box.

All tourists great and small

Both Blakeborough and Heavisides provide evidence of the popularity of a visit to the Topping around 1900. Blakeborough wrote of the large numbers from Teesside coming for the Trinity Fair, Heavisides wrote of the many hundreds who accomplished the climb to the summit on Whit Monday. Whitsun is seven weeks after Easter, Trinity three weeks later. A fascinating postcard appeared at this time, purporting to show a group of visitors at the summit. All the surviving copies of this card have been hand-tinted, a process carried out in Bavaria where costs were low enough for the coloured cards to compete with the conventional monotone varieties. The image of this card has been widely used as evidence of early twentieth century tourism, but all is not as it appears at first sight, as can be seen below.

Old wine in new bottles

As we move into the twentieth century there are ever more books on North Yorkshire and Cleveland. These generally repeat what has gone before, with little evidence of original research. Typically, there would be something on the view, the Prince Oswy legend, Ord's theories about the pits, quotations from the Cottonian manuscript and Margery Moorpout's immortal words about the Topping being the biggest hill in all Yorkshire. There was sometimes little regard to accepted wisdom or actual fact. A good example of this rather careless approach was in *Yorkshire Moors and Dales* by A P Wilson, appearing in 1910. He managed to pick up one of the least likely derivations of the name Roseberry, and went on to make some entirely unsubstantiated claims. There is no evidence for his opinion that a hill fort was situated at the summit, with Britons hurling huge rocks down on their enemies. And it is simply untrue that many ancient weapons of flint and brass have been found on the sides of the hill: in any event brass only really appeared in Roman times. Two years previously J S Fletcher in *The Enchanting North* claimed that the Topping was 'barely eleven hundred feet in height, though some writers have written of it as being half as high again'. The greatest published height seems in fact to be the 1488ft originally given by Graves in 1802, well short of Fletcher's implied 1650ft.

The picture clearly shows a group of people standing at a gap in a line of iron railings. Closer examination reveals that the lady on the right, looking remarkably calm, is virtually standing on thin air. More telling is the relative size of the figures compared with the railings. The heavy iron stanchion at the end of the railings in the foreground is still standing today, and is about forty-two inches in height. This would make the people just over three feet tall! Clearly the group has been added after the photograph was taken; perhaps to liven up what would have been a comparatively dull picture. The very presence of the railings suggests that large numbers of people did crowd onto the summit, and that the risk of accidents prompted the then owners to erect the fence.

The heavy iron stanchion at the end of the railings in the foreground is still standing today. The iron bar, between the stanchion and the trig point, is from the 1902 Coronation bonfire.

A more accurate guide was *Tramping In Yorkshire* by Alfred J Brown, published in 1932. In it he described his ascent of the Topping from Captain Cook's Monument on Easby Moor:

> 'Roseberry is a mountain apart, standing isolated and aloof from the Cleveland chain. Small it is – and it is only 1,057 feet (against the 1,064 of the neighbouring Monument) – it *looks* like a real mountain; a kind of miniature Alp, though it is as green as an apple.'

Rather surprisingly, the early twentieth century books make virtually no mention of possibly the most obvious structures on the Topping at that time, the summer house and Roseberry ironstone mine. The latter omission is strange in that the presence of the mining activity could hardly remain unnoticed. Apart from the surface buildings and machinery on the south side, the tramway ran right round the south and western sides, with an incline down through Newton Woods. Of course the British have always tended to see industrial sites as unwelcome blots on the landscape rather than as providers of work, products and wealth. It might be this attitude that led to the omission of Roseberry Mine. Ironically, now that it has closed and virtually vanished without trace, it is a major source of interest to visitors.

At a time when guides and gazetteers were largely based on old material, a notable exception was *The King's England* series by Arthur Mee. He was an exceptional journalist with an immense love of England's green and pleasant land. In 1936, when he was sixty-one, Mee engaged a team of researchers to carry out what he saw as 'the first census of the ancient and beautiful and curious historic possessions of England since the motor car came to make it possible'. The North Riding guide appeared in 1941 with a pessimistic introduction stating that it had been completed 'in the early months of the Hitler War and is a picture of the county as it was before the aerial bombardment of the Island', and therefore that it stood as a record of Yorkshire 'before the Blitzkrieg'. The references to Roseberry Topping may have contained nothing new, but this beautifully written and well-informed work must have inspired many to visit Cleveland and climb the Topping in the early post-war years.

Modern guide books

The closing decades of the twentieth century witnessed an explosion in the number of guide books to North Yorkshire and the North York Moors. Few new books referred to the historic region of Cleveland, probably because this honourable name had been appropriated by Teesside. Some books latched onto the popularity of the television series 'Heartbeat' set around Goathland. This new breed of guide books tended to focus on leisure pursuits rather than take any real interest in the area. So, for example, there were books of walks, books of pubs, and books of walks from pubs. Most were a re-packaging of old writings, sometimes including ideas that had long since been discredited. Occasionally one comes across something apparently new about Roseberry such as the assertion that 'A fine medal of Henry VIII was also found on the hillside'. Unfortunately there is no known evidence to support this statement.

A good example of a contemporary guide book is *Inside the North York Moors* by the knowledgeable local writer, and champion of all Yorkshire, Harry Mead. He devotes five pages to the Topping, unusually explaining its geology before going on to traditional topics, and adding some more original references to ironstone mining, fox hunting and the county boundary which split Roseberry in two.

The treatment of Roseberry in some supposedly themed books can be little different from a more general publication. *In Folk Tales from the North York Moors* Peter Walker, a popular writer and creator of 'Heartbeat' under the name of Nicholas Rhea, spends less than half his chapter on the Prince Oswy legend. The remainder is standard guide book material.

Errors made by one author are understandable but, because others use previous books and articles, rather than go back to primary sources, these errors can be repeated in later publications. An example is Margery Moorpout's famous quotation from *The Register Office*. This tends to appear nowadays as 'It's t'highest hill i' all Yorkshire' whereas Joseph Reed seems to have actually written 'It's t'biggest hill i'all Yorkshur'. The reader can decide whether such criticism is important or merely pedantic.

Books that combine easy reading with plenty of illustrations have become popular, sometimes published in the name of a well-known personality. An early example of this genre was the extremely popular *James Herriot's Yorkshire* of 1979. Alf Wight gave a minimal description of Roseberry as 'an interesting hill with trees on its lower slopes and a bare pointed summit which makes it look like a little volcano' printed immediately above a large photograph. In this case the picture was certainly worth more than his twenty-two words.

Modern tourism

Just as the railways revolutionised personal travel in Victorian times, so did the motor car in the twentieth century. At first motoring was only for the wealthy and cars were comparatively rare. Even by 1909 there were only two car owners in Stokesley. Yet the possibility of being able to travel where and when you wished was irresistible. Particularly after the Second World War car ownership blossomed and the rail network declined. Pinchinthorpe Station closed in 1964 as part of the cut-backs blamed on Dr Beeching, but demanded by the government in order to stem British Railways' huge operating losses.

Today, most travellers arrive at the foot of Roseberry by car, although Newton is on a regular service bus route, and the National Park operates a special Moors Bus. Increasing car parking along the grass verges of the Great Ayton to Guisborough road caused problems. The National Park Authority realised that a proper car park was required and in 1979 purchased some land adjacent to the roadside beside the track leading to Newton Woods and the Topping. Construction began and the car park was completed in 1981. A mobile toilet unit had to be installed until the permanent toilet block could be completed two years later.

> ... most travellers arrive at the foot of Roseberry by car ...

A reminder of the golden age of touring by motor car. This Morris Cowley Two-Seater, complete with dickey seat, was first registered in Durham in 1930 as UP 3744. The original catalogue claimed that the car, priced at £162 10s, offered 'roomy accommodation for two persons, leaving room which some folk find sufficient for a third.' In the photograph, taken in August 1930, the driver has left his two passengers on the front seat, confirming the catalogue's claim.
Photograph supplied by the Northern Echo and Darlington & Stockton Times, car identified by Harry Edwards, Morris Register Club Historian.

the beauty of the Topping . . .

. . . hides a darker side

known to far fewer . . .

accidents and rescues

The darker side of the Topping

Behind the beauty of the Topping, familiar to so many through cards, calendars, prints and paintings, hides a darker side known to far fewer. The exposed rock face on the western side is unstable with loose rocks. Fortunately, the massive rock fall of 1912 happened when nobody was on the slopes, but there was a fatality connected with the rock fall. An ex-president of the Cleveland Naturalists' Field Club, Mr Henry Simpson, attended a meeting at Roseberry on 15 June 1912, specially convened to examine the state of the Topping after the rock fall. Although in poor health, Simpson managed to ascend to the summit. He died six weeks later, and his obituary in the proceedings of the club commented 'Although possibly he should not have undertaken this feat in his then state of health, one cannot help admiring the enthusiasm that permitted him to take his last look at one of the finest views of the Cleveland district, of which he was so sincere and ardent an admirer'.

Apart from the 1912 collapse, there have been many lesser falls and some close escapes. Mary Bainbridge recalls her mother and some friends walking up to Roseberry after chapel one Sunday in the 1930s. They sat down to talk and admire the view. A sudden noise from above made them look up, and to their horror they saw a large rock tumbling down the slope towards them. They sat motionless, frozen to the ground, when just at the last minute the boulder swerved and crashed past to the side of them. To this day Mary says that she avoids going near the Topping.

There have been several fatalities. A favourite hobby of young lads used to be collecting birds' eggs, and the rocky face of the Topping was a good place for jackdaws' nests. On 21 May 1933 Peter Hammond and a friend were out bird nesting when Peter lost his grip and fell to his death. A similar fate befell Sidney Rolfe in 1947, although this accident may have been on the side of Cliff Rigg. After this second fatality the possibility of placing notices warning of the risk of climbing the rock face was raised with the Parish Council, but no action was taken. Then in 1948 Eric Jones from Middlesbrough had a lucky escape when climbing on the hill with two friends. Part of the rock broke away and Jones fell, suffering head injuries. He was carried down the hillside on an improvised stretcher by a party of boy scouts, and was admitted to North Ormesby Hospital.

Although bird nesting has become a thing of the past, newer activities have brought other risks. Recently a youth was seen at the summit tying a length of polypropylene rope around the base of the trig point. On being asked what he was doing, he announced his intention of abseiling down the rock face. He was then asked if he would mind being photographed. 'Why?' he enquired. 'So that there is a picture to show at the inquest' was the reply! This had the desired effect and the abseil was abandoned.

Adults are generally more safety conscious, but the exertions of climbing the hill can take their toll, even among the physically fit. In the 1960s a Nunthorpe doctor recorded the times of his regular runs from the Newton car park to the summit and down again. One day he collapsed and died on the slopes. The most recent fatality was Benny Dowson, who was found on the path near the summerhouse in November 1992. Benny was in the habit of exercising his lurcher, and perhaps doing the odd bit of gentle poaching, very early in the mornings. One morning he was found lying on the ground, with his dog baring its teeth at anyone who approached. The ensuing recovery of poor Benny's corpse turned out to be a near farce. The emergency services were called from Aireyholme Farm, and the police arrived first. It was raining hard, but the officer attending said that he had no Wellington boots and that it would be best to wait for the ambulance. The ambulance crew duly arrived, and although they had no boots either they did struggle up to the body with a stretcher. Having pronounced Benny dead, they then said that they couldn't take his body away because if they put a corpse into their ambulance the vehicle would need sterilising before further use, and they weren't going to do that. Also the death would need official confirmation and as it was a Saturday they wouldn't be able to get hold of a doctor. In sheer disbelief Charles Phalp of Aireyholme Farm called the Cleveland Search and Rescue Team, and within minutes they were at the scene, with their own doctor and a proper body bag. Benny was finally carried down with dignity.

Aircraft crash

Only two aircraft have crashed in Great Ayton. A Lockheed Hudson from Thornaby Aerodrome hit the side of Easby Moor in the early hours of 11 February 1940, with the loss of three of its crew of four. Twenty years later to the day, the Middlesbrough Evening Gazette carried an article describing how Michael Procter lost his life when his Percival Proctor G-ALUJ crashed in Newton Wood around midday on 10 February 1960. Procter, a Leeds businessman and member of the Yorkshire Aero Club, had taken off from Yeadon Airport near Leeds with the intention of flying to Newcastle. When his aircraft ran into thick fog in the vicinity of Roseberry, he apparently tried to return to Yeadon. Two farm workers, Thomas Featherstone and Brian Little, noticed the aircraft flying low overhead, and when the fog lifted a couple of hours later they saw a white streak in the hillside of Roseberry Topping. The Proctor had gone into the pine trees at the upper edge of Newton Wood, near the summerhouse.

That morning Charles Phalp had been muck spreading in the field alongside the upper edge of Newton Wood. He remembers it as a really thick misty morning. When he returned to the farm house there was a phone call asking if he had seen an aircraft crash. The police had been told that a plane had disappeared from radar screens in the Roseberry area, but they didn't know whether it was a military or civilian aircraft, its size or how many people were on board. Charles arranged to meet the local policeman, Andy Patterson, and they set off across the fields in the fog. Visibility was so bad that they couldn't even see the rocks of the Topping. When they came across the tip of a wing they thought that the plane must have crashed quite high up, so they went up to the summerhouse area but found nothing. Then, as they dropped down through the gate into Newton Wood, Charles saw someone lying on the ground looking just as if he was asleep in his overcoat. The wreckage of the aircraft was scattered among the trees.

Just as with the Hudson crash twenty years before, souvenir hunters were soon drawn to the site. The police erected a makeshift tent at the scene, roped off the site and mounted a guard; by now it was snowing. In a couple of days Messrs Scholefield and Jameson from the Air Accidents Investigation Branch drew up at Aireyholme in their big Rover car, and emerged into the Yorkshire snow with the remark 'It's been a hell of a ride up the jolly old long dog' (referring to the old A1 road).

Jameson went off to interview witnesses while Scholefield asked Charles to give him a hand with a large wooden box which they carried up to the crash site. The box opened out to reveal a mobile investigation laboratory, with a protective tent and even a small heater. Charles dragged the Proctor's engine up the slope with a length of rope, and Scholefield started to carefully strip the engine down. Every nut and bolt was taken apart. The only fault revealed was that the drive shaft to the vacuum pump, driving the instruments' gyroscopes, had sheared some time before the crash. This would have meant that the artificial horizon on some instruments would have been out of action. Bill Peberdy, who had been taught to fly by Michael Procter, remembered him as a very able pilot. He felt sure that Procter would have been able to cope with this, although it would make flying more demanding. Peberdy had heard the news of an aircraft crash on the wireless, and phoning around some friends soon revealed that his old instructor had been at the controls.

Charles offered to get rid of the bits and pieces, but to his amazement Scholefield then proceeded to reassemble the engine. With the preliminary field investigation complete, the two investigators headed back down the A1. Charles had been told to put a match to the remains of the fuselage, but it proved most reluctant to burn. He had hoped to salvage the wheels for use on the farm, but found them too badly damaged. Only the de Havilland Gypsy Queen Mk II engine was saved. Mr 'Stevo' Stephenson, a woodwork teacher at Stokesley School, had it displayed there on a specially-built stand for many years. The Proctor had been built for the RAF in 1942 and was transferred to the civil register as G-AGLC in 1951. It was sold to French Morocco in 1953, registered as F-DADK, and returned to Britain in 1956.

The official accident investigation report gave the cause of the accident as navigational error, accompanied by the brief summary of events:

> 'Aircraft took off from Leeds Airport for Newcastle on a private flight. Pilot decided to go to RAF Ouston as Woolsington's weather was bad. The A T Controller on duty at Leeds received a message from the aircraft that it was returning to base because of weather and this was the last message received from it. Local police were released (sic) of wreckage in the vicinity of Roseberry Topping in the North Riding of Yorkshire and subsequent investigations showed that the pilot had flown into this high ground in conditions of low cloud and bad weather.'

Rescues

As more people took to the moors, inevitably some found themselves in difficulties. The only source of rescue was the National Park volunteer wardens, who soon complained that they couldn't take on this additional responsibility. So in 1965 two specialist search and rescue teams were set up, one covering the eastern moors from Scarborough, and the Cleveland team covering the western moors. Today the Cleveland team has some fifty members, all volunteers, on call twenty-four hours a day, seven days a week.

A typical rescue will often start with a call-out to a specified rendezvous point. From here a small first response team, including a team doctor, paramedic and possibly a search dog, will set off to locate the injured person. They carry comprehensive medical supplies, provide emergency first aid, decide what rescue equipment is needed, and tend to the casualty until the backup team arrives with the appropriate rescue equipment. At the same time, and unless the rescue needs helicopter support, one of the team's Land Rover ambulances will drive as near to the scene of the accident as possible. The casualty will then be carried down on a specialist mountain rescue stretcher to the waiting Land Rover, driven to the county ambulance, and so on to hospital.

Search and Rescue anecdotes

Roseberry is a favourite place for search and rescue practices, sometimes involving an RAF rescue helicopter. On practice occasions it is usual to use up old equipment, for example, flares that are approaching their use-by-date. At one practice the helicopter was approaching, and an old flare was set off to alert the helicopter crew to the rescue position. Instead of emitting orange smoke, a large flame shot out. In the ensuing excitement the flare was accidentally thrown away, unfortunately landing in a hedge. The weather had been dry, and the hedge started burning.

The Cleveland Search and Rescue Team at Carlton Bank, with Roseberry Topping in the distance

Then the helicopter arrived overhead, and the resulting down draft fanned the flames into a conflagration!

Of course the team often find themselves on the slopes of the Topping responding to emergency situations; in a typical year about one in ten of all calls come from here. Given the popularity of the Topping this isn't really surprising, and in addition to the casual walkers there are two annual races to the top, sponsored walks, a diversion from the Cleveland Way and even organised parties on the summit. One party was in full evening dress! Although they have had to deal with two fatalities here since their formation in 1965, both from heart attacks, most incidents are less serious. However, there is no doubt that the Topping can be a dangerous place for the unprepared, the unwary or the plain unfortunate. Over the past ten years the team has been called out to deal with numerous cases of broken bones, usually legs or ankles. Some incidents are somewhat more unusual. After Millennium Eve celebrations on top of Roseberry, they were in attendance when a man collapsed with malaria and was brought down safely. It subsequently transpired that he had recently returned from abroad. And some incidents are quite bizarre. During the Armada beacon celebrations a young man, absolutely paralytic with drink, was carried down from the summerhouse. The team's Land Rover was quietly driven up to his house, where the blue flashing lights were accidentally switched on as they pulled up, bringing an alarmed mother rushing to the door. The youth was taken inside and dropped onto a bed. He momentarily came to, uttered a quick 'Thanks very much' and instantly collapsed back into unconsciousness.

Recently, the team undertook an unusual task, reversing their normal role by carrying someone up to the summit. Rosemary Berks of Darlington had been disabled with polio from childhood, but nevertheless had managed to live an active life. She had only one unfulfilled ambition, to go up Roseberry Topping. As a surprise for her fiftieth birthday the team carried her to the summit, accompanied by her family, and arranged a champagne party at the summit.

Animal antics

Incidents can involve animals as well as people. Sheep can appear to be stranded on inaccessible ledges, although quite why they often leap off as the rescuers approach is

The Cleveland Search and Rescue Team hold frequent exercises on Roseberry, sometimes in conjunction with helicopter support
Photo: Cleveland Search and Rescue Team

not clear to the Team! On one occasion the records show a sheep vacating its crag 'in spectacular fashion with a dive that would have won an Olympic gold medal'. For some reason the Team called this animal Baasil. This particular incident happened just a few weeks after the foot and mouth disease outbreak of 2001. Before attempting to rescue the sheep, the team phoned the British Mountaineering Council's technical department to ask about the decontamination procedures for ropes and equipment possibly in contact with the disease. After a long pause the answer was a baffled 'Well, we've never been asked that before'.

Perhaps the strangest animal rescue involved a family out on the Topping and an inquisitive young bullock. The story is related by Charles Phalp.

'About seven o'clock one evening a kid came down to the farm; he was quite agitated and told me that he had been sitting on the footpath with his mother. Puffing and blowing he said "Can you come quick, my mother can hear a cow bellowing underneath the ground". He was really insistent, so I had to go with him. I told his mother that she would just be hearing the cows over towards Little Roseberry, but she said "Just listen" and sure enough I could hear this muffled cry from underneath the ground. I couldn't see how anything could have got under the ground, but there had to be an explanation. There are old mine workings under Roseberry, although the drift entrances had all been filled in. I went down to the bottom of the slope and looked around. About fifteen or twenty yards from where the main shaft had gone into the hillside there was a hole. It wasn't that big and was among the bracken. The ground must have slipped away after heavy rain, making a hole for the bullock to slip into. I didn't know what the hell to do. In desperation I phoned the Cleveland Search and Rescue lads. Three or four of them turned out and one let himself down the hole. "You'll have to come with me" he said. I thought that it was my animal and that I would have to show willing, so they stuck a helmet on my head, tied a rope round me and lowered me down. I followed him down and we had gone in about twenty or thirty yards and there was the bullock staring straight back at us, lit up by our lamps. When he saw us he took off down the shaft, knocking props out as he went. I said "We are going to have to forget about it, it's not worth risking anybody's life over. I will see if we can get someone with a gun." But the Rescue lad said "Hang on a minute; we will see what we can do. There's no way the animal can get out the way he came in, because he'd fallen down the hole. But if we go a bit further down and dig another hole we might get him out". By now it was dark and I said I wouldn't be able to get anyone with a digger, but he said they would dig by hand, and the next thing I knew was that he'd put a call out and fifty people with spades turned up in minutes. I don't know where they all came from. They all started digging down and within an hour they were in and had made a ramp from the mine working to the outside. We got a bag of meal for the calf and brought its mother a bit closer. She was bellowing with all her might. Then we got back into the mine shaft near where the bullock was and sat quietly, switching our lights off. Bit by bit he came closer and eventually we were able to get behind him. Then he was out up the ramp like a shot. He was a very lucky animal.'

20 Who owns the Topping?

Boundaries and ownership

It was not practicable to cover the complete ownership history of Roseberry Topping here. This chapter concentrates on the period from the mid-twentieth century when ownership and boundary changes took place that significantly affected Roseberry. Prominent among these were the designation of the National Park, the formation and later abolition of the County of Cleveland, the splitting of the hill between two counties, and the acquisition of most of Roseberry by the National Trust.

Historic boundaries

For centuries the administrative divisions within the northern counties were 'wapentakes', equivalent to the 'hundreds' of the southern counties. The term was derived from a method of voting at assemblies by a show of weapons. Within a wapentake lay the ecclesiastical parishes and townships, which became civil parishes after 1832. It was usual for a parish to contain a variety of terrains, from low water meadows to high moors, thus enabling it to be as near self-sufficient as possible. So it is not surprising that the flanks of Roseberry Topping were shared by the parishes of Ayton and Newton, with the boundary running over the summit. The wapentake boundary between Langbaurgh West and Langbaurgh East also passed through the summit.

The area of the ancient manor of Newton was smaller than the parish, but also extended to the summit of Roseberry. Manor court proceedings included the practice of riding round the manor boundary, often known as beating the bounds, which would have included a ride up to the summit by the court officials and 'as many of the inhabitants of Newton as chose'. Successive generations of the Staveley family of North Stainley, near Ripon, were lords or ladies of the manor of Newton and at the end of the eighteenth century the estate was in the hands of the delightfully named Miss Roseberry Mary Staveley.

Hands off Yorkshire

Whilst the Topping's various parishes were in the North Riding of Yorkshire, boundaries hardly seemed to matter. All this was to change as national governments in the second half of the twentieth century recognised inefficiencies in the established order, which had been set long before the rise of large urban areas and mass communications. This was at a time when large organisations were thought to be the most effective and efficient. In private industry this may have been the case, although the experience of post-war nationalisation might have led one to ask if this maxim really did apply to government control.

Lord Redcliffe-Maud's commission duly recommended in 1969 that local government should be organised into fewer and larger units, bringing town and country together. One of these units was to be based on Teesside, which itself had only come into existence the previous year. This new unit would include sixteen parishes then in Stokesley Rural District, among them Great Ayton, with its share of Roseberry Topping. Harold Wilson had broadly accepted the Redcliffe-Maud recommendations, but the 1970 general election brought Edward Heath to Number Ten. His new Conservative government was much less enthusiastic and abandoned the general plan, although some of the detailed recommendations did go forward, including that for an enlarged Teesside.

Many of the smaller communities to the south of Middlesbrough had no desire to be part of Teesside. Their antipathy was driven by feelings of identity, and by politics and economics. In Great Ayton a 'Help Keep Ayton in Yorkshire' campaign soon got underway. June Imeson, a local councillor, brought three influential MPs to the village. They viewed the prominence of Roseberry Topping from Gribdale, agreed to support Ayton's case, but declined to ascend to the summit. In a triumph for parochial democracy, on 25 January 1972, it was decided to let Ayton remain in Yorkshire. One of the Labour politicians involved, Denis Howell, had sympathy with the broad case, but claimed the opposition had overstated matters. He accepted that the people of Ayton had more affinity with Stokesley than with the urban sprawl of Middlesbrough, but felt it was offensive to say that 'these people have escaped from Teesside once, as if Teesside is a place from which everyone automatically ought to escape'.

There was jubilation in the village, with the ringing of church bells, but dismay in Teesside. This had wrecked the concept of bringing town and country together, and there were even suggestions that Teesside should join with Durham and Hartlepool. In the event Hartlepool was forced into an arranged marriage with Teesside, to give birth on All Fools' Day 1974 to the 'County of Cleveland', a bizarre title given that 'Cleveland' is derived from the Old English for a hilly district whereas the new county had virtually no hills. Most of the proper Cleveland Hills remained in North Yorkshire.

Deciding that Ayton would be left in Yorkshire meant that the county boundary now followed the line of the boundary between Newton and Ayton, right across the middle of Roseberry Topping. So the 'biggest hill in all Yorkshire' was divided between Teesside and Yorkshire, in an act recalling James Gillray's famous etching from 1805, 'The Plumb-pudding in Danger'. In this cartoon Pitt and Napoleon are seated at the dining table slicing up the world, as represented by a large steaming pudding. This time the knife went right through the middle of the Topping.

In 1805 James Gillray drew one of the most famous political caricatures of all time, with Pitt and Napoleon dividing up the world, shown as a steaming plum pudding. In this new version Roseberry Topping is divided up between the Teesside business executive and the Yorkshire squire.

Cartoon created by Ian Wilson, with apologies to James Gillray

If Redcliffe-Maud had favoured centralised bureaucracy over local identity, the tables were turned in the 1990s when John Major asked John Banham to look into further local government reform. Banham focussed on the question of local identity and found, not surprisingly given its brief history, that few people identified themselves with the County of Cleveland. There were no questions about efficiency or costs, and the County of Cleveland was duly abolished on its twenty-second birthday in 1996, to be replaced by four smaller unitary authorities. The northern half of the Topping then found itself in the new council of Redcar and Cleveland, where it remains to this day.

Once the county boundary had been drawn across Roseberry, other boundaries followed, including the parliamentary constituencies for Westminster and Brussels. In practice, given that the hill is owned by the National Trust and lies within the North York Moors National Park, the political divisions have had little obvious effect. It is perhaps significant that the latest popular series of Ordnance Maps have virtually obliterated all trace of administrative boundaries while giving prominence to the boundary of the part of the Topping owned by the National Trust.

Cleveland County unfairly maligned?

The track records of the counties of Cleveland and North Yorkshire, at least regarding Roseberry Topping, might suggest that Cleveland was not entirely the ogre imagined. When much of the Roseberry Topping land situated within Cleveland came up for sale in 1984, the council funded part of the purchase price, enabling the National Trust to acquire the land. After this they made significant financial contributions to the maintenance of the area. In contrast, when Roseberry land in North Yorkshire came up for sale, the council appeared to take no interest.

In 1988 Cleveland refused to part-fund a study into a motorway across the North York Moors, linking Cleveland with the M11 in Cambridgeshire, because of the impact the road would have on the National Park. North Yorkshire decided to contribute, arguing that the motorway would boost industry and tourism. Then in 1993 it was Cleveland that organised the task of laying a new zig-zag footpath up the western slope of Roseberry Topping.

It would perhaps be fair to say that during its brief life of only twenty-two years Cleveland showed more commitment to Roseberry Topping than other local authorities, before or since.

Ownership today

The National Trust owns the upper slopes of Roseberry Topping, and an arc of moors and woods from Newton Moor in the east to Cliff Rigg Wood in the south. This area was gradually acquired from 1984 to 1998, through purchases and donations.

Ernest Sydney Bradley, of Newton Grange Farm, put almost 245 acres of land on the market in August 1984. At the time, he claimed that 'EEC advice was to get rid of redundant assets'. The land included the northern part of Newton Wood, the northern and eastern slopes up to the summit of the Topping, Roseberry Common and part of Newton Moor. The selling agents were Messrs Albert Walker of Middlesbrough, and their advertisement read as follows:

> 'North Yorkshire Moors National Park, the prominent local landmark and beauty spot known as Roseberry Common. Together with woodland and small moor extending in all to 245 acres. To be sold by private treaty as a whole or in three lots. Further details available at the agent's Guisborough office.'

Note that the estate agents were careful not to call the land 'Roseberry Topping', a distinction not always made in the numerous press articles of the time. In fact the sale did not include the summit, which was part of the Cleveland Lodge estate owned by Sir Wilfred and Lady Fry. The southern boundary of the land upwards from Newton Wood was the Newton Manor boundary, marked out by a dry stone wall running from east to west over the summit. A substantial part of this ancient boundary wall had been carried away in the 1912 landslip.

It was by no means clear who would purchase the land. The National Trust was short of money, and coyly issued a statement:

> 'Obviously the National Trust is taking an interest in Roseberry Topping but we don't look at the purchase as being the only answer to its salvation. We see ourselves more as a back stop for the acquisition of properties such as this. We don't want necessarily to stand in the way of any public body which might want to acquire it.'

After three months of behind-the-scenes negotiations a deal was agreed in December whereby Cleveland County Council, the National Park and the Countryside

Commission would contribute to the purchase by the Trust. Part of the Trust's share of the cost was covered by bequests from Miss Hobson and Mrs Salter. The total cost was not disclosed. In response to press questioning, all that their regional information officer, Miss Tiffany Hunt, would say at the time was 'It is a significant purchase for the National Trust. We paid a fair price'.

The remaining twenty acres of Newton Wood were bought in 1986 with grants from the Countryside Commission, the National Park and a bequest from a Mrs Fisher.

In the early 1990s the Trust acquired the quarry and woods at Cliff Rigg from Syd Bradley and Christopher Willis of Snow Hall Farm, Newton-under-Roseberry. This was soon followed by the purchase of two small plots of land at Nettle Hole and Newton Wood from Lady Fry at Cleveland Lodge in Ayton.

In July 1988, after the death of her husband Sir Wilfred, Lady Fry had become the owner of the 'southern face' as she preferred to call it. It was widely believed that the Trust owned the entire Topping, and people felt free to roam over the whole area. This annoyed Lady Fry and, at the time, she was reported as saying 'I have told the Trust that I'm fed up with people being led to think it is the sole owner. But even in all the publicity given to the public appeal to finance footpath repair work on Roseberry Topping, it was never made properly clear that it doesn't own the whole lot'.

However, in 1997, Lady Fry generously donated the summit and the upper part of the southern slope, some ten acres, to the National Trust. The following year the Trust was able to purchase the southern part of Newton Wood from H S Petch and Son Ltd of Whitegates Farm. By now, the National Trust owned most of what would commonly be regarded as Roseberry Topping and its immediate surroundings. But the area where the summerhouse is situated, the lower southern slopes including the Roseberry Mine site, and all the arable land remained in the Cleveland Lodge estate.

When Aireyholme Farm, part of the Cleveland Lodge estate, came on the market following the death of Lady Fry in 2001, many people believed that the National Trust might purchase it. However, one of the Trust's main criteria was whether the site would suffer if the property were to be held by other parties. No doubt mindful that the tenant farmers at Aireyholme, Charles and Freda Phalp, would remain and continue their careful stewardship of the land, the Trust did not make an offer. Instead, Aireyholme was sold to an absentee landlord in West Yorkshire. Thus the arable fields and the lower southern slopes, including the summerhouse and the Roseberry Ironstone Mine site, all part of Aireyholme Farm, remain in private ownership. The land is worked by the second and third generations of the Phalp family as tenants.

The National Trust

The National Trust was founded in 1895 to look after places of historic interest or natural beauty permanently for the benefit of the nation, across England, Wales and Northern Ireland. One of its aims, particularly relevant to Roseberry Topping, is to show leadership in the regeneration of the countryside. It is a registered charity, and is dependent on members, visitors, volunteers, partners and benefactors. The Trust has been hugely successful in protecting our heritage. It has been able to mobilise enormous resources, develop skills and expertise in all types of conservation, and to open a huge range of properties and landscapes to the public. It is rightly the envy of other European countries, although there are a few people in England who disagree with aspects of its policy and its management style.

Above: Extract from Ordnance Survey Explorer OL26, original scale 1:25,000. The purple line denotes the extent of the National Trust ownership.
© Crown Copyright and/or database right. All rights reserved Licence no 100046071

In the spring of 1985, within months of this first acquisition, an appeal was launched by the Trust for £20,000 to preserve and conserve the Topping. David Bellamy, well-known for his concern for the environment, asked 'Why not plant a tree for £10 or maintain a metre of footpath for £5?' The appeal was successful, and work started on the repair of eroded surfaces, fences and walls, and the control of bracken, using young people on the government's Manpower Services Commission scheme. One of their first tasks was the paving of the path up from Newton-under-Roseberry. At this time the distinctive but discreet National Trust signs were erected at the side of footpaths where they entered Trust land.

National Trust reorganisation in the 1990s saw the appointment of Mark Bradley as warden with specific responsibilities for the management of land at Roseberry. He is one of a team of wardens based at Ravenscar who look after the Trust's Yorkshire and Cleveland coastal estate. Mel Cunningham is now the property manager of this estate, following on from Bob Dicker who was the manager at the time of the acquisition. The role of the warden is to take day-to-day responsibility for delivering the National Trust's objectives for the property and maintaining or improving its condition. Repairs to footpaths, walls, fences and stiles need to be organised and visitors' safety ensured. Arrangements must be made with tenant farmers who rent grazing on Trust land. And it is down to the warden to take whatever steps are needed, in conjunction with the Trust's specialist advisers in fields such as ecology and archaeology, to conserve the essential characteristics of the Topping; all those things which make Roseberry Topping, Roseberry Topping.

Another aspect of the warden's job is to help people enjoy and understand the landscape which has become accessible to everyone through the Trust's ownership. Of course, this is the aim of the physical management of Roseberry, but activities away from the Topping's slopes are also vitally important. There is support for research and publications, projects with local schools, and presentations to local societies. Roseberry is only one of the National Trust's properties calling on Mark Bradley's time. Fortunately, he can rely on hundreds of hours of unpaid assistance from the National Trust Volunteers.

Opposite: The boundary between Aireyholme Farm and the National Trust land at Roseberry Common is also the boundary between agricultural landscape and the wild moorland

Different interests

The two owners of the Topping and its surroundings thus have quite different interests. The aim of the National Trust is to look after special places for ever, for everyone. There is open access across their part of the Topping, although they would naturally prefer visitors to keep to footpaths. Much of their stewardship of the Topping has been to minimise footpath erosion, as ever-increasing numbers make their way to the summit.

In contrast, the agent for the owner of Aireyholme expects his tenants to manage a profitable farming business, difficult enough in this challenging environment. Crops are grown and animals grazed in the enclosed fields around Roseberry. The only public access is on designated rights of way. It remains to be seen how the removal of the Common Agricultural Policy's subsidies on production, and the radical change to payments based on countryside stewardship, will affect this part of the Topping.

The North York Moors National Park

The North York Moors National Park was designated in 1952 and became independent of North Yorkshire County Council in 1997. Its western boundary runs along the railway line from Great Ayton Station, and then up the A173 Ayton to Pinchinthorpe road. Thus Roseberry Topping and Newton Wood are entirely within the Park. However, the National Park Authority does not as a rule own land, but works with landowners and others to achieve its statutory purposes which are to:

- Conserve and enhance the natural beauty, wildlife and cultural heritage.
- Promote opportunities for the understanding and enjoyment of the special qualities of the area by the public.
- Seek to foster economic and social well-being of the local communities. This became a duty under the 1995 Environment Act.

The North York Moors National Park Authority is based in Helmsley. Roseberry Topping falls within the area of a senior National Park ranger, currently Frank Pickles, who is supported by an area ranger and a number of volunteer rangers. Their main activities around the Topping have been to maintain dry stone walls and to take measures to combat footpath erosion, working closely with the National Trust and the Phalps at Aireyholme Farm.

Roseberry's wildlife

Introduction

As might be expected it is Newton Wood, rather than the adjacent moorland, which hosts the majority of species. A full survey of all the local flora, birds, butterflies and moths, animals, insects and fungi in the area would be a complete book in itself, so this chapter is very much a summary. Most of the important species present are described and illustrated, but some are absent for reasons of space. These include insects, those essential woodland recycling agents, and also molluscs and reptiles. In general only English names are used; occasionally scientific names are added. The history of Newton Wood, as revealed from old maps and documents, is also briefly considered.

Newton Wood, a haven for bluebells

Newton Wood is probably the finest example of remaining acidic oak woodland in Cleveland. One of the National Trust's first activities here was a bluebell survey involving the pupils of Roseberry School in Great Ayton.

In the spring, the carpet of bluebells spreading out beneath the vibrant greens of new tree foliage is a spectacular sight. A walk through Newton Wood at bluebell time is, without doubt, one of the highlights of the new season. Tim Smit of the Cornish Eden Project has put it this way:

> 'I never feel more alive than when walking in bluebell woods. The triumph of spring over winter, the resurgence of life following a long sleep and the awakening of something primal deep within that can be best described as love - love of life.'

The bluebell is Britain's favourite wild flower. In a recent poll by *Plantlife* magazine to find a wild flower emblem for each county, twenty per cent of all counties chose the bluebell. As a result it was selected as the national wild flower emblem. Whatever the complex requirements needed by bluebells, the conditions in British woods seem to be most suitable, since nowhere else in the world do these flowers grow as they do here. The number of bluebell plants in British woods has been estimated as representing between one-third and one-half of the total world population. Until the twentieth century all bluebells found in our woodlands would have been our native species, known botanically as *Hyacinthoides non-scripta*. But since the seventeenth century the Spanish bluebell has been grown in gardens, and can hybridise with our native bluebells. It is feared that this hybrid could replace the native populations in sites where the Spanish bluebell has appeared, often by careless tipping of garden bluebells in the vicinity of woodland. So far there is no evidence of the hybrid bluebell amongst the Newton Wood native population, and it is to be hoped that this will continue.

Unfortunately, another threat to the bluebells is that of being crushed. Plants have been trampled by visitors, often merely to seek a better view for the inevitable photograph. Large dogs have rolled among the plants and even trials bikes have been ridden through them.

' Blue, darkly, deeply, beautifully blue '

Robert Southey 1774 – 1843

Other herbaceous plants

In addition to bluebells, Newton Wood provides a wide range of flora in early spring when the woodland floor is well lit prior to the growth of the tree canopy. There are good populations of other characteristic flowers of the woodlands. Wood sorrel, with its delicate, veined white flowers and triple leaves, can be seen in the drier areas, along with dog's mercury, an all-green plant which flowers in March. The great wood-rush, wavy bittercress and greater stitchwort may also be found. By mid-April several fern species, including the ubiquitous bracken, begin their growth from underground rhizomes. The male fern, scaly male fern (similar to male fern but with dense golden scales on the stalks) and broad buckler fern are all present.

Near the middle of Newton Wood there is a wetter area which, although fairly narrow at the top of the wood, broadens considerably as it moves downhill towards the edges of the cultivated fields. Different plants frequent this area; most obvious to the casual walker is ramsons or wild garlic, with its strong scent pervading this part of the wood during the early spring. Other plants favouring these damp conditions are giant horsetail, marsh marigold with its large yellow flowers, and opposite-leaved golden saxifrage, a short, yellow-flowered perennial.

1 Broad buckler fern, common within Newton Wood

2 Ramsons, with its garlic-like odour, prefers the damper regions of Newton Wood

3 Giant horsetail, abundant in the damper area

4 Harebells on the slopes above Newton Wood

Opposite: Bracken and rosebay willowherb on northern slopes

Photos: 1-3 Alan Bunn; 4 JC

By early summer, bracken dominates many areas of the woodland. Smaller plants such as red campion, enchanter's nightshade and wood dock struggle to survive on path edges and in some open glades. One flowering plant rises above the bracken, the foxglove. From June its brilliant pinkish purple, and occasionally white, flowers provide a blaze of colour.

From early July bracken also dominates the slopes of Roseberry, in spite of intermittent attempts to control its growth. But before the bracken takes over, other moorland plants such as wood sorrel, tormentil, bilberry and rosebay willowherb can be seen. Rosebay willowherb is also known as fireweed, having become relatively common on the sites bombed in the two World Wars of the twentieth century. Prior to this it was a scarce woodland plant.

Trees

The dominant trees in Newton Wood are oak species. The great majority are hybrids between sessile oak *Quercus petraea*, as the major parent, and English or Pedunculate oak *Quercus robur*. This hybrid is known as *Quercus x rosacea*. In the damper area well-established ash and sycamore trees dominate. These trees create numerous saplings, forming dense undergrowth which causes a problem for the National Trust staff. Removal of these saplings is part of the Trust's continuing maintenance programme for the woods. Other trees present in the wood include rowan, various conifers, hazel, hawthorn, wild plum and wych elm.

Until the start of the twentieth century some of the slopes above Newton Wood, at the level of the summerhouse, were wooded. An 1886 pencil sketch, with Ayton Banks Farm in the foreground, showed a belt of fir and pine trees stretching right across the Topping from the summerhouse to Roseberry Common. Ironstone mining and the 1912 land slip removed the majority of these trees, and only the occasional gnarled hawthorn remains today. However, on the eastern slopes, now that sheep grazing has virtually ceased on Roseberry Common, rowan and silver birch are beginning to establish themselves.

Birds

As with plants, the majority of bird life is found in Newton Wood.

A pair of fulmars Photo: Peter Grainger

A notable exception is the fulmar, which surprisingly nests on the upper cliff face of Roseberry Topping itself. Fulmars, tube-nosed seabirds, usually choose sea-cliff nesting sites such as Huntcliffe at Saltburn-by-the-Sea, but for some time now they have also bred intermittently on inland rock faces such as Highcliffe near Guisborough and Roseberry Topping.

In the spring, migrant warblers, including garden warbler, redstart, blackcap, willow warbler, wood warbler and chiffchaff, join the resident birds of Newton Wood. Singing males can be heard around the wood, although evidence of breeding is more difficult to ascertain. The wood has been a successful breeding site for tawny owls and the great spotted woodpecker. In 1979 a pair of redstarts reared young and this species slowly increased in number until in 1998 nine pairs were reported. The site became Cleveland's principal breeding area for this species but, unfortunately, redstarts have not bred here in the last two years.

On the moorland area around Roseberry occasional sightings of whinchat and ring ouzel have been reported, and tree pipits have been seen showing off their display flight. In May and June quail may be heard calling from the fields below the Topping near Newton-under-Roseberry and Pinchinthorpe, although this species is very elusive and rarely seen.

Butterflies and moths

Butterflies such as commas and the small, large and green-veined whites are present throughout the period from spring to autumn. Others, including the ringlet and meadow brown are mostly visible in July. Perhaps the most rewarding sight in the woods is the purple hair-streak. These butterflies spend most of their day perched in the tops of oak trees. In flight the purple upper-wing patches of both sexes are visible from above, but the more common view is of the silvery undersides as the butterflies fly around the top of an oak tree. Oak tortrix moths, whose caterpillars seriously defoliate oak trees, have a wing-span of twenty millimetres. They can be seen during August. In April and May the spring usher and pale brindled beauty moths are also visible. The bramble leaf-miner, with an eight millimetre wingspan, can be recognised by its yellow stripe on each wing.

Purple hair-streak Photo: Peter Waterton

Meadow brown Photo: Peter Grainger

Mammals

The environment of Newton Wood provides ample food and good cover for several of Britain's wild mammal species. Unlike birds, flowers and butterflies, mammals are not generally seen by the casual visitor to the woods. Many mammals are nocturnal in their habits. Sometimes however, their presence can be detected by the signs they leave; tracks, hairs, droppings and their burrows and nests.

There are some exceptions of course. Probably the most commonly encountered mammal is the grey squirrel. It is highly likely that prior to the twentieth century the red squirrel would have been present, but then it was displaced by the more versatile grey squirrel. Rabbits are also commonly seen in the fields and grasslands around the woods, and there is a strain having a much darker fur than usual in the locality. The brown hare, much chased by sporting gentlemen in past times, is present in good numbers. Numerous molehills can be seen everywhere, although their owners are rarely encountered, preferring their subterranean darkness to the daylight.

Thick undergrowth in the woods provides cover for the secretive roe deer, which nevertheless is not such an unusual sight for the quiet, early morning observer. The previous passage of a fox through an area is given away by the characteristically pungent smell emitted to mark its territory. At quieter times, particularly in the evening moonlight, foxes themselves can be seen.

There are several disused badger setts on the hillside. Sadly, and in spite of being protected by their own Act of Parliament since 1992, these animals are still persecuted for so-called sport. Badgers are also now facing a new threat from farmers, rightly concerned about the spread of bovine tuberculosis.

The presence of numerous gnawed nut shells is indicative of small rodent activity. Recently the Great Ayton Wildlife Society organized a live capture-and-release exercise, using Longworth traps, to find out which rodents were responsible. Traps were set over a forty-eight hour period in September 2005 at seven sites in the area. Twenty-seven animals were caught and released; bank voles, wood mice and common shrew. The latter was not as abundant as its name might suggest, for on this occasion just a single animal was caught.

Bats can be seen flying along the edge of the woodland at dusk, but electronic bat detection equipment would be required to positively identify the species present.

Fungi

Although fungi can be observed during any season in Newton Wood, the autumn is more traditionally recognised as the best season to search for them. The fungi occur in a wide range of sizes and differing sites. The damp area in the middle of the wood, where ash and sycamore have been felled, provides suitable places for fungal growth. One of the most obvious fungi is the Jew's ear which grows for most of the year on the living and dead wood of elder. Its brown gelatinous fruit-bodies are edible. Dead moll's fingers, aptly named from its black finger-like growths, lives on sycamore tree stumps and logs. The related candle snuff or stag's horn fungus is similar but with white growths. Turkeytail produces fan-like growths on dead wood and, although not edible, is used in Chinese herbal medicine.

Jew's ear fungus

Dead moll's fingers

Man's influence

As described in another chapter, the eastern slopes of Roseberry are marked by a great many pits, generally associated with mining activities. In the region of the pits around the 240m contour foxgloves can be seen growing, whereas they are not to be seen in the surrounding ground. It is possible that the seed for these plants was long-buried before being brought to the surface by mining activities. Another plant which takes advantage of a distinctive environment provided by these pits is the broad buckler fern. This fern appears to have found a niche amongst the bracken about half-way up the western edges of these pits; it is not frequently found amongst the bracken on the surrounding open moorland.

The wood's history

Most visitors to Roseberry would probably think that Newton Wood had existed since time immemorial, which incidentally is legally defined as since 1199. However, there is evidence that only a few hundred years ago the wood was smaller than today. The 1646 map by Joan Blaeu showed woodland, but its boundaries were not precise. That tireless diarist of the mid-eighteenth century, Ralph Jackson, mentioned Newton Wood on several occasions. The Jeffreys' map of 1771 depicted woodland in the area and, although the boundaries cannot be taken as accurate, it appeared to be positioned in the area of the summerhouse. Tuke's map of 1787 (below), and three early nineteenth century maps, the latest being 1817, all showed the wood as being smaller than today. The trees finished about 100 metres south of the end of the lane from the Newton car park.

Yet a later nineteenth century map, the Newton-under-Roseberry tithe map of 1837, showed the same extent of woodland as exists at present.

So it can be deduced that, before 1817, the oaks at the northern end of Newton Wood, nearest to Guisborough, either did not exist or were not sufficiently mature to be recorded as woodland. By 1837 they were large enough to be so recorded. The Newton-under-Roseberry manorial records of 1802 contain a reasonably accurate map of the estate, including the woodland area. At this time the wood was spread over four parcels of land, two belonging to the manor estate and two to

Mr Spence, a freeholder of Newton.

The nature of Newton Wood changes from north to south. The northern section is dominated by hybrid oaks, fairly regularly spaced and with none showing characteristics of coppiced trees. The damp middle part of the wood consists of sycamore and ash trees. The southern section is principally hybrid oaks, less evenly spaced than at the northern end. Several of the trees here show evidence of coppicing, where the timber would be harvested by cutting back to almost ground level, after which the tree would grow several trunks from the base. The age of an oak when coppiced can be estimated from the diameter of its base, and the ages of the trunks growing from the base from their diameters. The sum of these two figures yields the total age of the tree, and the latter figure is the approximate time since the oak was last coppiced. At the southern end of the wood coppiced oak bases have diameters of up to three feet. The majority of the larger oaks in the wood have trunks with diameters of twelve to twenty-four inches when measured at about six feet from ground level.

Alan Mitchell has suggested that an oak in a good woodland site with a twelve inch diameter trunk will be between forty-eight and seventy-two years old. Rather than apply this directly to Newton Wood, we can use data obtained from a felled oak on the southern edge of the wood. An average diameter of only twelve and a half inches had been achieved after ninety-two years, as measured by the annual growth rings. This is equivalent to a significantly lower growth rate than that suggested by Mitchell, implying that conditions in the wood are not ideal. Applying the new data to the other oaks within Newton Wood, those with twelve inch diameter trunks would be about 100 years old, and those with twenty-four inch diameter trunks would be about 200 years old.

So we may conclude that the vast majority of larger oak trunks are between 100 and 200 years old, with occasional trees older than 200 years. Some of the coppiced trees in the southern part of the wood were estimated as over 300 years old.

Summarising the above data, it seems that from map evidence the oaks at the northern end of Newton Wood are those remaining from trees planted sometime in the early nineteenth century. The southern end of the wood is older, and shows evidence of coppicing, with the last coppicing taking place between 100 and 200 years ago. Leather tanning, which used large quantities of oak bark, was well established in Great Ayton in the mid-seventeenth century. The oak bark would be obtained from coppiced oaks, and it seems likely that oaks from the southern end of Newton Wood would have been used for this purpose. In the middle of the eighteenth century Ralph Jackson recorded in his diary the planting of sapling oaks to create oak plantations on the Eston hills, and he noted later that the bark from 'thinnings', taken out twelve years after planting, was suitable for tanning of leather. After some years further thinning would take place, increasing the spacing between trees. The trees at the northern end of Newton Wood show a regularity which indicates a planted, rather than a natural, wood. It seems possible that this part of the wood was established early in the nineteenth century specifically to supply oak bark for the leather tanning industry. The demise of the tanning industry around 1850 meant that these oaks were not used for their intended purpose, and they were left to grow into the un-coppiced oaks seen today in this part of the wood.

… other trees present … include rowan, hazel, hawthorn, wild plum and wych elm …

The Topping today

Today's visitors - walkers

Most visitors to Roseberry Topping are walkers. They arrive from all directions: from Newton Wood, from Guisborough, down from the moors via Little Roseberry, or from Aireyholme Farm. The three main paths are all paved and stepped with sandstone blocks and paving. Some of those on foot are intent only on the ascent to the summit, but others will have more distant destinations. The Cleveland Way, from Helmsley to Filey, was officially opened in 1969. From Gribdale Gate the route hugs the wall on the western edge of Great Ayton Moor before turning to the east to cross Hutton Moor towards Guisborough. At this point the original guide advised that 'enthusiasts will cross the gap to climb Roseberry Topping, returning the same way', a two-mile extension to what for most would be their third day's hiking.

Mention must be made of sponsored walks, many of which have used the Topping. One novel approach recently, favoured by a group of sixth-formers from Stokesley, was to climb to the top from Newton sixteen times, equivalent to ascending Mount Everest from Base Camp.

Today's visitors - runners

Although most people climbing the Topping stop at the summit to admire the view, a few have no time to stand and stare. There are several fell-running events during the year that include the ascent to touch the trig point on the summit, before speeding down the punishingly steep descent. The most famous race is the annual one from Newton-under-Roseberry car park to the summit and back. This has a long history, going back to 1953, the year of the coronation of Queen Elizabeth II. The record time of ten minutes and twenty seconds, set in 1992 by Robin Bergstrand, will not easily be broken. It is claimed that later stone paving on the main paths slows the descent, but the fact remains that he was an excellent athlete, being challenged by a close rival. In the same year that Robin set the record for Roseberry he came third in the mountain-running world championships. He recalls 'I went up the tourist path to the summit, and then jumped off the edge and ran down the scree, picking up the tourist path at the gate and following it down through Newton Woods'. The ladies' record of thirteen minutes and thirty-six seconds by Gilly Hale has stood since 1990. Gilly remembers

how she was determined to capture the record, setting herself successively faster target times each year until she achieved it.

Several other fell races pass over the summit of the Topping: the Guisborough Moors Race, the Gribdale Gallop and the Guisborough Three Tops. Top runners average over nine miles per hour in these events.

For those who find insufficient challenge in this sort of race, the 109 mile Cleveland Way Relay, organised by the Cleveland Orienteering Klub, requires navigational, as well as athletic, abilities. Teams consist of up to sixteen runners, and must include at least one female member. The race starts by Filey landing stage at 5:00am, ending in Helmsley market place before the fish and chip shop closes. Another long distance race, the 56 mile Cleveland Classic, is no longer staged. This used to be held by the Friends of Botton Village for many years, and started in Great Ayton with an ascent of the Topping.

Many other orienteering events are organised around the slopes of the Topping and through Newton Wood, but the courses do not normally include a control point at the summit.

Today's visitors - riders

Specialised mountain bikes, designed to be used in off-road conditions, began to appear in the 1980s. Combining the simple appeal of the open countryside with the advanced technology of the machines, this new leisure activity became immensely popular. However, since the mid-1990s interest has declined slightly, with a revival of road cycling. On the Topping, as generally in the countryside, mountain bikes are restricted to bridleways and so cannot ascend to the summit. None the less, many enjoy pedalling their machines past Aireyholme and on to Little Roseberry along the bridleway.

Horses are, of course, also restricted to bridleways, and so the area is not as popular with horse riders as other parts of the surrounding countryside. On a more exotic note, it is now possible to ramble round the Topping in the company of a llama. The animals are not ridden, but provide a novel alternative to a rucksack, carrying loads that can even include champagne picnics.

Today's visitors - climbers

Rising to a height of some sixty feet, the distinctive summit rocks of 'The Matterhorn of Cleveland' have offered an obvious challenge to generations of rock climbers. But the potential for good climbing is limited by the soft nature of the rock, previous cliff collapses and a growing reputation for looseness and instability. There are a few recorded climbs, although of the dozen or so on the main face all have, at some time, been affected by rock falls and over half have been lost entirely.

The first known ascent of the main face was by Geoff Fixter and Eric Marr in the late 1950s. Their route, 'The Chimney', followed a cleft between the main face and a pillar leaning against it, and remained popular until the pillar collapsed in May 1979 taking this original route, and several other subsequent ones, with it to the boulders below. Perhaps the most impressive route of ascent was that first made by Tony Marr and Johnny Adams when they climbed the wide crack on the left of the main face in 1967. Steep and strenuous, this route waited some ten years for a second ascent and remains the hardest recorded route on the face. Two, more approachable, crack lines were climbed by Chris Woodall and partners in the 1980s. On a subsequent night-time ascent of one of these, the leading man shouted down that he wasn't happy with the quality of the rock. Reassuring comments from below led him to continue, reaching the top and bringing up the rest of the party, but within a fortnight a significant part of the climb had collapsed.

To the south-east of the main face there is a more stable area of rock which, although not as high, offers less serious outings, where success or failure is more to do with ability then luck. It was here that Roseberry Topping's first recorded climbs were made by Arthur Barker and his brother in the 1930s and, in contrast to many of those on the main face, they can still be enjoyed today. Further routes have been recorded in the years since then and provide a couple of hours' entertainment in a fine, peaceful and secluded position only a few yards from the often crowded summit.

Whilst so promising from afar, the grand cliff of Roseberry Topping offers relatively little to the rock climber, except distant views towards the far superior crags of Hasty Bank and Highcliff Nab.

' In solemn silence on his misty throne
Sits, towering over all – the landscape's king '

Cleveland John Reed Appleton 1868

Today's visitors - flyers

With more amenable sites in the vicinity, notably the edge of Easby Moor by Captain Cook's Monument, few people take to the air from the summit of Roseberry. Enthusiasts of radio-controlled model aircraft have occasionally been spotted, but so far not the intrepid users of hang gliders or parascenders. The first aeroplane in the vicinity of Roseberry may have been the aircraft that ran out of fuel and landed in a field just outside Ayton in 1918. Nowadays, flights to and from Durham Tees Valley Airport regularly pass over the Topping, giving passengers the chance to look down on the summit.

Looking after footpaths

With so many visitors, Roseberry Topping would inevitably suffer unless some effort was made to look after it. Before the National Trust took over the area, maintenance work was minimal since the area was considered as agricultural land. Under the care of the Trust matters improved considerably, and by July 1995 they had spent £500,000 on improvements and planned to spend another £500,000 over the following four years. Much of their stewardship has been to counter footpath erosion using different techniques. On parts of Little Roseberry the path was temporarily diverted to allow natural regeneration of the usual path, but this method was clearly impracticable on the main paths to the summit where stone would be needed. Stone could be transported in vehicles up the bridleway beyond Aireyholme Farm, but from there vehicle access would be impossible. The solution has been to use a helicopter.

On Tuesday 21 September 1993 a helicopter began to airlift 200 tonnes of stone in big polyester fibre bags up to the western slopes. A new zig-zag path was laid out and paved, giving particular attention to the drainage and to replanting at the sides of the new path. The cost of over £30,000 was met by the Countryside Commission, and the work was carried out by Cleveland County Council in conjunction with the North York Moors National Park and the National Trust. The skilled task of laying a path that would be easy to walk on and blend in with its surroundings was entrusted to Pathcraft of Scotland, who had experience of similar work on Ben Nevis. They used stone from a redundant drystone wall in Kildale, which originally had been quarried almost 200 years earlier at Ingleby Greenhow from the same stratum as the sandstone that caps Roseberry.

Left-over stone was taken back down by helicopter in January 1994 and used on part of the bridleway down Little Roseberry, where previous attempts to encourage natural regeneration of the path had failed under the onslaught from boots and bikes.

The path from Roseberry Common to the summit was paved in 1999, again using a helicopter to carry stone to the site. The entire lifting job was completed during one working day in May. Dave Close, a former farm worker who had been healing erosion scars around the National Park for six years, was in charge. The procedure was to dig out the worn path to a firm base, level it and lay the paving. Additional small steps were incorporated after walkers claimed that sloping paths were more difficult to walk on. This time the stone used was a mixture of redundant dry stone walling stone and large slabs specially quarried. The cost was met through use of Landfill Tax Credits, an imaginative scheme allowing companies operating landfill sites to divert some taxation to environmental projects. Biffaward, an environmental fund set up by Biffa Waste Services, donated £33,660. The required ten percent matched funding of £3,366 was met by the National Park, and ICI plc supplied some of the stone.

Left: Stone, for surfacing paths, being carried to the Topping by helicopter in May 1999

Photo: courtesy of the Northern Echo and Darlington & Stockton Times

Right: Llamas were employed in 2004 to transport stone to repair walls at Little Roseberry

Photo: Wellington Lodge Llama Trekking of Staintondale, Scarborough

Repairing walls

Dry stone walls form an important feature of the Roseberry landscape. They were built using stones found in the vicinity, generally well rounded boulders from the end of the last Ice Age, with some more angular pieces of sandstone from more recent rockfalls. Walls around Roseberry were not constructed as well as the familiar limestone dry stone walls of the Yorkshire Dales, and generally require more maintenance.

Work restoring walls has been undertaken in several campaigns, initially using young trainees on Manpower Services Commission schemes, and later employing professional wallers. As with paving stones, transporting materials to their point of use was a problem. In March 2004 this was tackled in an unusual manner by using llamas, from Wellington Lodge Llama Trekking near

Scarborough, to carry stones in panniers. Although the stretch of walling being repaired, at Little Roseberry, could be reached by four-wheel-drive vehicles, the llamas did much less damage to the surrounding moorland. And they guaranteed lots of press coverage.

The Trust did have ambitious plans to restore the old dry stone wall up from Newton Wood, marking the boundary between Great Ayton and Newton-under-Roseberry. This had largely been destroyed in the 1912 rockfall and replaced by a wire fence. Work was started but unfortunately abandoned after problems with the contractor and with the ground conditions.

As well as repairs to walls there have been improvements to fencing, gates and stiles, with newer stiles incorporating special gates at ground level for elderly or infirm pet dogs.

Moor and woodland management

Many people might imagine that open moorland could be left to look after itself, but such a policy would result in a tangle of dense undergrowth on all but the well-used paths. Bracken is always a problem, since it grows to six feet in height by the end of the season, making life impossible for other moorland plants such as heather. There are several methods of bracken control, spraying being the most effective, and the National Trust sprayed large areas of the Roseberry slopes in 1998 to dramatic effect. The bracken, however, has since returned.

The best way of generally managing vegetation on open moorland is by selective grazing with sheep. This is the practice on large parts of the North York Moors, along with the cycle of heather burning. In the recent past the slopes of Roseberry were grazed by sheep, but this has now ceased because of potential difficulties with the large number of visitors using the same ground. The inevitable results are beginning to be visible. There is considerable growth of scrub, particularly on Roseberry Common. Quite large rowan and birch trees have established themselves on the eastern side of the Topping, along with some gorse, elder and holly. Whether this area eventually becomes quite well wooded remains to be seen; in the nineteenth century much of the slopes above Newton Wood were covered with trees, although these were mainly conifers.

Newton Wood itself was probably developed during the eighteenth century as an oak plantation to provide bark for the leather tanning industry. As such, it would have been tended, as any other agricultural crop. Active management of the wood probably ceased some two hundred years ago when the local tanning industry declined. Oaks now have to compete with species seen as having lesser environmental value, such as sycamore and ash. The National Trust has carried out selective removal of such saplings, and some replanting. Until recently, fallen branches and trees may have been removed, but now it is appreciated that decaying timber provides habitats for many insects, apart from encouraging fungi. This is why dead wood can be seen lying on the ground throughout the wood.

Will Taylor

art and literature

23

Roseberry's literary appearances

This chapter looks at Roseberry Topping's appearances in poetry and literature; its descriptions in more factual works are covered in the chapters on the antiquarian authors and on tourism. We concentrate here on two eighteenth century authors, the dramatist Joseph Reed and the poet Thomas Pierson. There is a brief resumé of some of the many other writers who have given Roseberry a mention. Among these pages on literature are illustrations showing how some artists have portrayed Roseberry.

Famous lines by Joseph Reed

Joseph Reed was born in Stockton-on-Tees, probably in 1722. His parents were strict Presbyterians, steeped in Calvinist doctrines; anything to do with plays and acting was the devil's handiwork. It is therefore surprising that young Joseph's talents turned towards play-writing as he grew up. With his elder son already working in the family rope-making business, Joseph's father decided that his younger son should have a 'good education'. However, this was brought to an end when Joseph's brother died, and he had to take up the family business. Then, in 1754, he moved to London, where he established a thriving rope factory. Throughout this time Joseph continued to write. Before he left Stockton he had already published a farce, *The Superannuated Gallant*, but this was never performed on the stage.

Joseph Reed is chiefly remembered for his play *The Register Office*, in which the immortal character of Margery Moorpout appears. A register office in those days was not concerned with births, deaths and marriages, but was in effect a private employment agency. It would

Illustration from an early text of *The Register Office* by Joseph Reed. Sadly, the character of Margery Moorpout, who was born beside Roseberry Topping, is absent. Instead we see Mrs Doggerel demonstrating her dubious acting skills to Gulwell, with her daughter looking on.

184 ART AND LITERATURE

Alec Wright lived in Stokesley and worked as an artist from 1920 to 1978. Often described as Cleveland's best known painter, he had a flair for watercolour and pen sketching. Wright made numerous pen-and-ink sketches of historic buildings and local views, and a series of much admired watercolours of famous Cleveland scenes as evidenced here. The scene below left is on scraperboard. This is an unusual medium where a black surface is scraped away to reveal white underneath.

Pictures reproduced by permission of Billingham Press Ltd and Studio Print, Redcar

find jobs for those who were able to pay a fee. In the play, Gulwell, the rascally proprietor, systematically defrauded his clients by offering to find them impossibly attractive jobs, the reality being very different. As an example of his bogus employments, Gulwell instructed his secretary Williams thus:

> 'Stay, you must write an advertisement for the Daily, any time this afternoon will do, of an employment to be disposed of in Ireland, of a thousand pounds per annum, which requires little learning or attendance and may be executed by a deputy.'

The play introduced a number of characters in search of work, a Frenchman, a Scotchman [sic], a young army officer, an Irishman, a would-be author and her daughter, and Margery Moorpout, a pure and honest Yorkshire girl. The Irishman was expecting a good job in the West Country, whereas Gulwell was planning to ship him a good way further west, to America, and there turn him into an indentured servant. Fortunately, the Irishman uncovered the plot, and Gulwell received his comeuppance.

Margery Moorpout was the real heroine of the play. Her surname was dialect for a fledgling grouse, and commonly used as an epithet for women from the moors. Margery's simplicity and honesty shone throughout the scene in which she appeared. She was proud of her Yorkshire origins, and told Gulwell that she had been born and bred at Little Yatton [*Ayton*], beside Roseberry Topping. When he asked where this was, Margery was taken aback that not everyone knew the Topping. Ever since then it has become near-obligatory in articles about Roseberry to include part of her response:

> 'Sartainly, man, ye knaw Roseberry? Ah thowght onny fual hed knawn Roseberry. It's t'biggest hill i'all Yorkshur. It's aboon a mahle an' a hawf heegh, an' as cawd as ice at t'top on't i' t'yettest day i'summer: that it is.'

There may be a grain of truth in her comment on temperature, for when the play was written, Britain was experiencing much colder summers and winters. Margery explained that she had been forced to leave Ayton because the village squire had pursued her, morning, noon and night, with the intention of having his wicked way with her. She, being virtuous, would have none of this. Now it so happens that we know the identity of the squire of this period. He was Thomas Skottowe, although nothing is known about his proclivities so far as young women were concerned. Nevertheless, Reed was laying himself open to a charge of libel, since he knew that the squire could be easily identified. In the event there was no legal action, perhaps hinting at some truth in Reed's lines. Incidentally, it was Thomas Skottowe who gave James and Grace Cook a house and position at Aireyholme Farm, paid for the education of Grace's son James, and later paved the way for his successful naval career.

The two-act farce was first performed on 25 April 1761, at the Theatre Royal, Drury Lane. This was during the reign of the great actor and manager David Garrick, although he himself did not perform in *The Register Office*. The play seems to have been generally well received, since it was staged at intervals for a number of years at Drury Lane and was still in print during the early nineteenth century. An early biographer of Garrick described it as follows:

> 'The author is certainly a man of genius; his farce of *The Register Office* contains a variety of Characters aptly drawn; and it has accordingly met with great and deserved approbation.'

The prompter, Richard Cross, was more sparing in his praise. In his diary he observed 'A new farce (*The Register Office*) wrote by one Reed, a ropemaker, brought out by Mr. Foote – went off tolerable – hissed a little at the end'.

That same Samuel Foote, a good actor and a rival to Garrick, had earlier promised Reed to bring out his play at the Haymarket Theatre. Foote stole one of Reed's characters, Mrs Snarewell, and incorporated her in a play of his own. However, he seems to have made his peace with Reed and eventually produced *The Register Office* at Drury Lane. What the London audience made of Margery's dialect is unclear; it would also be interesting to know how the London actresses coped with it. There were probably no voice coaches in those days.

Reed's farce originally ran foul of the Lord Chamberlain's office, as it contained much profanity and double entendre. Two of the original characters, Lady Wrinkle and Mrs. Snarewell, had to be removed. The latter was 'warm in her praise of the comfort she has received from Mr Watchlight, who was called twice from his bed in the night and was so earnest in his ejaculations'. It is perhaps surprising that this was considered unacceptable in that robust age. But then Reed could be censorious in his own right. In his adaptation of Henry

Jean Battey (1906 – 1999) was a Quaker who lived and worked in Great Ayton. In her 1980's dramatic etching, Roseberry towers impressively above the buildings of Aireyholme Farm.

Henry James Robson was fifty-one when he started sketching scenes in rural Cleveland whilst on holiday and at weekends. He was living in Stockton with his wife, Isabel, and daughter, Mary, and is described in the 1891 census as a 'steam crane and iron founder'. The two sketches here are typical of his work, and have been taken from *Victorian Cleveland Sketchbook*

Below left: View from the summerhouse. The conifers were not on the first Ordnance Survey map and, from the evidence of 1910 photographs, had disappeared by that date. Perhaps the trees were planted to provide timber for the ironstone mine.

Below right: View from the lane beyond Gribdale Terrace, looking over Ayton Banks Farm. The buildings of the first Roseberry Ironstone Mine can be seen in the centre of this sketch.

Permission to reproduce sketches granted by David B Wilson, Stockton-on-Tees

Fielding's *Tom Jones*, which opened in 1769, Reed 'very judiciously stripped Jones of his libertinism, and legitimated him'.

The leading role in Thomas Pierson's epic

The epic poem by Thomas Pierson was one of the earliest published works taking Roseberry Topping as its theme. It was published in 1783 and titled simply *Roseberry Topping, A Poem*. Although it had little to say about the hill itself, the work was important in placing Roseberry in a decidedly romantic context, right at the summit of ancient Cleveland. Pierson didn't climb to the top for exercise or to admire the view, but to be inspired. Other writers in the eighteenth and early nineteenth centuries also tended to take this quasi-religious view of the Topping, and it was only with the emergence of tourism in the nineteenth century that writers adopted a more objective approach, concentrating on geographical and historical features.

Not much is known about Thomas Pierson. In his introduction to the 1847 edition of the poem, John Walker Ord quoted from an entry in the 1782 *Biographia Dramatica* which described Pierson as formerly a blacksmith, a watchmaker and a schoolmaster at Stokesley. Ord was enthusiastic about the poem, but limited his praise of Pierson to noting that, although he was 'among the uneducated or uncultivated poets', he deserved a better reputation. He also wrote detailed notes, nothing less would be expected from Ord, to pin down some of Pierson's high-flown language. Pierson, who died in 1791, produced only one other work, a play, which was published three years after the poem. Apart from any literary talent, he may well have been remembered for his extraordinary wig.

At the start of the work, Pierson is standing on the summit. It is clear that he has come to praise Roseberry. We can imagine him lifting that unruly wig from his eyes, mopping his brow, and gazing out in awe and rapture at the view.

'Of Atlas mount let poets *Antique* sing,
Whose summit bare supports the bending sky;
Of Roseberry's rude rock I deign to write,
The height of Toppin, and it's oozing rill.'

There are only a few references to the mountain itself: the 'oozing rill' where Prince Oswy perished and, later in the poem, 'a Druid's ancient hut, a half demolished cell'. To the east, north and west there is unstinting praise for the unfolding panorama, in severe contrast with the prospect to the south, beyond Broughton. Here we see what at least one eighteenth century man thought about the moors.

'Those hills, like posterns, lead to caverns dire,
To dreary deserts, bogs, and broken roads,
Impervious Glens, Pits fathomless, and foul:
O'er precipice, morass, by Westerdale,
By Castleton, the *pathless* desert leads:
To Farndale-Gill the *Wilderness* extends,
From thence to WHITBY, or to SCARBRO' *spreads*.'

There are other contrasts, some quite extreme. At the Carlton alum works, which had ceased operating a few years previously, 'a chasm hideous chasm pours red rubbish thence'. On the other hand, Guisborough's ruined priory resembled Athens, or even 'Solomon's fam'd temple, splendid-built, magnificent'.

He wished others would ascend Roseberry, so that they might benefit from the experience.

'This rocky mount, pyramidal and steep,
Fit spot, fair feat of *sage* philosophy,
Let ev'ry sophist climb, sometimes ascend,
This rural feat may curious thoughts employ;
The wise Philosopher may travel here,
Search Nature's secrets, see her wonders great,
In every stone, each pebble, speck *minute*,
The shaggy woods, the precipice below,
Art, science grows – in that small village mean,
Even dirty Newton, fixed in the vale.
The grave Astronomer may wander *far*,

THOMAS PIERSON,
THE AUTHOR OF "ROSEBERRY TOPPING."

"That Wisdom lieth in a wig
I'm sure it is no lies;
For Pierson's wig it was so big
It covered both his eyes!"

Thomas Pierson, the author of an epic poem on Roseberry Topping published in 1783. This illustration is reproduced from an 1847 edition with notes by John Walker Ord, who presumably wrote the lines about Pierson and his wig.

Robery Leslie Howey (1900 – 1981) was the son of Staithes Group artist John William Howey. In the post-war years he began working in pastel, then pure watercolour, progressing to mixed media work and oils. His later work was distinguished by striking light effects. Although he is probably best known for his views of Whitby, he produced many pictures of Roseberry Topping.

These two paintings have been reproduced as prints by his son, David Howey.

The planets mark, or view the Atmosphere,
Tell each new Star, the Sun and Moon behold,
The sapphire-arch illum'd with golden gems,
Learn horizontal lines, see worlds around,
Celestial Orbs, or *Things* upon this Earth.'

Although today it is all too easy to dismiss Pierson's heroic style as contrived and excessively florid, the poem contains some interesting facts about the state of Cleveland at that time. For example, there was a wide variety of fish in the rivers, but at Ayton anglers attacked his beloved paradise of Cleveland - 'with rods, with nets, rapacious sportsmen kill, so greedy of their prey, the brooks they drain'. Pierson seems to have nurtured a prejudice against fishermen in general. He later denounced those along the coast for swearing, lying and cheating, and for turning to swindling and smuggling along with their fishing. There are descriptions of the abundant wildlife, and of the verdant Cleveland Plain with its cornfields and orchards, grazing cattle and lambs. His attitudes to animal welfare appear surprisingly modern, with sharp criticism of horse racing at Hambleton, game shooting on the moors and fox hunting around Aireyholme.

Time and again Pierson turned to the many country houses that were such a feature of the eighteenth century landscape. He never mentioned their owners by name, but invariably heaped lavish praise on them, perhaps hopeful of their future patronage of his literary efforts. The praise may not always have been justified, as many of the owners, like the rest of us, no doubt had their faults. But Pierson's eulogies may also have been slightly tongue-in-cheek. Perhaps, as a well-read schoolmaster, he was familiar with the art of satire, which was flourishing in the eighteenth century. He might have been looking down both literally and satirically on the residents of the Cleveland Plain below.

Sir Charles Turner of Kirkleatham, referred to only as 'The Baronet', was credited with much agricultural knowledge. Yet his attempts in 1773 to reclaim open moorland at Kempswithen, mentioned by Pierson, were expensive and ultimately unsuccessful.

At Normanby Hall, Ralph Jackson was described as a gentleman and a widower, with many qualities: sober, mild and courteous (since Jackson's wife had died in 1781, Pierson's poem must have been written in the period 1781 to 1783). Jackson was certainly not always that sober. We know from his diaries that in May 1764, after dinner, he went to the Cock Inn at Guisborough where he met Augustine Skottowe. The pair of them drank sour punch from six until nine, when he took Skottowe back to Normanby. Once there, the drinking continued and Jackson later recorded 'I became so intoxicated as to be totally deprived of sence'.

At Busby Hall 'the gentleman blessed with consort fair, but childless still' was William Marwood. The Marwoods had long been at Busby Hall, but William was not really a true Marwood. Jane Marwood should have inherited the estate, but she had eloped with a handsome Dutch officer billeted with the family at the time of the Jacobite rebellion in 1745. This resulted in her being disowned by her mother, who passed the estate to a distant cousin on the condition that he changed his name from William Metcalfe to William Marwood.

The occupants of Ayton Hall were described as a family of frugal worth, hardly a fitting description for William Wilson, who had retired as Commodore of the East India Company's fleet, with a personal fortune.

Pierson completed his virtual tour round Cleveland and beyond in his home town of Stokesley. In contrast to his previous unbridled delight, he was troubled by a moral decline in this market town, no doubt due in part to its many inns and ale houses.

'It's present state, alas! is *changing* still,
Varies and turns as luxury and pride
Increase and fall, as mirth and sloth *abound*,
Where sensual riot, *merriment* obscene,
Employ the Day, and revel thro' the Night;
Justice too *little* rules, no order guides,
But *stiff opinion* ev'ry Man protects.'

It is probable that Pierson's dislike of Stokesley also had a more personal basis. The gentlemen of Stokesley did not exactly fall over themselves in pledging to buy his book. John Jackson, of Hutton Rudby, wrote 'The most virulent abuse falls on the gentlemen of Stokesley, who it appears have not subscribed liberally to his work', concluding that Pierson would not have treated Stokesley as harshly if 'ten righteous subscribers instead of four had supported him'. Perhaps more importantly, Pierson had been found wanting as the village schoolmaster, and was replaced by a stranger, perhaps better qualified to teach 'sublime philosophy and science deep'.

Eclipsing his concern for Stokesley, Pierson saw greater threats hanging over England. Yet all could be

Will Taylor (1942 – 1998) lived at Ainthorpe, near Danby. He was intimately acquainted with the countryside in all its seasons and captured its changing moods in his landscapes, whether through the immediacy of his pen-and-ink drawings or the atmospheric grandeur of his lino-cuts. Due to his special technique of blending inks onto the lino-cut before printing, each print was unique. Some of his pictures have been used on the covers of a series of Celtic Christian books by Canon David Adam, former vicar of Danby. Will Taylor's prints are reproduced by permission of Norma Taylor.

saved by the Navy, a prophetic wish as Trafalgar would be little more than twenty years away. National pride restored, England's green and pleasant land might then become a fit abode for the gods. In the final pages of his poem, Pierson has to leave the summit to make way for Jupiter and his entire retinue, who have forsaken Mount Olympus to take up residence above Roseberry Topping:

> 'Yet, see! what glorious Form descending comes,
> With lustre comes, 'tis Jove, *perhaps*, that shines,
> Has Ida or Olympus quickly left,
> His late abodes, to view this famous Isle,
> To grace this Toppin with his senate wise?
> 'Tis even so – I see their God-ships come,
> Let me depart, with ardour quit the mount,
> To give their Lord-ships room to take their seats.'

Ebenezer Elliott

Ebenezer Elliott was born in 1781. He took over his father's iron foundry in Rotherham and, when the business went bankrupt, moved to Sheffield and became a successful dealer in iron. He was vehemently opposed to the Corn Law, and wrote radical poetry in support of his views. There is a statue in his honour in Weston Park, Sheffield, coincidently also the current home of the Roseberry Bronze Age hoard. Elliott's poetry included a few lines on the Topping:

> 'When Cook, a sailor's boy, with aching eye,
> Gazed from the deep on oft climbed Roseberry;
> While trembling as she listened to the blast,
> His anxious parent sea-ward wishes cast,
> And fervent prayer was mute, but not suppressed,
> Though love was resignation in her breast;
> Why didst thou not – thou happiest name of joy –
> Bid her cheered spirit see that deathless boy
> Bear round the globe Britannia's flag unfurled,
> And from the abyss unknown call forth a world?'

A mention by Sir Walter Scott

Sir Walter Scott single-handedly created the romantic view of the Scottish Highlands through a series of world famous novels. One of his lesser-known works was *The Pirate*, published in 1822. This tale was set in the Shetlands (Zetland), and involved a shipwrecked pirate and his relations with the family who befriended him. Local knowledge for the plot came from Scott's friend, the sheriff of Orkney and Zetland. There are several intriguing references to North Yorkshire. The pirate is named as Captain Clement Cleveland, although he came from Bristol. Another character in the book is a farmer, Jaspar Yellowley, who had been born at the foot of Roseberry Topping. In a footnote, Scott explained that the islands of Orkney and Zetland were bought by Sir Lawrence Dundas in 1766, his son, Lord Dundas, holding the islands at the time Scott wrote the book.

John Walker Ord

John Walker Ord is chiefly remembered for his *History and Antiquities of Cleveland*, covered in the chapter on the antiquarian writers. However, he published many other works, including *The Bard and Minor Poems*, a collection of poetry, published in 1842, in which was included a sonnet *To Roseberry*:

> 'Cleveland, each Yorkshire vale salutes thee king,
> And thou art watch-tower for the roaring sea;
> Hundreds of ship-wrecked tars have looked to thee
> As through the howling billows they did swing:
> Thou soarest aloft, as with an eagle's wing,
> Elate with looks of mountain sovereignty.
> Spring's earliest clouds rest on thy forehead free,
> Spring's youngest flowers commence their blossoming
> Within thy bowers:- to thee the birds first sing!
> And thou hast joyous pastures, verdant plains,
> Groves for thy subjects, mountains for thy slaves;
> Yea, the fierce storms salute thee, mighty thing:
> Within thy cliffs the lordly eagle reigns –
> Cliffs coeternal with the winds and waves!'

Joseph Taylor

Roseberry has the distinction of being the first poem in a collection of some sixty poems by Joseph Taylor of Leeds. The collection was published in 1841 by subscription, mostly from people in the West Riding, with a few from Cleveland. In truth Taylor's poem had little connection with Roseberry and, like the rest of the collection, was more to do with the Christian faith. The general tenor is clear from the subjects of some other works in the collection: temperance, the torments of hell, and the weaknesses of man. Taylor was loaned a copy of John Graves' *History of Cleveland* by the author's son, and he quoted from it in a series of footnotes. There were references to Cook, 'the bright meteor from the lowly vale', and to the supposed druid's altar at the summit where, he claimed, victims stained the mountain dew with their blood. As with other poems about the Topping, plagiarism creeps in. If Taylor didn't have his own copy of Graves he certainly had Gray's *Elegy in a Country Churchyard*, written almost a hundred years earlier. Compare Taylor's 'The peasant singing on his homeward way, The distant lowing of the patient kine' with Gray's 'The lowing herd wind slowly o'er the lea, The ploughman homeward plods his weary way'.

John Ryley Robinson

The Victorian era produced a number of romantic poems featuring Roseberry Topping. One such was *Rosebury Topping* by John Ryley Robinson, who was born in Dewsbury, in the West Riding, in 1829. He clearly had a love of the Cleveland area, and of Roseberry Topping.

> 'Oh! How indelibly a lovely view
> Imprints itself upon our memory.
> For who can climb thy summit, and from thence
> Behold that prospect, so enchanting, spread
> Before his wondering gaze, nor feel its power
> To cheer the mind and elevate the soul?'

Robinson went on to describe the views from the summit, a rural scene 'of Cleveland, with its smiling fields of corn, its meadows with its flocks and herds', contrasting with the smoke cloud over Middlesbrough. He was not, however, a starry-eyed environmentalist, but an economic realist, as can be seen by these lines:

> 'And though the furnaces upon its banks
> At times pour forth such volumes of dense smoke,
> Which sadly mar the prospect, and obscure
> The view beyond, we bear with them, because
> We know that they turn our iron into gold,
> Developing our hidden wealth, and build
> Such towns as Middlesborough, which we see
> Whilst standing here, and wonder at its growth.'

The poem contains five lines which once again seem to demonstrate that plagiarism is nothing new:

> 'Cover'd with ships, whose glitt'ring sails are seen
> Now, fully bosom'd by the wind, and now
> As eddying to the breeze, in various shades
> Contrasting with each other, they present
> Fresh source of pleasure to the raptured sight.'

Compare these lines with an extract from the narrative of a gentleman quoted by Graves in 1808:

> 'To the east we had the first view of the sea, covered with ships, whose glittering sails, now fully bosomed to the wind, now edying to the breeze, formed various shades contrasted by the sun-beams, as they stood in different directions, and presented a pleasing variety to the enraptured sight.'

The son of a Methodist preacher, Robinson concluded his poem by reminding us that everything we see from the summit was created by God who 'if we serve Him faithfully, will raise our souls to dwell with Him in endless bliss.'

Henry Heavisides

Henry Heavisides was born in 1791 in Stockton-on-Tees. The later writer, Michael Heavisides, does not seem to have been related to him. Henry Heavisides spent some time working for William Pratt, the Stokesley printer and bookseller, and wrote a few lines on Roseberry which he likened to Mont Blanc; most other writers have preferred the Matterhorn.

> 'The storm-beaten cone,
> Seen afar on the billowy main,
> That stands in magnificence lone,
> The lofty Mont Blanc of the plain.'

John Reed Appleton

John Reed Appleton was born in Stockton in 1824. He published *Cleveland, A Poem in Blank Verse* in 1868. Unusually, this poem described the weather on Roseberry Topping throughout the four seasons of the year. It began:

> 'Lo! Roseberry - with stately head erect
> Gorgeously gilded by the setting sun
> In solemn silence on his misty throne
> Sits, towering over all – the landscape's King
> While the bright clouds, as courtiers, stoop and kiss his robe.'

At other times wild storms lashed the hill.

> 'In far, far other moods
> I've seen him frown when heavy clouds have lain
> Upon his breast, and vivid lightnings gleamed,
> And from afar the muttering thunder roll'd
> And wildest storm flew crashing through the dark'

George Markham Tweddell

Tweddell was one of the great characters of nineteenth century Cleveland. He was one of three illegitimate sons of Elizabeth Tweddell, his father being a grandson of

Archbishop Markham of York. Tweddell was said to have adopted the name of Markham later in life to remind the Markham family of their indiscretion. He was a printer and publisher, a shopkeeper and schoolmaster, and a poet. With his radical views and inability to manage his finances he never achieved the literary reputation enjoyed by his wife, who wrote dialect poetry under the name of Florence Cleveland. However, he did write some lines on Roseberry:

> 'Who has not heard of Roseberry?
> The favourite hill of every Cleveland bard,
> Of Roseberry's rude rock I deign to write,
> The height of Topping and its coming rill.'

James Milligan

To end our brief survey of nineteenth century literature associated with Roseberry Topping, mention might be made of a long descriptive poem by James Milligan, *The Hills and Vale of Cleveland*, published in 1881. The lightness of his touch contrasts favourably with the grandiose phrases, ornate rhetoric and pious exhortations of his fellow writers:

> 'Oft during the warm summer months
> Gay parties may be seen
> Wending their way up Rosebury,
> As blithe as king or queen.
> To enjoy themselves they each strive:
> Thus play some harmless games,
> While others on Rosebury rocks
> Delight to carve their names.
> Some love to sit beside the well
> And sip from its clear spring,
> And think of the ancient legend
> Poets are wont to sing.'

Milligan, who lived in Great Ayton, went on to romanticise about Aireyholme Farm, and the young James Cook walking along Cliff Rigg, near to where his parents' cottage stood.

Gertrude Bell's letters

Gertrude Bell was a well-educated, independent and adventurous woman. The Bell family made their fortunes in the iron industry on Teesside, and Gertrude's grandfather founded Bell Brothers at Port Clarence iron works. She was familiar with North Yorkshire; soon after her birth in 1868 her father had built Rounton Grange near Northallerton as their new family home. Gertrude became an Alpine mountaineer, an Arabic scholar, an archaeologist, and an agent for British Intelligence in the First World War. She twice travelled round the world, recording her experiences in a series of letters. Her letter of 12 March 1903 was written in the Governor's House in Singapore, where it was uncomfortably warm and humid. She ended thus:

> 'And it's all like a vapour bath. The slightest exertion, writing a letter even, makes you as hot as if you had been up Roseberry Toppin on the hottest summer day.'

A modern romance

There is very little mention of Roseberry Topping in novels. However, one example is in *Cleveland View* by D L Leach, published in the 1940s. It is set, as the title suggests, in the Cleveland area, in the years immediately prior to the start of the Second World War, and can be best described as a light romance.

What may surprise the modern reader is the extensive provision of public transport services at that time. Although the characters in the book had cars, they chose to take the bus from Hutton Rudby to Great Ayton 'the place the village people called affectionately amongst themselves "Canny Yetton", a mile and a half from the summit of Roseberry Topping'. From there they walk on to Roseberry.

> 'The three of them, Maisie and Paul and Judith, had taken this short cut to Roseberry Topping. Getting down from the Ayton bus at Cleveland Lodge, they had turned eastwards off the beaten track, and climbed upwards through the beautiful plantations. The climb was steep; sometimes they came out into a short, flat strip of grassland perched high above the road; from here there showed lovely vistas of patchwork country lying below. Slowly they mounted, skirting along the edge of a cornfield until they reached a gate at the end of the last coppice.
>
> Here there was short springy moorland grass beneath their feet. Maisie sat down on the flat grass plateau land and gazed at the view; the basket and books were dumped down while Paul and Judith climbed the last steep bit to the high point of the Topping. Slight steps had been cut in the hard wind-bitten earth, and an iron spike driven in here and there to give a hold across the steep point itself.
>
> It had its reward to give after the last steep tussle. Judith caught her breath as she saw the vast beauty below, the still greater charm as she beheld an interrupted(sic) view wherever she turned her gaze. She tried to call out to

' Gorgeously gilded by the setting sun … '

Cleveland John Reed Appleyard 1868

Paul, who stood a shade below holding her left hand, while she clutched the iron spike in her right, "I feel on top of the world, I feel like the Queen of Space!" He looked and smiled, seeing her lips moving, but the wind, which was carrying her words swiftly away, was drumming hard into his ears; he could only nod his head and smile back. The wind blew cold and hard even on this, the hottest of days, upon this highest spot of all the Clevelands.

They half-climbed, half-slid down from the steep Top, and walked back to the long flat stretch of grass on the lower plateau, where Maisie lay peacefully enjoying the view.'

Whodunit?

The *Piper of Dreams* is something of a curiosity among books connected with Roseberry Topping. In order to set the scene for this book we need to start with another book, *Masquerade*, which has nothing to do with our hill. This was a puzzle book, written by Kit Williams, and published in 1979. It invited readers to find a golden hare, buried somewhere in the British Isles. The book contained fifteen beautiful illustrations, each of various people and animals, with a message round the border of each picture. The secret was to draw lines from the characters' eyes through their claws or fingers to the border, where specific letters would be identified. These letters were then rearranged to form a word and the sequence of fifteen words gave the clue as to the exact spot where the golden hare could be found. The initial letters of each word spelt out 'Close by Ampthill' where the hare was buried. When it was published the book created a frenzy of interest. The hare remained in the ground for over two years and was eventually discovered, not by someone solving the clues, but by a cad with a metal detector who had elicited some extra clues from Kit William's girlfriend. The proper solution was worked out a few months later by two physicists.

The huge success of *Masquerade* led to a number of imitations, but none captured the public imagination to anything like the same extent. One of these later books was *The Piper of Dreams*, published in 1982. It was written to raise funds for the National Society for the Prevention of Cruelty to Children. The story, by Terry Pitts Fenby, explained how a goblin named Peter Pumpkin acquired the Pied Piper's magic flute. In exchange for the return of his flute, the Pied Piper gave the goblin a series of clues leading to a hidden golden coffer. Poor Peter could not

The Piper of Dreams by Terry Pitts Fenby, with illustrations by Bill Bruce, reproduced by permission of Hodder & Stoughton Ltd. A disguised Roseberry Topping can be seen rising up up out of the sea.

read, and so enlisted the help of readers of the book to solve the mystery. A real golden flute had been buried near Captain Cook's Monument on Easby Moor, within sight of Roseberry Topping. Although there were many clues relating to the north-east, to Captain Cook and to Easby Moor, one of Bill Bruce's illustrations gave the game away. This was a representation of Roseberry Topping and Little Roseberry, looking from the south-west. In spite of sea levels having apparently risen to cover a good deal of Newton Wood, the scene was recognised by many people, even some living outside the boundaries of Yorkshire. So the golden flute was found all too soon, and the charity's income from the book fell far short of expectations. Clearly the strength of the image of the Topping in people's minds had been seriously underestimated.

Today's literature

It is apparent from what has been said that Roseberry Topping, by reason of its isolated position and unusual shape, holds a peculiar fascination for all who climb it or view it from afar. Robert Holman, the contemporary playwright born in 1952, in a letter to the author, describes his boyhood, living on a farm near Nunthorpe. On a hill near the farm he could see all the chimneys and billowing smoke clouds of Teesside's heavy industry, (this being shortly before the Clean Air Act of 1956 had taken full effect). Behind him the view of Roseberry Topping and the Cleveland hills was a complete contrast. Even at that tender age the difference between the two landscapes made a huge impact on him and has informed a lot of his work as the years have gone by. It was Holman who said that:–

> ' so long as Roseberry Topping stands, so long will its special place in the affection of people endure '

'... Roseberry Topping ... our mountain of the imagination ...'

references

References are presented here, chapter by chapter. Within chapter headings, references are generally listed in order of publication date. Where a reference appears several times, the full reference is given only at the first appearance. Subsequent references are restricted to author and date (with the number of the chapter containing the full reference).

Chapter 1   Looking at the Topping

The History of Cleveland
   Rev John Graves
   F Jollie and Sons, Carlisle, 1808
   Reprinted as ISBN 0903169045
   Patrick and Shotton
   Stockton-on-Tees, 1972

Chapter 2   The origin of the name

Graves, 1808 (1)
The Origin of Pagan Idolatry
   Rev G S Faber
   F Rivington, London, 1816
History of Whitby and Streoneshalh Abbey Vol II
   Rev George Young
   Clark and Medd, Whitby, 1817
The History and Antiquities of Cleveland, comprising the Wapentake of East and West Langbargh, North Riding, County York
   John Walker Ord
   Simpkin and Marshall of London
   W Tait of Edinburgh and
   W Braithwaite of Stokesley, 1846
   Reprinted as ISBN 0903169053
   Patrick and Shotton
   Stockton-on-Tees, 1972
People's History of Cleveland and its Vicinage
   George Markham Tweddell
   Tweddell and Sons, Stokesley, 1877
History of Cleveland Ancient and Modern
   Vol I and Vol II
   Canon J C Atkinson
   Barrow-in-Furness, 1874
   Reprinted MTD Rigg Publications
   Leeds, 1993
History of Cleveland Ancient and Modern
   Volume II (Part Two) hitherto unpublished
   Canon J C Atkinson, 1893-4
   MTD Rigg Publications, Leeds, 1993
The English Dialect Dictionary
   Edited by Joseph Wright
   Oxford University Press, 1898-1905
Yorkshire Wit, Character, Folklore and Customs
   Richard Blakeborough
   Oxford University Press, 1898

Roseberry Topping
   R B Turton
   Yorkshire Arch Journal Vol 22, 1913
Place-names of the North Riding of Yorkshire
   English Place Name Society, Vol V
   A H Smith
   Cambridge University Press, 1928
Guisborough Cartulary
   Surtees Society, Volume 86

Chapter 3   Landscape and geology

North Eastern Daily Gazette
   Tuesday 14 May 1912
North Eastern Daily Gazette
   Thursday 16 May 1912
The Herald
   Saturday 18 May 1912
Roseberry Topping in Fact and Fiction
   J J Burton
   Proceedings of the Cleveland
   Naturalists' Field Club 1920-1925
   Vol III, Part IV
   Edited by Ernest W Jackson
   Jordison & Co Ltd, Middlesbrough, 1926
T'ills was Fallin' Down, the great landslip of 1872
   Brian Marsay, Bilsdale Study Group, 2005

Chapter 4   Prehistoric Roseberry

Early Man in North-East Yorkshire
   Frank Elgee
   Frank Elgee, 1930
The Chambered Cairn and adjacent monuments on Great Ayton Moor, North-East Yorkshire
   R H Hayes
   Scarborough & District Arch Society
   Scarborough, 1967
Historical Atlas of North Yorkshire
   Edited by Robin A Butlin
   ISBN 1 84103 020 1
   Westbury Publishing, Otley, 2003
The Archaeology of Yorkshire,
   an assessment at the beginning of the 21st century
   Edited by T G Manby, Stephen Moorhouse and Patrick Ottaway
   ISBN 1 9035 6405 0
   Yorkshire Arch Society, Leeds, 2003

Chapter 5   The Bronze Age hoard

Account of some Ancient instruments
   John Hixon
   Archaeologia Aeliana Series 1, Vol 2,
   Newcastle-upon-Tyne, 1832
An Account of certain Bronze Instruments, supposed to be Druidical Remains, found beneath a large Rock on the South Side of the Top of Roseberry in Cleveland
   G S Faber
   Archaeologica Scotia Vol 4
   Society of Antiquaries of Scotland, 1857
Ten Years Diggings in Celtic Saxon Grave-Hills
   Thomas Bateman
   J R Smith, London, 1861
   Reprinted as ISBN 0903485 48 6
   Moorland Publishing Company, 1978
Ord, 1846 (2)
The Ancient Bronze Implements, Weapons, and Ornaments of Great Britain and Ireland
   John Evans
   Longmans, Green, & Co, London, 1881
Elgee, 1930 (4)
Egglescliffe – A Short History of the Village
   Rev A T Dingle
   ISBN 0 903169 10 X
   Edited by Robert Ward
   Patrick & Shotton, 1973
Prehistoric and Roman Archaeology of North-East Yorkshire
   Edited by D A Spratt
   ISBN 1 872414 28 1
   CBA Research Report 87
   Council for British Archaeology, 1990
The Bronze Age – a time of change
   Nyda Roberts
   ISBN 0952355205
   Signal House Publications, 1994
Bronze Age Copper Mining in Britain and Ireland
   ISBN 0747803218
   William O'Brien
   Shire Publications Ltd, 1996
Butlin, 2003 (4)
The Residents of Tanton Hall, Stokesley
   J Beryl Turner
   Unpublished paper October 2003

Manby et al, 2003 (4)

Chapter 6 Sight lines or leys

The Old Straight Track
    Alfred Watkins
    Methuen, London, 1925
    Reprinted as ISBN 0349137072
    Abacus, Tunbridge Wells, 1974
Lines on the Landscap; Leys and Other Linear Enigmas
    Paul Devereux and Ian Thompson
    ISBN 0 7090 3704 X
    Robert Hale Limited, London, 1989
On the Straight and Narrow
    Paul Grantham
    Published in *The Voice of the Moors*
    Issue 52
    North Yorkshire Moors Association
    1998
www.leyhunter.com
www.smr.herefordshire.gov.uk

Chapter 7 Farming on the slopes

General View of the Agriculture of the North Riding of Yorkshire
    Mr Tuke, junior
    W Bulmer and Co, London, 1794
The Finance (1909-1910) Act Valuations
    Valuation Office Field Book
    IR58 58926
    National Archives, Kew
National Farm Surveys of England and Wales, 1940-1943
    Ministry of Agriculture & Fisheries
    MAF 32/1087/430
    National Archives, Kew
Making of the English Landscape
    W G Hoskins
    Hodder and Stoughton, London, 1955
A Survey of the Agriculture of Yorkshire
    W Harwood Long
    MA Thesis, University of Durham
West Cleveland Land Use, circa 1550 to 1850
    P K Mitchell
    Ph D Thesis, University of Durham, 1965
Farming in Yorkshire – a regional survey
    Bill Cowley
    ISBN 0 85206 130 7
    Dalesman Publishing Company Ltd, 1972
Butlin, 2003 (4)
The Rudds of Marton
    Beryl Bass
    ISBN 0 9730029 0 5
    Earth-Net Publications,
    British Colombia, 2001

Chapter 8 Fox hunting

The Ballads and Songs of Yorkshire, transcribed from private manuscripts, rare broadsides, and scarce publications; with notes and a glossary
    C J Davison Ingledew
    Bell and Daldy, London, 1860
Bards and Authors of Cleveland and South Durham and the Vicinage, Part 4
    George Markham Tweddell
    Tweddell and Sons, Stokesley, 1865
The Cleveland Hounds as a Trencher-fed Pack
    A E Pease
    Longmans, Green, and Co, London, 1887
Men, Horses & Sportsmen
    William Scarth Dixon
    Jonathan Cape, London, 1931
Northern Sport & Sportsmen
    J Fairfax Blakeborough
    Yorkshire Press, Stockton-on-Tees and
    Hunter & Longhurst, London, 1912
The Spirit of Yorkshire
    J F and R Blakeborough
    B T Batsford Ltd, London, 1954
Memorable hunt for Cleveland
    Darlington & Stockton Times
    15 November 1971

Chapter 9 The antiquarians

Britannia
    William Camden
    London 1607
    Translation of Camden on
    www.philological.bham.ac.uk/cambrit/yorkseng.html
Library of Sir Robert Cotton, Julius, shelf F, volume VI
    The British Library, London
Graves, 1808 (1)
Beauties of England and Wales Volume XVI: Yorkshire
    John Bigland
    John Harris, London, 1812
Young, 1817 (2)
A Picture of Whitby and its Environs
    Rev George Young
    R Rodgers, 1824
Ord, 1846 (2)
Atkinson, 1893-4 (2)
Tweddell, 1877 (2)
Old Cleveland Writers and Worthies
    William Hall Burnett
    Hamilton Adams and Company
    London, 1884
The Alum Farm
    Robert Bell Turton
    Horne & Son Limited, Whitby, 1938

Chapter 10 Myths and legends

Camden, 1607 (9)
Cottonian manuscript (9)
Yorkshire Holy Wells and Sacred Springs
    Edna Whelan and Ian Taylor
    ISBN 1869939093
    Northern Lights 1989
Rural Sketches and Poems
    John Walker Ord
    Simpkin and Marshall, London and
    W Tait, Edinburgh, 1845
Ingledew, 1860 (8)
Bards and Authors of Cleveland and South Durham and the Vicinage, Part 9
    George Markham Tweddell
    Tweddell and Sons, Stokesley, 1866
Yorkshire Legends and Traditions, as told by her Ancient Chroniclers, her Poets and Journalists
    Rev Thomas Parkinson
    Elliot Stock, London, 1888
T'Hunt o'Yatton Brigg
    Richard Blakeborough
    Yorkshire Dialect Series No 9
    The Yorkshire Publishing Press, Stockton-on-Tees and Hunter & Longhurst,
    London, 1899
County Folk-lore, Vol II,
Examples of Printed Folk-lore concerning the North Riding of Yorkshire, York and the Ainsty
    Mrs Gutch
    Published for the Folk-lore Society by
    David Nutt, London, 1901
Yorkshire Notes and Queries
    Edited by Chas F Forshaw
    Bradford and Elliot Stock, London, 1906
Burton, 1926 (3)
Witches in Old North Yorkshire
    Mary Williams
    ISBN 0 907033 54 7
    Hutton Press Ltd, 1987
Marvels, Magic and Witchcraft in the North Riding of Yorkshire
    David Naitby's Bedale Treasury
    David Kirby
    ISBN 0955076900
    Summerfield Press, 2005

Chapter 11 Trinity fair

The Cleveland Repertory & Stokesley Advertiser
    Vol III, No 6, 1 June 1845
    Extracts transcribed by Beryl Turner,
    Stokesley Local History Study Group, 2004
Rhymes and Sketches to illustrate the Cleveland Dialect
    Florence Cleveland (Mrs G M Tweddell)
    Tweddell and Sons, Stokesley, 1875

Great Ayton, Stokesley & District, Past and Present; with a Chapter on Bilsdale and its Hunt
    John F Blakeborough
    T Woolston, Middlesbrough, 1901

Yorkshire Fairs and Markets
    Publications of the Thoresby Society, Vol XXXIX, 1939

The Cleveland Village Book
    Cleveland Federation of Women's Institutes, 1991

Chapter 12   Smoky beacons

The Ralph Jackson Diaries
    Cleveland Archives, Middlesbrough
    also on www.historic-cleveland.co.uk

The Local Records of Stockton and the Neighbourhood or A Register of Memorable Events, chronologically arranged, which have occurred in or near Stockton Ward and the North-Eastern Parts of Cleveland
    Thomas Richardson
    William Robinson, Stockton, 1868

The Watering Places of Cleveland; being descriptions of these and other attractive localities in that interesting district of Yorkshire
    Samuel Gordon
    Webster, Redcar, 1869
    Republished MTD Rigg Publications, Leeds, 1992

Beacons of East Yorkshire
    John Nicholson
    Hull Literary Club
    A Brown and Sons, Hull and Simpkin, Marshall and Co, London, 1887

Old Yorkshire, Vol 1
    Edited by William Smith, 1889

Yorkshire
    Gordon Home
    A & C Black Ltd, 1908

Notes on Great Ayton Celebration 16 May 1911 (held in Great Ayton Library)

Beacon Fire on Roseberry Topping – Lightning Floodlights Hills and Villages
    Darlington & Stockton Times 12 May 1945

Programme for the Celebrations of the Coronation of Edward VII in 1902.
    Darlington & Stockton Times 11 March 1953

To Escape the Monster's Clutches
    Compiled by M Y Ashcroft
    ISBN 0 906035 04X
    NYCC Records Office Publication No. 15, November 1977

The Wonders of Yorkshire
    Marie Hartley and Joan Ingilby
    JM Dent & Sons Ltd, London, 1959

Round and About The North Yorkshire Moors
    Tom Scott Burns and Martin Rigg
    MTD Rigg Publications, 1988

The Beacons of North-East Yorkshire
    David Brooke
    The Ryedale Historian No 14, 1988-9
    Helmsley Archaeological Society

A Brief History of Danby Beacon
    Ray Barker
    The Danby Beacon Reunion September 1993

The Confident Hope of a Miracle, the true story of the Spanish Armada
    Neil Hanson
    ISBN 0 385 60451 3
    Doubleday, 2003

Chapter 13   The mystery of the summerhouse

The Gentleman's Magazine
    Vol 57, January to June 1787
    Vol 61, January to June, 1791
    Vol 73, January to June, 1803
    Vol 91, July to December 1821
    Vol 94, July to December 1827

Graves, 1808 (1)
Young, 1817 (2)
Gordon, 1869 (12)
Ashcroft, 1977 (12)

Captain Cook's Monument in Cleveland
    Cliff Thornton
    Cook's Log Vol 21, 1548-9
    The Captain Cook Society, 1998

Preliminary Report on Excavations & Fieldwork 1999 at Ham Green
    Avon's Gardens Trust and Bristol & Avon Archaeological Society

Follies
    Issue 57, Spring 2004 Vol 15 no. 2
    ISBN 0963-9004
    The Folly Fellowship

The Archaeology of Roseberry Topping
    Stephen J Sherlock
    Moorland Monuments Ed. Blaise Vyner
    ISBN 1 872414 559
    Council for British Arch, York, 1995

Unpublished Wilson family correspondence made available by Chris Barrow of Leicester.
Unpublished letter from Cliff Thornton to Graham Lee, 27 April 1998

Chapter 14   Industry on Roseberry

Plan of Workings in Main Seam Roseberry Mines, Great Ayton, Yorkshire
    Surveyor's Certificate No 543, 1929
    National Archives, Kew, London

The Mineral Tramways of Great Ayton
    R Pepper and R J Stewart
    ISBN 0 9507169 5 2
    Narrow Gauge Railway Society, Peterborough, 1994

Roseberry Ironstone Mine
    Richard Pepper
    Cleveland Ironstone Series, Peter Tuffs, 1999

Chapter 15   Roseberry's Pits

Graves, 1808 (1)
Young, 1817 (2)
Young, 1824 (9)
Ord, 1846 (2)
Gordon, 1869 (12)
Atkinson, 1874 (2)

Memoirs of the Geological Survey of the United Kingdom
    The Jurassic Rocks of Britain, Vol 1
    C Fox-Strangways
    HMSO, London, 1892

Atkinson, 1893-4 (2)

Forty Years in a Moorland Parish
    Rev J C Atkinson
    Macmillan and Co, 1892

The Early History of the North Riding
    William Edwards
    A Browne and Sons, 1924

Burton, 1926 (3)
Elgee, 1930 (4)
Blakeborough, 1954 (8)

Letter in The Dalesman
    Raymond H Hayes
    Vol 22, December 1960

Sherlock, 1995 (13)
Pepper, 1999 (14)
Butlin, 2003 (4)

Gaelic place-names in North-East England (3)
    William Pearson
    Bulletin of the Cleveland & Teesside Local History Society, 89, Winter 2005

Chapter 16   A Topping radio programme

'Fine Prospects' script
    BBC Archives, Reading, Berkshire

Chapter 17   Roseberry on historic maps

Yorkshire Maps and Map-Makers
    Arthur Raistrick
    ISBN 0852060114
    Dalesman Books, 1969

Ordnance Survey maps – a concise guide for historians
    Richard Oliver
    ISBN 1 870598 24 5
    Charles Close Society, 1993

Butlin, 2003 (4)

Chapter 18   Tourism and the Topping

A Tour through the Whole Island of Great Britain 1724-26
    Daniel Defoe

History, Directory & Gazetteer, of the County of York; with a variety of commercial, statistical, and professional information: also, copious lists of the Seats of the Nobility and Gentry, of Yorkshire
    Edward Baines
    Vol II East and North Ridings.
    Edward Baines, Leeds Mercury Office, and Hurst and Robinson, London, 1823
Ord, 1846 (2)
A Month in Yorkshire
    Walter White
    Chapman and Hall, London 1858
Guide to Hotels & Furnished Lodgings in Farmhouses, Seaside & Country Villages in Northumberland, Cumberland, Westmoreland, Durham & Yorkshire
    North Eastern Railway, (early 1860s?)
Walks in Yorkshire:
I In the North West, II In the North East
    W S Banks
    W R Hall, Wakefield and J Russell Smith London, 1866
Gordon, 1869 (12)
Atkinson, 1873 (2)
Burnett, 1886 (9)
Jackson's Cyclist's Guide to Yorkshire
    Tom Bradley
    Richard Jackson, Leeds, 1896
Beautiful Cleveland and just beyond its Borders. With Digressive Notes on some Short Tours in the Cleveland District
    Hood & Co Ltd, Middlesbrough, 1897
A Guide to Great Ayton, Roseberry, Captain Cook's Monument, and District, also local stories (including a Chapter by R Blakeborough)
    John F Blakeborough
    Hood and Co Ltd, Middlesbrough, 1900
Blakeborough, 1901 (11)
The Enchanting North
    J S Fletcher
    Eveleigh Nash, London 1908
Yorkshire Moors and Dales
    A P Wilson
    A Brown & Sons, 1910
The Romans in Cleveland
    Frank Elgee
    Hood & Co Ltd, Middlesbrough, 1923
The King's England, Yorkshire North Riding
    Edited by Arthur Mee
    Hodder and Stoughton, London, 1941
The Cleveland Way
    Alan Falconer
    HMSO, London, 1972
The Story of Cleveland
    Minnie C Horton
    ISBN 0 904784 09 6
    Cleveland County Libraries, 1979

James Herriot's Yorkshire
    James Herriot
    Michael Joseph, London, 1979
North York Moors National Park Reports
    NYM National Park Authority
    Helmsley (1979-80 to 1985-86)
Round and About the North Yorkshire Moors, A Glimpse of the Past
    Tom Scott Burns
    MTD Rigg Publications, 1987
Rambles in Cleveland and Peeps into the Dales on Foot, Cycle and Rail
    M Heavisides
    MTD Rigg Publications, Leeds, 1988
The County Cleveland Village Book
    Cleveland Women's Institutes, 1991

Chapter 19   Accidents and rescues

Proceedings of the Cleveland Field Club Vol. III
    Edited by Rev J Cowley Fowler
    A Brown & Sons, Hull, 1913
Preliminary Field Inquiry Report Ref. C.707
    Scholefield and Jameson
    Air Accidents Investigation Branch
The Tom Kirby newspaper files
    The Library, Great Ayton
Evening Gazette, 11 February 1960

Chapter 20   Who owns the Topping?

Newton Old Estate
    Microfilm 1945, frames 145 and 147
    North Yorkshire County Records Office, Northallerton
The County Borough of Teesside – a souvenir of its formation
    Norman Moorshom, 1968
Report of the Royal Commission on Local Government in England 1966 to 1969
    HMSO, London, 1969
Minutes of the Seventeenth Meeting of the Local Government Standing Committee
    25 January 1972, HMSO
Roseberry Topping
    Bill Cowley
    The Dalesman, Vol 45, 1984
Cleveland's Matterhorn
    William Reginald Mitchell
    The Dalesman, Vol 49, 1987
Reports of the Local Government Commission England 1992 to 1996
Local Government Act 1992
The Cleveland (Structural Change) Order 1995
The Cleveland (Further Provision) Order 1996
Pepper, 1999 (14)
Ayton Happenings – Past Village Events
    Malcolm Race
    Christchurch, Great Ayton, 2000

Chapter 21   Roseberry's wildlife

Ralph Jackson Diaries (12)
Newton Tithe records and Manorial records
    NYCC Record Office, Northallerton
Collins Field Guide - Trees of Britain and Northern Europe
    Alan Mitchell
    ISBN 0 00 2192136
    Collins Publishers, London, 1974
The History of the Countryside
    Oliver Rackham
    ISBN 1 84212 440 4
    Weidenfeld & Nicholson, London, 1986
Great Ayton A History of the Village
    Dan O'Sullivan
    ISBN 0 9508858 3 5
    Second Edition, 1996
Plantlife Magazine
    Spring 2003 and Summer 2003
    Plantlife International, Salisbury

Chapter 22   The Topping today

Chapter 23   Roseberry Topping in literature and art

The Register Office
    Joseph Reed
    Bell, London, 1761
Roseberry Topping
    Thomas Pierson
    Stokesley, 1783
The Pirate
    Walter Scott
    Archibald Constable & Co, Edinburgh, Hurst, Robinson & Co, London, 1822
The Bard and Minor Poems
    John Walker Ord
    London, 1842
White, 1858 (18)
Gordon, 1869 (12)
Tweddell, 1865 (8)
The Hills and Vale of Cleveland
    James Milligan
    Middlesbrough, 1881
Burnett, 1886 (9)
Striding through Yorkshire
    Alfred J Brown
    Country Life Ltd, London, 1938
Cleveland View
    D L Leach
    Macdonald and Co, London, 1943
The Piper of Dreams
    Terry Pitts Fenby and Bill Bruce
    ISBN 0 340 28606 7
    Hodder and Stoughton, Sevenoaks, 1982
Gertrude Bell Archive, www.gerty.ncl.ac.uk

index of names

Because subject matter is arranged in specific chapters, this index is restricted to people. Rulers and monarchs, national and international figures have been left out of this list, but fictional characters have been included.

Adam, David *(20th century vicar of Danby)* 191
Adams, Johnny *(rock climber)* 178
Appleton, John Reed
   (19th century Stockton poet) 193
Atkinson, Canon John Christopher
   (19th century vicar of Danby and historian)
   22, 70, 74-75, 82, 101, 124, 144, 148

Bainbridge, Mary *(Stokesley resident)* 157
Banham, John *(20th century businessman)* 164
Banks, W S *(West Riding author)* 148
Barker, Arthur *(pioneering rock climber)* 178
Bateman, Thomas *(19th century
   Derbyshire barrow-digger)* 47, 50-51
Battey, Jean *(Great Ayton artist)* 187
Bell, Gertrude *(early 20th century traveller,
   scholar and secret agent)* 194
Bellamy, David *(environmentalist)* 94, 166
Bergstrand, Robin *(fell-runner)* 176
Berks, Rosemary *(resident of Darlington)* 160
Bigland, John *(19th century author)* 76
Bird, William *(18th century antiquarian)* 122
Blakeborough, Richard *(19th century
   historian, from Guisborough)* 82-84, 87, 150
Blakeborough, John Fairfax *(son of Richard Blakeborough,
   author)* 86-87, 125, 130-131, 150, 152
Blaeu, Joan *(17th century map-maker
   from Amsterdam)* 135, 173
Bradley, Ernest Sydney *(sold part of
   Roseberry to National Trust)* 164-165
Bradley, Mark *(National Trust warden)* 166
Brewster, Rev John *(19th century
   historian, from Stockton)* 98-99, 101
Brown, Alfred J *(author, 1932 rambling guide)* 154
Bruce, Bill *(book illustrator)* 196
Burton, George A *(son of J J Burton, and
   manager of Roseberry Mine)* 92
Burton, Joseph James *(owner of Roseberry Ironstone Mine
   and local historian)* 36, 80, 110-111, 124-125, 128
Butler, J Theobald *(wrote to the local press in 1912)* 36
Burnett, WH 74

Camden, William *(16th century author and
   historian)* 22, 51, 70, 72, 74, 76, 79-80, 134, 144
Campion, Robert
   (erected Captain Cook's Monument in 1827) 99
Carr, John *(18th century architect)* 16
Cartwright, Mr *(artist employed by
   G S Faber)* 48-49, 51, 53
Cass, Moll *(Bedale witch)* 84
Cecyll, Theodocca *(1595 graffiti)* 73

Chaloner, Thomas the younger *(probable
   recipient of the Cottonian manuscript of 1604)* 70
Chaytor, Hugh *(joint first owner of
   Roseberry Ironstone Mine)* 109
Chaytor, William *(19th century deputy
   Lord Lieutenant of the North Riding)* 91
Chilton, William *(early 19th century owner
   of Middlesbrough farm)* 67
Clark, Estra *(20th century poster artist)* 147
Cleveland, Florence *(pseudonym of Mrs G M
   Tweddell, 19th century dialect poetess)* 86, 194
Clifford, Maria *(mistress of
   Bartholomew Rudd the younger)* 99
Close, Dave *(stone paver)* 180
Close, Roland *(20th century archaeologist)* 40
Close, Gordon *(Great Ayton gamekeeper)* 94
Coates, John *(1817 graffiti)* 73
Colebrook, Sir George *(18th century speculator)* 115
Colling, Charles & Robert *(18th century cattle
   breeders, from County Durham)* 61
Cook, James *(later Captain Cook, 18th century
   navigator)* 14, 49, 98, 131, 186, 192, 194, 196
Cotton, Sir Robert Bruce *(17th century antiquarian)* 70
Coulson, John *(17th century Lord of
   the manor of Great Ayton)* 61
Cowley, Bill *(20th century Cleveland farmer and writer)* 63
Cuit, George
   (18th century artist, from Richmond) 14, 61, 98
Cunningham, Mel *(National Trust manager)* 166

Daysh, Professor G H J
   (ex-Armstrong College, Newcastle) 130-131
Defoe, Daniel *(18th century traveller and author)* 144
Dicker, Bob *(National Trust manager)* 166
Dixon, Garbut *(1817 graffiti)* 73
Dodds, Joseph *(joint first owner of
   Roseberry Ironstone Mine)* 109
Dowson, Benny *(1992 fatality)* 158
Duck, Susan
   (wife of Bartholomew Rudd the elder) 99
Dundas, Lieutenant Colonel Lawrence
   (First Earl of Zetland) 103, 192

Edwards, William *(20th century head
   of Middlesbrough High School)* 124-125
Elgee, Frank
   (20th century Cleveland archaeologist) 51, 53, 125
Elliott, Ebenezer *(19th century poet)* 74, 192
Evans, John *(19th century archaeologist)* 47, 51

Faber, Rev George Stanley *(19th century
   rector of Long Newton)* 22, 44, 49, 51-52

Featherstone, Thomas
   (witnessed 1960 aircraft crash) 158
Fenby, Terry Pitts *(modern author)* 196
Fisher, Mrs *(National Trust benefactor)* 165
Fixter, Geoff *(rock climber)* 178
Fletcher, J S *(20th century travel writer)* 152
Fry, Lady Anne *(wife of Sir Wilfred Fry)* 164-165
Fry, Sir Wilfrid *(20th century owner of Cleveland Lodge
   Estate, Great Ayton)* 97, 164-165

Garbutt, Nanny *(Great Ayton witch)* 82-83, 131
Gordon, Samuel *(19th century author)* 91, 103, 123, 148
Graves, Rev John *(19th century historian)* 15, 17, 22, 49,
   70, 72, 74, 76, 79, 80, 82, 98, 101, 144, 148, 192-193
Greenwood, Christopher, also his brother, John
   (19th century map-makers) 138, 140
Gulwell, P *(Cleveland huntsman)* 67

Hale, Gilly *(fell-runner)* 176
Hansill, Thomas *(19th century owner
   of Roseberry Topping in Jamaica)* 19
Hammond, Peter *(fatal fall in 1933)* 157
Heaviside, Thomas *(19th century Stokesley printer)* 15
Heavisides, Henry *(19th century Stockton poet)* 193
Heavisides, Michael *(early 20th century
   Stockton author)* 150, 152, 193
Hixon, John
   (19th century Skelton attorney) 49, 52-53
Hobson, Miss *(National Trust benefactor)* 165
Hodskinson, Joseph *(18th century surveyor)* 138
Holman, Robert *(modern playwright)* 197
Hondius, Jodocus *(17th century Flemish engraver)* 134
Hood, Harold *(20th century Middlesbrough photographer
   and printer)* 83
Howey, David *(son of Robert Howey)* 189
Howey, Robert *(20th century artist)* 189
Hudson, H W
   (owner of a Stockton confectionery business) 17
Hunt, Tiffany *(National Trust, York)* 165

Imeson, June *(councillor from Great Ayton)* 163
Ingledew C J Davison *(19th century
   collector of songs and ballads)* 66-67

Jackson, George *(19th century
   landowner, owner of Aireyholme Farm)* 47, 52, 62
Jackson, John
   (19th century master at Rudby school) 66, 190
Jackson, Rachel *(sister of Ralph Jackson and wife
   of William Wilson)* 98
Jackson, Ralph *(18th century landowner and diarist, from
   Normanby)* 23, 90, 98-99, 101, 173-174, 190

Jameson, Mr (Air Accident investigator) 158
Jefferys, Thomas (18th century map-maker) 137-138, 173
Jones, Eric (accident in 1948) 157

Kitching, Alfred Edward
(20th century landowner, from Great Ayton) 92

Langstaffe, Mary (victim of Nanny Garbutt, a witch) 82
Leach, Mrs D L (20th century author) 194
Little, Brian (witness to 1960 aircraft crash) 158
Longlands, John (Jamaican landowner) 19
Mankin, Richard (17th century petty criminal) 61
Marr, Eric (rock climber) 178
Marr, Tony (rock climber) 178
Martin, Arnold
(20th century tenant of Aireyholme Farm) 110
Martin, Robinson (early 20th century
tenant of Aireyholme Farm) 92
Marwood, William
(19th century landowner, from Busby Hall) 190
Mason, Mary (mistress of Thomas Bateman) 51
McCraken, Anya (National Park architect) 97
McDonald, Tom (19th century Tasmanian prospector) 115
Mead, Harry (local historian, from Great Broughton) 154
Mee, Arthur (20th century journalist and author) 154
Milligan, James (19th century poet) 194
Mitchell, Alan (tree-dating expert) 174
Mitchell, Dr Peter K
(geographer from the University of Durham) 62
Moorpout, Margery (character from Ayton in an 18th
century play) 74, 130, 152, 154, 184, 186
Moro, Anthony
(one of Rev Graves' 'learned men' on fossils) 72
Mudd, Hester (Rosedale witch) 84
Mudd, Mary (character in a story about witches) 83
Mulgrave, Lord (responsible for local
defences against Napoleon) 91, 98

Naitby, David
(19th century Bedale collector of folklore) 84
Newgill, Nancy (Rosedale witch) 84
Nicholson, William (19th century Egglescliffe
market gardener) 47, 49, 50-52

Ogilby, John (17th century map-maker) 135-137
Ord, John Walker (19th century historian)
17, 22, 47, 49-53, 70, 73-76, 79, 101, 107, 119,
123-125, 144-146, 188, 192
Oswald, King of Northumbria
(father of Prince Oswy) 79, 80, 82
Oswy, Prince (drowned in the Roseberry Well legend)
70, 73, 79-80, 82, 131, 152, 154, 188

Parkinson, Rev Thomas
(19th century vicar of North Otterington) 82
Parrington, Thomas
(19th century Cleveland huntsman) 67
Patterson, Andy (local policemen) 158
Pearson, William
(place-name historian, from Stockton) 23, 128

Pease, Sir Alfred (19th century historian) 66, 125, 127
Pease, Joseph (19th century Quaker businessman,
from Darlington) 108
Peberdy, Bill (friend of Michael Procter) 159
Pepper, Richard
(20th century industrial archaeologist) 107
Petch, Harold S (local farmer) 165
Pevsner, Nikolaus
(20th century architectural historian) 16, 27
Phalp, Charles and Freda (current tenants of
Aireyholme Farm) 64, 94, 158-159, 161, 165-166
Phalp, Mark (son of Charles and
Freda Phalp, also a farmer) 64
Phipps, Constantine (the second Lord Mulgrave) 98
Pickering, Edgar (Cleveland huntsman) 67
Pickles, Frank (National Park ranger) 166
Pierson, John (19th century tenant of Aireyholme) 62
Pierson, Thomas (18th century Stokesley poet)
74, 148, 188, 190, 192
Pinder, Ray (of Great Ayton) 139
Pratt, William (19th century Stokesley printer) 193
Primrose, Archibald Philip (Fifth Earl of Rosebery,
better known as Lord Rosebery) 17, 19, 115
Primrose, Harry (Sixth Earl of Rosebery) 19
Procter, Michael (died in 1960 aircraft crash) 158-159

Redcliffe-Maud, Lord (20th century politician) 162-164
Reed, Joseph
(18th century Stockton playwright) 154, 184, 186
Rhea, Nicholas
(pseudonym of Peter Walker, a local author) 154
Richardson, Thomas (19th century Stockton historian) 90
Ripley, Robert (17th century petty criminal) 61
Robinson, John Ryley
(19th century poet from Dewsbury) 150, 193
Robson, Henry (19th century artist, from Stockton) 187
Rogers, William (17th century engraver) 134
Rolfe, Sidney (1947 fatal accident) 157
Rudd, Bartholomew the elder (18th century landowner,
from Marton Hall) 61, 99
Rudd, Bartholomew the younger (son of Bartholomew
Rudd the elder) 61, 98-99, 115
Rudd, Edward John (grandson of
Bartholomew Rudd the younger) 115

Salter, Mrs (National Trust benefactor) 165
Saxton, Christopher (16th century map-maker) 133-135
Scholefield, Mr (Air Accident investigator) 158-159
Scott, Sir Walter (19th century author) 192
Sherlock, Stephen (archaeologist) 119, 121, 127
Simm, Gary (landlord from Stokesley) 16
Simpson, Henry (local historian) 157
Simpson, Johnny (character in a story about witches) 83
Skottowe, Augustine (son of Thomas Skottowe) 190
Skottowe, Thomas (18th century landowner,
from Great Ayton) 99, 101, 186
Smit, Tim (founder of Eden Project in Cornwall) 168
Smith, A H (place name historian) 22
Smith, Brian (modern archaeologist) 55-56
Smith, Charles (19th century map-maker) 138

Smith, Michael
(18th century landowner, from Marske) 99
Smith, Tom (character in a story about witches) 83
Speed, John (17th century map-maker) 134-135
Spence, Mr (19th century landowner, from Newton) 174
Staveley, Mrs (19th century owner of
the manor of Newton) 108
Staveley, Roseberry Mary (18th century
owner of the manor of Newton) 162
Stephenson, 'Stevo' (teacher at Stokesley School) 159
Suggitt, Peter (owner of Suggitt's
ice-cream business in Great Ayton) 17
Swan, Mrs Myra (wrote to the local press in 1912) 34

Taylor, Joseph (19th century poet) 192
Taylor, Will (20th century Danby artist) 191
Thomas, Mr
(19th century owner of Pinchinthorpe Hall) 123
Thornton, Cliff (president of the Captain Cook Society) 98
Tresham, Francis (possible author of the Cottonian
manuscript of 1604) 70
Tugman, Rev E (early 20th century vicar of Newton) 87
Tuke, John (18th century author) 58, 138, 173
Turner, Sir Charles
(18th century landowner from Kirkleatham) 190
Turton, Major Robert
(20th century historian, from Kildale Hall) 20, 70
Tweddell, George Markham (19th century Stokesley
publisher and author) 15, 66-67, 76, 82, 86-87, 148, 193

Walker, Peter N
(author, creator of 'Heartbeat' stories) 154
Warburton, John (18th century map-maker) 137
Watkins, Alfred
(20th century historian, from Herefordshire) 56
White, Walter
(19th century journalist, from Berkshire) 148
Whitely, Martha (mistress of Edward John Rudd) 115
Wight, Alf (better known as James Herriot, of Thirsk) 154
Wilde, Oscar (20th century playwright) 19
Wilfrid, Saint (7th century abbot of Ripon) 80, 82, 107
Williams, Kit (modern author) 196
Willis, Christopher (local farmer) 165
Wilson, A P (20th century travel writer) 152
Wilson, William junior (son of William Wilson) 103
Wilson, Commodore William (18th century
landowner, from Great Ayton) 97-99, 103, 190
Winifryd or Winifred, Saint
(nun beheaded for protecting her virginity) 82
Withington, Rev R (19th century vicar of Great Ayton) 92
Woodall, Chris (rock climber) 178
Wright, Alec (20th century artist) 185
Wright, Old Gag Mally
(old resident of Newton) 86

Yellowley, Jasper (Scott character born at
Roseberry Topping) 192
Young, Arthur (18th century agriculturalist) 58, 73
Young, Rev George (19th century historian, from Whitby)
22, 82, 98, 119, 112-123, 125

acknowledgements

We, the Great Ayton Community Archaeology Project, are grateful to all who have assisted with the research for this publication, and would apologise for any omissions. We all appear on page 199, apart from Joan Groves and Peter Watson who were unable to be present for the photograph. Len Groves and Bazz Lewis sadly passed away before this book was published.

The Howey summer scene on page 189 is available as a print from David Howey of Yarm on 01642 898182.

David Adam of Belford for information on Will Taylor's lino-cuts
Richard Allenby for information about the Proctor aircraft crash
Mary Bainbridge of Stokesley
Chris Barrow of Leicester for Wilson family correspondence
The Battey family for the Jean Battey picture
Nicola Beech of the British Library for access to the Christopher Saxton map
Sir John and Lady Bell of Arncliffe Hall
Robin Bergstrand of the Fell Runners' Association
Billingham Press Ltd for Alec Wright picture
Tom Scott Burns for harvest photograph
Kevin Cale of Community Archaeology Ltd for archaeological advice and support
Derek Capes of Great Ayton for additional material on wildlife
John Clarke and staff at the National Railway Museum, York
The Cleveland Naturalist Field Club
Cleveland Search and Rescue Team, especially David Little, Gari Finch, Steve Glasper
Robin and Carol Cook of Swainby
John Coverdale of Ingleby Greenhow for additional material on fox hunting
Karen Culverwell of the Air Accidents Investigation Branch, Aldershot
Jenny Duke for photograph of stone on sledge
Linda Edgar, Administrator of the Dalmeny Estate
Harry Edwards of the Morris Register Club
Vic Fairbrother of Guisborough for additional material on birds
The Follies Fellowship for information in connection with the summerhouse
Mr and Mrs Garbutt of Great Ayton for photograph of 1902 bonfire
Rose Gibson of Leeds City Council Library for access to the John Warburton map
Peter Grainger of Middlesbrough for wildlife photographs
Gilly Hale of Great Ayton
Alan Halfpenny of Guisborough
Robert Holman, playwright
David Howey of Yarm for access to the work of Robert Howey
Ivy Hynes of Great Ayton
June Imeson OBE of Hambleton District Council
David Jackson of the A J Jackson Collection for photograph of the Percival Proctor
Lynda Kelly of Kelly Books Ltd, Tiverton for the historic Radio Times
Ian Lawrence of Middlesbrough for additional material on wild flowers
Graham Lee of the North York Moors National Park Authority
Alistair Mackenzie of the Cleveland Orienteering Klub
Terry Manby of Market Weighton for professional archaeological support
Andrew Martin and Margaret Wilson of the National Museums of Scotland for locating Faber's papers
Harry Mead of Great Broughton for extracts from his newspaper cutting files
Alan Myers and James Mackenzie of Middlesbrough for additional material on literature
Mark Newman of the National Trust for his introduction and additional material
Tony Nicholson of the University of Teesside for advice on various historical matters
Ordnance Survey of Southampton for a licence to reproduce extracts from OS maps
Jenny Parker and staff at the Middlesbrough Reference Library
David Parry of the North East Hill Running Association
Ben Pearce of Seamer for the information on rock climbing and photograph of David Bellamy
Sue Pearce of Great Ayton for additional proof reading
Bill Pearson of Stockton-on-Tees for place name derivations
Bill Peberdy of Scarborough for his memories of Michael Procter
Denis Peel of the Society of Antiquaries of Newcastle-upon-Tyne for finding John Hixon's papers
Irene Pepper of Nunthorpe for access to the late Richard Pepper's archives
Charles and Freda Phalp of Aireyholme Farm for additional material and reminiscences
Freda Phalp of Aireyholme Farm for photographs inside Roseberry Ironstone Mine
Marjorie Rolfe of Great Ayton
Peter Rowe at Tees Archaeology, Hartlepool for aerial photographs
Ken Sedman Dorman Museum, Middlesbrough for photographs of the hoard replicas
Chris Sheppard of Leeds University Library for access to the Godfrey Bingley Collection
Pradeep Sihota of the British Geological Survey
Alan Simpson of Great Ayton
Andrea Smith of the Society of Antiquaries in Scotland in connection with Faber's original papers
Brian Smith of Eaglescliffe for additional material on sight lines
Julie Snelling of the BBC Written Archives Centre, Reading for original radio script
Staff at the Archives of the Northern Echo and Darlington & Stockton Times
Staff at the City of York Reference Library
Staff at the North Yorkshire Library Service
Staff at the Stockton-on-Tees Reference Library
Studio Print of Redcar for permission to use Alec Wright pictures
Keith Sweetmore and staff at the North Yorkshire County Records Office
John Taylor and staff of the Great Ayton Library
Norma Taylor of Danby for access to the work of Will Taylor
The Teesmouth Bird Club
Julian Temple of the Brooklands Museum
Cliff Thornton, Capt Cook Society for additional material about the summerhouse
Peter Tuffs of Guisborough for photographs of Roseberry Ironstone Mine
Beryl Turner of Stokesley
Blaise Vyner for aerial photographs
Wakefield Art Gallery for permission to reproduce the work of George Cuit
Peter Waterton of Great Ayton for images of butterflies
Richard Webber of Bristol for information on the Ham Green House gazebo
Kate Webster at Hachette Children's Books
John Weedy of Lancaster for the image of Lord Roseberry from the Illustrated London News
Wellington Lodge Llama Trekking of Staintondale
David Wilson of Stockton-on-Tees for permission to use the sketches by Henry Robson
Peter Wood of Moorsholm for flights in his WW2 Auster spotter aircraft
Gill Woolrich of the City of Sheffield Museum for information on the Roseberry hoard
The Yorkshire Garden Trust for research in connection with prospect houses

...NSIS · EPISCO-
...VS · PARS

(Map of northern England showing part of the Bishopric/Yorkshire region. Notable place names visible include:)

Rivers and coast (top): Holme, Bellosis, Billingham, Norton, Stockton, Middleburghe, West Cothm, Kirklethum, Lasenbye, Yerbye, Wilton cast, Lockenbye, Eston, Normanbye, Toccote, Vplet

Upper region: Arsm, Leuenthorp, Stansby, Acklam, Ormesbye, Marton, Tollesbye, Gasburgh, Huton, Pinchinthorp, Newton Eaton, Dunsbury tappin hill, Thornabye, Preston, Eggesclif, Estabys, Barwick, Staynton, Maltbye, Nunthorp, Kildale, Newbye, Hilton, Middleton, Semere, Stokesley, Ingleby, Easby, Batersbye, Bay

Middle left: Persbrig, Ouer Cunsley, Darlington, Middleton george, Neusam, Worsall, Yarum, Kirkleuenton, Crathorne, Rudby, Dromonbye, Kirkby, Broughton, Inglebye, Nether Cunsley, Clyffe, Manfeld, Blackwell, Nysam, Nether Dunsley, Sockborn, Ouerdunsley, Skuterskill, Sazay, Busbye, Carleton

Central area: Epplebye, Cleesbye, Stapleton, Hurworthe, Croftbrig, Eryholme, Davton, Smeton magna, Girsbye, Hornbye, W. Rugton, E. Rugton, Pottoo, Whartlton cast, Swaneby, Arneclyffe, Aumondske, Bilsdale chap, Sct Johns, Aldburghe, Stanwik, Melsonbye, Newton, Burten, Kneton, Sedbury, Myddleton, Hawnabye, Long Cowto, Smeton pua, Appleton, Wisk flu

Middle: Skeby, Mouton, Vekerbye, N: Cowton, S. Cowton, Birtbye, Welbury, Snylesworthe, Richmond, Easbye, Skorton, Huton conyers, Dighton, E: Harlesey, Harlesey cast, Montgrace ab:, Osmotherbye, Brunton, Ellerbeck, Arden, Brough, Cowborn, Catterik, Bolton, Ellerton, Kiplin, Danbye wiske, Sigston cast, Thirlbye, Hauxby, Kirkby fletheham, Langton mag:, Brunton, Sigston, Arncliffe, Hippeswell, Burghhall, Killerbye, Tunstall, Skotton, Fletcham, Fencotes, Yafford, N. Alverton, Codbek flu, Ouersilton, Carleto

Lower middle: Appleton, Hornbye cast, Allathorn, Hunton, Patrikbrunon, Hackforthe, Langthorp, Askew, Thirntost, Ynderby steple, Morton, Romanbye, Lanmouthe, Nether Silton, Kebek, Helme, Oldbiland, Riuis ab, Sproxton, Osuold, Bedall, Leming chap:, Gatenbye, North Otteringto, Thornton in y more, Thornton in the beanes, Burrobye, Vesall cast, Newbiggin, Kirkbye knoll, Boltbye, Kerrbye, Srauton, Ampleford, Cowlyn, Burrall, Firbye, Egilly, Thakeston, Burniston, Newby, S. Otterington, Thornton m y strete, Thornbarghe, N. Kiluinton, The mont of Sct Johns, Thurlbye, Feliskirk, Ellington, Watlas, Thorprow, Pickall, Maunbye, Kirkby, Newsom, S. Kiluinton, Willowb flu

Lower area: Thornton youre flu, Snape, Well, Cauthorp, Brakenburgh, Thrvsk, Sutton, Kilborn, Masham, Clyston, Thornbergh, Kirtlynton, Ynderbye, Sandhuton, Bagby, Thirkleby, Biland ab:, Healey, Burton, Neserfeld, Middleton, Baudrebye, Catton, Carleton, Skiptonbridge, Graswith, Sowrbye, Carleton, Curewould, Newbrugh, Swinton, Hilton, W. Tanfeld, E. Tanfeld, Wath, Melmerbye, Suttonhongroue, Topclif, Bridforth, Husthwate, Daulton, Eldmyre, Huton, Sesey, Thormanby, Owston, Bransby, Kettlesmore, Thorp, Asserley, Norton hall, Raynton, Crake cast, Sterf

Bottom: Kirkby malshed, Gaughby, Bushopto, Castleton, Huton, Disforth chap:, Cundall, Thornton bridge, Kaskill, Marton ab:, Larton, Mysbie, Studley, Rippon, Hewick, Marton, Braferton cu Helperbye, Esingwowlde, Stillington